THE WEST
IDEOLOGY
OTHER ESSAYS

Andrew Gamble

BRISTOL
UNIVERSITY
PRESS

First published in Great Britain in 2021 by

Bristol University Press
University of Bristol
1-9 Old Park Hill
Bristol
BS2 8BB
UK
t: +44 (0)117 954 5940
e: bup-info@bristol.ac.uk

Details of international sales and distribution partners are available at
bristoluniversitypress.co.uk

© Andrew Gamble 2021

British Library Cataloguing in Publication Data
A catalogue record for this book is available from the British Library

ISBN 978-1-5292-1704-9 hardcover
ISBN 978-1-5292-1705-6 paperback
ISBN 978-1-5292-1706-3 ePub
ISBN 978-1-5292-1707-0 ePdf

Cover design: Liam Roberts
Image credit: Liam Roberts
Bristol University Press uses environmentally responsible
print partners.
Printed and bound in Great Britain by CMP, Poole

For my grandchildren

Joni, Nye, Louis, George, Ceinwen, Ivy
and Emyr

Contents

Preface   vi

Introduction: An Intellectual Journey   1
Notes on the Essays   16
1   The Western Ideology (2009)   23
2   Neo-liberalism and the Tax State (2013)   39
3   Ideas and Interests in British Economic Policy (1989)   59
4   Hayek on Knowledge, Economics and Society (2006)   81
5   Marxism After Communism (1999)   101
6   G.D.H. Cole and the History of Socialist Thought (2002)   121
7   Social Democracy in a Global World (2009)   141
8   The Quest for a Great Labour Party (2018)   161
9   Oakeshott's Ideological Politics (2012)   181
10   Oakeshott and Totalitarianism (2016)   201
11   The Drifter's Escape (2004)   215
Epilogue: The Western Ideology Revisited   237

Notes   245
Acknowledgements   263
Index   265

Preface

These two volumes of essays would not have happened without the patient encouragement and sound advice of Stephen Wenham at Bristol University Press. I must also thank, for some very useful comments on the original plan, Helen Thompson, Ben Clift, Simon Griffiths, Colin Hay, Magnus Feldman and Ben Rosamond.

So many people have helped and shaped me over the last sixty years. Many of them are mentioned in the pages which follow, but by no means all. One of the greatest influences upon me has been my students, both research students and undergraduates, as well as my colleagues at Sheffield and Cambridge, and in the wider academic community and the public policy world. Most of the essays collected here had their origins in those engagements over the last forty years.

My family has supported me in so many ways through this time, and these essays are dedicated to them, and in particular to my grandchildren.

Introduction: An Intellectual Journey

My first published essay was entitled 'Everlasting capitalism'. It appeared in 1968 in a student magazine at Cambridge and discussed Herbert Marcuse's *One Dimensional Man*, and his argument that all radical alternatives to capitalism had disappeared in the West. Published in 1964 *One Dimensional Man* was one of the first books I encountered when I started at Cambridge the following year. A friend gave it to me to read and it led to intense discussions. It opened a window for me into the world of European critical theory and confirmed my growing interest in political ideas, making me wonder whether Marcuse was right that history and ideology in the West had come to an end, and that there was no longer any possibility for radical dissent or radical change.

This book contains a selection of my articles and papers on political ideas and ideologies over the last forty years, They have been chosen to illustrate some of the main themes of my writing in intellectual history and the history of political ideas. In the companion volume to this one, *After Brexit*,[1] I have put together a selection of essays from my writings on political economy and British politics. Although there is inevitably some overlap in themes between the two books, they are intended to be self-standing, and hopefully the essays selected give each book an internal coherence. This Introduction is followed by notes on the themes of each essay.

The title essay of this collection is 'The western ideology' (Chapter 1). It was delivered as the Leonard Schapiro Lecture at the PSA Conference in Swansea in April 2008. By the western ideology I mean the doctrines which came to define western modernity. This was not just a struggle of ideas but also a struggle of states to determine who had the right to define what the West was, what modernity was and who best represented it. This struggle took place over several centuries between states and within states. In important respects it is still going on, but at various points in the last two centuries intellectual advocates of liberal modernity have declared that the battle is over and liberal modernity has won. The American and French Revolutions at the end of the eighteenth century were held by many contemporaries to represent the triumph of reason over superstition and liberty over tyranny. Hegel's enthusiasm for Napoleon knew no bounds. Napoleon was the incarnation of the world spirit. His victorious armies were sweeping away the old Europe and ushering in the new Age of Liberty – equality under the law and national self-determination.

It became a settled conviction of liberals in the nineteenth century that the Enlightenment principles which triumphed in the two great Revolutions were the principles which should order politics, economy and society. They accepted that there were many conflicts to come but the basic shape of the modern world had been settled, and there were no higher institutional or ideological alternatives. If human beings wanted progress, happiness and liberty they had to embrace and fight for the implementation and extension of liberal principles throughout the world.

Many contested the liberal juggernaut and in particular the idea that the principles of modernity were settled. Conservatives rejected the new western ideology because they rejected the Enlightenment and its conception of modernity and fought to defend what they could of Europe's *ancien régime* of hereditary right, feudal property and established religion. The tide of change initiated by the spread of capitalism, science and democracy steadily undermined these efforts and led to revolutions and internal reforms. A liberal international order with Britain as its champion gradually emerged, and liberal regimes were established in a growing number of states. But this was not the only battle which liberals had to fight. The nineteenth century saw major struggles between liberalism and socialism and between liberalism and nationalism. Socialism and nationalism both claimed to embody a higher form of modernity than liberalism, and to be the true interpreter of the western ideology. Internal struggles between classes and external struggles between states contributed in the first half of the twentieth century to two world wars and communist revolutions in Russia in 1917 and China in 1949.

From the standpoint of the liberal West and its two leading states, Britain and the United States, the challenges of nationalism and authoritarianism represented by Germany, Austria-Hungary and later Japan were decisively defeated, and the threat of Soviet and Chinese Communism successfully contained. After the Second World War, the United States assumed the leadership of the West and of the wider 'free world'. It organised a new liberal international order under its leadership, and fought a long 'cold war' with the Soviet Union. In the 1950s some US intellectuals confidently proclaimed the end of ideology, at least as far as the internal politics of the West was concerned, and some critics of the liberal versions of the western ideology like Herbert Marcuse agreed with them. But the turmoil of the next three decades then intervened.

A much greater watershed was reached in 1991 when Soviet Communism collapsed, leaving the United States and its western allies as undisputed victors. The proclamations of an end of history were this time even louder, and for a short time hopes for a new world order and 'One World', the regaining of a unified world system which had existed before 1914, were widely entertained. But history has returned again, particularly since the financial crash in 2008 and the austerity and political turmoil which have followed. This time it has taken the form of nationalism, both through the internal challenge to liberal and cosmopolitan elites and the rise of new nationalist great powers who are not eager to work within the rules of an international order they did not shape. The liberal rules-based international order has also been weakened by attacks from within, and by the evident decline in the capacity and the willingness of the United States to lead.

The western ideology has always been contested, and the order it created has often been criticised as tolerating, and in many cases being based upon, systematic inequalities and exclusions. It has also been extraordinarily resilient, in part by being associated with two hegemonic states, first Britain and then the United States. Economic liberalism has been a key component of the western ideology and, although by no means the only strand, at times it has been a dominant strand. Any discussion of contemporary political ideas and ideologies has to recognise the central role it has played in the western ideology, but it is important not to treat the western ideology monolithically as though it was a single doctrine. That ignores the never-ending contests to define and interpret its essential principles. No one doctrine has ever entirely captured it.

The title essay acts as a frame for the other essays in this collection. Some of them explore the character of economic liberalism and why it has been such a resilient form of political economy for two hundred and fifty years, one capable of mutating in many different ways and giving rise to a multitude of different schools and doctrines. The first group of essays explore some of these doctrines, particularly as expressed in the writings of Friedrich Hayek, one of the most important thinkers and interpreters of economic liberalism of the twentieth century. Some of his key ideas are explored in 'Hayek on knowledge, economics and society' (Chapter 4). His ideas on economic liberalism have such power and reach because as a form of political economy they are closely aligned with the fundamental institutions of the market order – households, markets and states. This is explored in the second essay, 'Neo-liberalism and the tax state' (Chapter 2). In this way, neo-liberalism continues much older ideological traditions of economic liberalism. Neo-liberals, including Hayek, liked to claim their version of economic liberalism as the only valid one, But other schools of economic liberalism, including Keynesianism, have always contested this. The complex interplay of ideas and interests in different standpoints in political economy is the subject of the third essay, 'Ideas and interests in British economic policy' (Chapter 3).

Other essays in this collection explore ideas which criticise liberal forms of the western ideology. The sixth essay on G.D.H. Cole (Chapter 6) explores his account of social democratic and Marxist ideas written in the era when both were at the peak of their appeal and influence, and economic liberalism was on the retreat. 'Marxism after communism' (Chapter 5) analyses the impact of the 'end of history' on both Marxism and social democracy, and what either might offer in a post-communist and post-socialist world. 'Social democracy in a global age' (Chapter 7) looks at some of the challenges facing social democrats in an era characterised by increasing economic, cultural and political interdependence. Chapter 8 explores the debate in the British Labour party over whether its purpose was the fulfilment or the rejection of the western ideology.

A very different critique of the western ideology comes from conservative thinkers. The two essays (Chapters 9 and 10) on Oakeshott examine his rejection of socialism but also his sceptical response to many accounts of liberal modernity, including Hayek's, where they involve turning the state into an enterprise to achieve particular social purposes. The final essay, 'The drifter's escape' (Chapter 11), explores strands of political and religious thought in Bob Dylan's song lyrics that reject ideas of progress in human affairs and the notion that politics might serve some higher good.

Intellectual and political influences

None of us can escape the contexts which form us – culturally, intellectually and politically. I was at school and then university in the 1960s amidst all the tumultuous events, both political and cultural of that time. I first became aware of politics through some of the defining moments at the start of that decade – the Cuban missile crisis (1962), the imprisonment of Nelson Mandela (1962), and the assassination of President Kennedy (1963). The shock of Kennedy's assassination was immense. Still at school, I was attending a lecture to be given by Isaiah Berlin at the University of Sussex on Machiavelli. Just before he was about to start a porter rushed in and shouted, 'If anyone wants to know the President of the United States has just been assassinated.' Berlin was impassive and after a short pause launched into his lecture. If we had had smart phones we would all have been on them. I remember nothing of the lecture but the memory of the moment when I first heard about Kennedy has never left me.

The first politics book I remember owning was *Political Ideals* by Bertrand Russell. I began paying close attention to British politics for the first time after the 'night of the long knives', when Harold Macmillan dismissed one third of his Cabinet in 1962, and I then watched with fascination the unravelling of the Government's authority during the Profumo affair in 1963. I still counted myself a Conservative at the time, but other thoughts were beginning to stir.

The first British election I really noticed, although at 17 too young to vote, was in 1964 when Labour under Harold Wilson gained a precarious four-seat majority. Labour's slogan 'Let's go with Labour and we'll get things done' would be regarded as far too prolix by today's spinmeisters, but it captured a national mood and helped end thirteen years of Conservative rule. It was one of the relatively few occasions in its history when Labour succeeded in generating enthusiasm around a message of national renewal. Living through a change of government with all the optimism and high expectations such events generate, particularly in the young, was exhilarating. It was reinforced by Lyndon Johnson's sweeping victory over Barry Goldwater in the US Presidential election of November 1964.

That moment of relative hope and optimism did not last. On going up to Cambridge in 1965, I picked up a copy of the Labour Club magazine *Forward*. It had a US soldier in Vietnam holding a flamethrower and declaring, 'I am canvassing on behalf of the Democratic Party.' I immediately enrolled in the Labour Club, which turned out to have only fifty members, half of whom were Fabians or other kinds of social democrat and half of whom were various varieties of Marxist. That all changed very rapidly. Within two years the Socialist Society, the successor to the Labour Club, had more than one thousand members. The second half of the decade saw intense disillusion with establishment parties and establishment politics, and the rise of radical movements, including the protests against the Vietnam War, the new feminism, and the libertarian counter-culture, all of which particularly attracted the student young, and transformed the way many in that generation thought and lived. The effects for good and ill are still with us. Such bursts of radical energy, which are cultural as much as they are political, do not happen very often. Living through such a moment, particularly when you are young, changes you in ways you do not fully understand at the time. Nothing is ever quite the same again.

I was first drawn into the study of politics through economics, sociology and the history of political thought rather than through political science or international relations. I chose to study economics at university for my first degree, although quite why I cannot remember: as it was not an option at my school, I had little knowledge of what was involved. I had taken A-levels in History, English, and Latin/Ancient History. But economics proved a good choice. In the 1960s the Economics Faculty at Cambridge was still dominated by great Keynesians like Joan Robinson, Nicholas Kaldor and James Meade, and still called itself the Faculty of Economics and Politics. There was no separate faculty or department of politics. The economics tripos was in those days a broad social science tripos, including papers on politics, sociology, and economic history, as well as on economic theory and applied economics. I took papers on British and US political institutions, the British industrial revolution, political sociology, sociological theory, Russian economic development, statistics, macro-economics and micro-economics. Joseph Schumpeter would have approved.

Parts of the course seemed deadly dull, hardly relevant to a world in turmoil or to the much more exciting world of ideas. Only much later did I learn to appreciate the importance of the marginal-cost pricing of road and rail. But Cambridge offered a wealth of other ways to learn and grow intellectually. At the height of the student protests an 'Anti-University' sprang up in Cambridge, a whole programme of alternative lectures and seminars with many speakers from outside Cambridge to provide the extra intellectual stimulus and real world involvement we felt we were not getting from our ordinary courses. Challenging orthodoxies and crossing boundaries is something the young often do, and should be encouraged to do. When Friedrich Hayek was a student at the University of Vienna he spent a lot of his time attending lectures and reading in subjects far removed from what he was supposed to be studying. As he commented many years later, in the University you were not expected to confine yourself to your own subject.

Over the course of my degree I became more and more interested in the historical and philosophical aspects of economics, and in the other social sciences. I was also reading widely in the history of political ideas, but papers in that subject were only offered by the Faculty of History and so were not available to me. After I graduated from Cambridge in 1968, I became one of the first students on a new MA programme in political thought in the Politics Department at Durham, which was taught by David Manning, a former student of Michael Oakeshott, and Henry Tudor, a former student of Herbert Marcuse. There were only five students on the course, which made for an intense and rewarding experience. I studied Marx and Marxism under Henry Tudor in much greater depth than had been possible before, while David Manning introduced me to the very different intellectual world of Oakeshott. On the first day of the course a fellow student, John Gibbins, thrust a copy of Oakeshott's *Experience and its Modes* into my hands and said, 'You will need this.' He was right. I had never encountered Oakeshott in my studies at Cambridge. That was now to change. To be immersed in two such powerful and contrasting all-encompassing systems of thought as those of Marx and Oakeshott had a profound influence on me. Oakeshott came to Durham in 1969 to give a talk to the department, and spent some time with the MA group. I experienced at first hand his personal magnetism and the fascination of his conversation about ideas.

I wrote my MA dissertation on the relationship between Marx and Adam Smith, and then returned to Cambridge with the offer of an SSRC studentship to undertake doctoral research under the supervision of Philip Abrams, a political sociologist and one of the architects of the new social and political sciences tripos. It was typical of the casualness of British universities at that time that I was offered the studentship without interview or even having to specify a topic. I spent the first six months considering and discarding a great array of subjects before finally deciding to study recent changes in Conservative ideas and policy. This proved to be a decision which shaped my subsequent academic career. The spur to this was Enoch Powell. His break from the Conservative leadership in 1968 and his articulation of a radical new vision – against immigration, against the EEC, against Keynesianism and social democracy, and for a politics of national identity and free market economics – fascinated me. It seemed to show the potential for a very different kind of Conservatism than the one represented by Macmillan, Butler, Heath and Macleod which had been dominant since 1945. I worked on this project during the Heath Government of 1970–74, a period of growing conflict, division and looming crisis. The project grew into a study of the governing and electoral strategies of the Conservative party since 1945, the politics of power and the politics of support, and the tension between them which I argued explained why the party was in such disarray and divided over its future direction. This study was published in 1974 as *The Conservative Nation*, and it gave me a research programme which has lasted until the present. In 1970 Thatcherism was no bigger than a small cloud on the Conservative horizon, any more than Brexit was in 2010. But within a few years both had permanently transformed the Conservative party. Powell's legacy for the Conservatives in both respects was profound.

The political and economic crisis of the 1970s was the most serious crisis capitalism had faced since the 1930s. The optimism of the golden decades of the 1950s and 1960s, when economic prosperity had returned and western democracies had strengthened, disappeared. There was a sharp political polarisation and new radical alternatives emerged on both left and right about the best way forward. Edward Heath lost two elections and then the Conservative leadership. Margaret Thatcher, who succeeded Heath in 1975, was to be a very different kind of Conservative leader to any since 1945. Labour moved back into government in 1974 but without a solid parliamentary majority or agreement on how to deal with the problems the British economy now faced.

The crisis influenced my writing in two ways. I continued working on Conservatism and on the ferment of ideas on the right in the 1970s, particularly the revival of economic liberalism and the debate on British decline. The 1970s saw a new intensity in that century-old debate in the British political class. Thatcher was to make the reversal of British decline a key manifesto commitment in 1979. She did not use the slogan 'Make Britain great again', but the thought was the same. At the same time, I made my first attempt to analyse the wider structural causes and consequences of a major economic crisis. I had been collaborating with Paul Walton on Marxist theory and Marxist political economy after we had met in 1968 in Durham, when Paul was studying for an MA in sociology. In 1972 we published *From Alienation to Surplus Value*, which won the Isaac Deutscher Memorial Prize. We devoted the lecture held to mark the prize to an analysis of the rapidly unfolding economic crisis, and this eventually turned into another book, *Capitalism in Crisis: Inflation and the State*, published in 1976.

In 1973 I was appointed to a lectureship in political economy at the University of Sheffield in the Department of Political Theory and Institutions. This was the department which Bernard Crick built. He became its first professor when the department was established in 1965, and David Blunkett (later Labour Home Secretary) was one of his students. When I joined the department there were two professors, Colin Leys and Howard Warrender, and ten other lecturers. I taught courses on the political economy of modern Britain and on Marx and his interpreters. It was a strange time in British universities, with fears being fanned in the media about left-wing cultural subversion of British institutions. A local newspaper discovered that the department was about to be accused on an ITV programme fronted by Lord Chalfont of having been taken over by Trotskyists, and splashed it across its front page. At the time the political enthusiasms of the lecturers covered all the ground from the far-right Freedom Association to Third World Marxism, but did not actually include Trotskyism. The people most offended by the accusation were the Conservatives in the department, of whom there were several. The offending line was struck out before broadcast after the Vice Chancellor spoke to someone in the ITV hierarchy. It was a first lesson in how the British establishment worked.

There were many things wrong with universities in the 1970s, but they gave their lecturers a degree of licence which seems a lost age now. I had complete freedom in what I taught and what I researched, and indeed whether I did any research at all. Nobody checked. Just being a lecturer, teaching your students and professing your subject was considered enough. If you did some research as well and published the occasional article that was a bonus. I revelled in the freedom. It gave me space to develop my teaching and research in the directions I chose and also to spend one day a week teaching political economy to day release classes of Yorkshire and Derbyshire miners, ICI shop stewards, and the Fire Brigades Union. Day release classes are long gone, but I am still grateful to the participants who taught me far more than I ever taught them. This was political economy from a different angle.

The 1980s saw the completion of my study of the politics of decline, published as *Britain in Decline* in 1981, and my increasing absorption in studying the politics of Thatcherism, which was published under the title *The Free Economy and the Strong State* in 1988. My work on Thatcherism was greatly advanced by the twelve articles I wrote between 1979 and 1990 for *Marxism Today*; more than any other journal, this took the lead in analysing the political, economic, and cultural consequences of the new Conservatism which was taking shape. Stuart Hall pioneered this analysis and was the first to call it Thatcherism.

Under the editorship of Martin Jacques, *Marxism Today* was transformed from the rather staid and little read theoretical journal of the British Communist Party into a broad journal of ideas and comment which was lively, eclectic, direct and challenging. It published a wide range of writers with very different political positions, and conducted interviews with politicians including many Conservatives. Martin was a brilliant and exacting editor. He was never satisfied and he always proposed radical changes to whatever you produced. He was generally right. One of the special things about *Marxism Today* was that the journal organised occasional discussion weekends for some of the regular contributors, who included Stuart Hall, Eric Hobsbawm, Bea Campbell, Charlie Leadbeater, Robin Murray, Lynne Segal and Geoff Mulgan. There were some memorable exchanges. One of them was Bea Campbell's very direct and blunt challenge to Eric Hobsbawm on his attitude to feminism. In its relentless critique of the politics of Labour and the wider Labour movement *Marxism Today* was often seen as the intellectual harbinger of New Labour. But while some of its contributors, particularly Geoff Mulgan and Charlie Leadbeater, became actively involved as political advisors to the Blair Government, others, including Stuart Hall and Martin Jacques, ultimately denounced New Labour for its caution in government. It had a project for the party, they argued, but not one for the country, and did not deliver the radical break with Thatcherism they had hoped for.

During the 1980s I also became involved in another significant collaboration, editing *Developments in British Politics* with Henry Drucker, Patrick Dunleavy and Gillian Peele, and later on with Ian Holliday and Richard Heffernan. This was a new kind of textbook and so successful that it became a series which is still going strong. I was involved for twenty years (1983–2003) up to *Developments 7*. Each book in the *Developments* series was an entirely new book with different contributors; this was hard work, but had the benefit that it forced us to keep abreast of the latest research and debates on all aspects of British politics. The idea for the series was the brainchild of Henry Drucker and Steven Kennedy. Steven was an inspirational publisher who was intellectually as well as commercially involved in all the books he commissioned. He made many things happen which otherwise would not and was a constant source of support and encouragement. One of the best things about *Developments* was the often sharp disagreements at the editorial meetings about British politics.

A new period opened in the 1990s marked by some profound geopolitical shifts – the opening of the Berlin Wall, the collapse of the Soviet Union, the reunification of Germany, the end of apartheid in South Africa, and the beginnings of the economic rise of China, India and Brazil. George H. Bush declared a new world order, and it became an era of high globalisation and an economic boom which was to last until the financial crash of 2008. Progressive forces regrouped and began to make advances across the western democracies, starting with Bill Clinton's election as US President in 1992. In Britain, the tide turned against the Conservatives after their fourth election victory in 1992. Labour won its biggest ever election victory in 1997 under Tony Blair. So overwhelming was the triumph that on election night Cecil Parkinson, once one of Margaret Thatcher's key lieutenants, when asked who should be the next leader of the Conservative party observed that at that stage of the night the party had yet to win a single seat.

In the run-up to that election victory attention began to be focused on public policy and reform, and what a progressive political platform might look like, and whether there were alternatives to the neo-liberal regimes of the 1980s. In 1993 I was one of the founders of the Political Economy Research Centre (PERC) at Sheffield. David Marquand became the first director, and we managed to persuade J.K. Galbraith to open it. He told us he would come, but that at his age he no longer fitted into the plebeian parts of aircraft. We wondered if he ever had. The University of Sheffield agreed to award him an honorary degree, which paid for his trip. It was a memorable occasion. Galbraith had an undimmed faith right to the end in a progressive political economy to counter the inequalities which capitalism created.

One of the important fruits of PERC was a new academic journal, *New Political Economy*, established in 1996, the result of a close collaboration with a number of colleagues – Tony Payne, Ankie Hoogvelt, Michael Dietrich and Michael Kenny. It became a focus for interdisciplinary and comparative work on political economy. PERC rapidly established a distinctive profile in research on political economy and public policy, and I became involved in a number of collaborative projects on stakeholding, on assets, on ownership and on the political economy of the company with a group of exceptional researchers and research students. One of the highlights for me was my collaboration with John Parkinson and Gavin Kelly on a Leverhulme project on the political economy of the company.[2] John was one of the most gifted public lawyers of his generation and made an immense theoretical and practical contribution to the reform of company law. He died very young, aged only 48, in 2004.[3]

I also began to write more on international politics in the 1990s. Another PERC collaboration with Tony Payne led to an edited book *Regionalism and World Order* (1996), and this revived a link with Mario Telo at Université Libre de Bruxelles (ULB). Mario and I had first met at a conference on Thatcherism at Bologna in the 1980s and I now began to participate in projects he organised on regionalism, multilateralism, the future of Europe and most recently multiple modernities. Mario's ability to create networks of scholars not just within Europe but across the world is unequalled, and he proved very successful in promoting intellectual engagement between scholars from different countries, different cultures and different intellectual traditions. Debating multiple modernities with academics from all over the world in Macao, the casino capital of China, was an experience impossible to forget.

I still remained very engaged with the study of British politics and in 1997 I accepted an invitation to become co-editor of *Political Quarterly* (PQ) with Tony Wright. Bernard Crick was still actively involved in the journal and the full PQ board had started to meet in the Savile Club in Mayfair, because Bernard was a member and could get a preferential rate. But the Savile barred women from being members and entering the club, so the meetings had to be held in an anteroom just by the main club entrance. When several members of the board objected strongly to meeting in a club which maintained such an archaic rule, Bernard explained that he was fighting hard to overturn it, and in the latest vote had come close to winning. The PQ board decided that the Crick version of the inevitability of gradualism was too slow and moved its meetings elsewhere. The rule is still in force today.

I was an editor of PQ between 1997 and 2012, the period of the rise and fall of the Third Way, the successes and failures of New Labour, the Iraq War and the financial crash. Other members of our editorial team were Jean Seaton, Donald Sassoon, Emma Anderson and Stephen Ball. *Political Quarterly* was founded in 1930 by Leonard Woolf, Kingsley Martin and William Robson, and later editors had included Bernard Crick, John Mackintosh, David Marquand and Colin Crouch. The aim of the journal has always been to publish articles on public policy written in plain English and which deal with issues of political importance. It has always been more than an academic journal and is the better for it. Editing it was one of the highlights of my career, and a pleasure too, particularly because of the opportunity to work with Tony Wright, who had an unequalled grasp of what understanding politics and engaging in politics involved. One of the assets of PQ was the quality and range of the members of its editorial board, and the opportunities which that provided for lively and stimulating debate and disagreement on current politics.

In 2008 a fourth period opened, in which we are still living. The financial crash in 2008 and the subsequent recession shattered western prosperity and confidence, and highlighted the growing power of non-western states. It ushered in a time of political upheaval and economic uncertainty. Neo-liberal ideas were widely discredited but still showed enormous resilience. Austerity took hold and many centre-left parties lost power to conservatives. But austerity did not bring recovery, and many deep-seated problems were not addressed. Political challenges when they did come were mostly from populist nationalists on the right. The liberal multilateral world order began to fragment as leading states, including the US under Donald Trump, began to challenge and disregard it.

I was fortunate in this period to become involved in *Policy Network* and worked closely with Roger Liddle, Patrick Diamond, Olaf Cramme and Charlie Cadywould on a variety of projects, including a pamphlet *Open Left: The future of progressive politics* (2018). *Policy Network* was the living embodiment of the ideals of an 'open left'. It promoted dialogue and discussion on progressive politics in a non-partisan and ecumenical spirit, and built networks across Europe and around the world. The seminars and conferences which these networks organised were noted for the open intellectual exchanges they fostered.

The period since the financial crash has been more reminiscent of the 1970s than the period in between, and my writing has returned to many of the themes and preoccupations with which I started. I also returned to Cambridge in 2007, joining the Department of Politics, where I linked up with some exceptional colleagues, including Helen Thompson, David Runciman, Geoffrey Hawthorne and John Dunn. With them and Christopher Hill I helped to establish a new Department of Politics and International Studies (POLIS). Cambridge is still an amazingly rich intellectual environment. Every lost intellectual cause in the world still has its advocates and devotees in Cambridge if you look hard enough. I enjoyed once again the depth and the eclecticism of its academic culture and supervising some exceptional undergraduates and research students. Cambridge has one of the richest traditions in the study of political thought in the world, and one of the highlights of my time in Cambridge was the opportunity to attend weekly The History of Political Thought seminar and engage with some of its leading figures, especially Istvan Hont with whom I established the Cambridge Centre for Political Thought, strengthening the institutional link between the Faculty of History and the Department of Politics and International Studies. If the old ideal of the university will survive anywhere it will be in Cambridge, although even there it faces formidable pressures.

After retiring from Cambridge in 2014, I rejoined the Department of Politics and International Relations in Sheffield, and became a professorial fellow in the Sheffield Political Economy Research Institute (SPERI), which had been established by Tony Payne as the successor to PERC. SPERI has a wonderful group of young researchers who are all engaged in innovative work which is helping to extend the boundaries of political economy in many different directions. It was good to be able to work closely with Tony again, since we were long-time friends and collaborators on intellectual projects as well as allies in negotiating university politics and building institutions. Tony once said to me that university politics was like white water rafting: highly risky, unpredictable and requiring lots of teamwork.

SPERI was a coming home for me since, in relation to the broad field of political studies, I have always regarded myself first and foremost as a political economist. My research interests and publications have been quite diverse, but a common thread is the attempt to use a political economy approach to study politics, exploring the complex interrelationships between state, markets and households, and the ideas, policies and institutions through which these relationships are expressed. Political economy currently has various meanings, but my own approach has been primarily historical, institutionalist, and comparative, and has also sought wherever possible to be interdisciplinary. I have collaborated with economists, lawyers, sociologists, geographers and historians as well as political scientists and international relations scholars.

British universities and politics as a subject of study have changed greatly over the course of my academic career. When I went to Cambridge in 1965 the proportion of school leavers going to university was 5 per cent. In 2019 it was over 50 per cent. In 1973 I joined a department at Sheffield of thirteen lecturers, all male. During the 1980s, this shrank to eight. Today the department has more than fifty academic staff and its gender balance has been transformed. In 1973 university departments saw their role as concerned primarily with teaching and scholarship, and student numbers were very low, allowing a large amount of individual tuition and support.

The UK higher education sector was fundamentally changed in the 1980s by a number of linked developments – the huge increase in student numbers in the 1990s, the charging of full fees to overseas students, the linking of funding to departmental research ratings, and more generally the application of the new public management doctrines to the public sector by Conservative Governments in the UK in the 1980s and 1990s. All university disciplines underwent often painful changes to fit in with the new dispensation. The changes dismayed many academics, not least disciples of Hayek and Oakeshott, like Kenneth Minogue and Shirley Letwin, who became some of the strongest defenders of a traditional ideal of the university. They intensely disliked the application of neo-liberal doctrines to universities, which, like Hayek, they thought should remain outside the market and beyond the state.

In order to survive it was necessary to adapt. Many academics would have preferred to be left alone to pursue their research and teach their students, but this was no longer an option. It was necessary to learn political skills, how to manage rapidly changing departments and a rapidly changing university environment. The main downside was the time that immersion in the new bureaucracy took. But it had its compensations. It provided me with practical lessons in how politics works in large organisations that I could never have acquired from books.

In the early part of the twentieth century there were only a handful of chairs in the UK in political theory or government or international relations. From very small beginnings politics as a subject has expanded rapidly from the 1960s onwards, and there has been a parallel development of international relations and increasing integration between the two. At the beginning of the twenty-first century, politics has become an established subject in every major international university. At the same time, there have been continuing controversies over where to set the limits to the discipline, between those who want to narrow it and professionalise it, establishing a core of agreed methods and theories, in order to prescribe what can and cannot be taught within it, against those who have wanted to keep alive a broader, more eclectic vision of political science. I have always temperamentally belonged to the second group. The idea of an academic discipline, as Stefan Collini reminds us, is an unstable amalgam of forces.[4] Disciplines are constantly being reshaped and reimagined, their cores disputed. Each new generation challenges some of the ideas held by the previous one, but there are certain principles which need to be observed if a discipline is to stay healthy and preserve the best parts of the tradition of study which it represents. In my inaugural lecture at Cambridge in 2008,[5] I identified four key ones – openness to other disciplines and other approaches; a focus on problems rather than methodology; a balanced curriculum which embraces as many approaches to the subject as possible; and an appreciation of the nature of political reasoning and the limits of politics. I have been lucky to work in departments both at Sheffield and Cambridge which have promoted that kind of ethos.

Notes on the Essays

This book has four themes.

Theme 1: Hayek and neo-liberalism

  1 The western ideology (2009)
  2 Neo-liberalism and the tax state (2013)
  3 Ideas and interests in British economic policy (1989)
  4 Hayek on knowledge, economics and society (2006)

Theme 2: Socialism and social democracy

  5 Marxism after communism (1999)
  6 G.D.H. Cole and the history of socialist thought (2002)
  7 Social democracy in a global world (2009)
  8 The quest for a Great Labour Party (2018)

Theme 3: Oakeshott and conservatism

  9 Oakeshott's ideological politics (2012)
 10 Oakeshott and totalitarianism (2016)

Theme 4: Politics and fate

 11 The drifter's escape (2004)

Theme 1: Hayek and neo-liberalism

This theme looks at economic liberalism and its growing importance in shaping policy from the 1970s onwards. 'The western ideology' (Chapter 1) was delivered as the Leonard Schapiro Lecture just at the moment that the financial crash was beginning to unfold in early 2008, although the most dramatic events were not to take place until September and October. Economic liberalism in varied forms has been central to the dominant interpretation of the western ideology and liberal modernity. The western ideology is defined as the doctrines which have legitimated and promoted the institutions of liberal modernity in the last two hundred years. This essay explores political conditions, such as the hegemony exercised for long periods by first Britain and then the United States, which made this possible. It examines the different strands which make up economic liberalism, focusing on the emergence of neo-liberalism as the dominant form of economic liberalism from the 1980s onwards, and particularly after the collapse of the Soviet Union in 1991 which removed a major ideological and political competitor. It asks whether these political conditions can be sustained.

'Neoliberalism and the tax state' (Chapter 2) was written after the financial crash for a collection edited by Vivien Schmidt and Mark Thatcher, and took shape in meetings in Boston and Paris. The theme of that book was why economic liberalism in general and neo-liberalism in particular had proved so resilient since the 2008 financial crash after so many of its ideas and policies had been discredited. This essay examines the different paradigms which have defined economic liberalism in the past, and the particular novel features of neo-liberalism and its various strands, including the Austrian School, Ordo-liberalism, economic libertarianism, public choice, monetarism, and supply-side economics. It looks at some of the deep roots of neo-liberalism in ideas about the relationship between households, states and markets, and how this relates to its ideas about the company as a corporate household and the state as a public household. The theory of the tax state became a key component of both economic liberalism and neo-liberalism in the twentieth century. This essay develops some of the arguments in my book on the financial crisis, *The Spectre at the Feast* (2009), and anticipates some of the arguments from *Crisis Without End?* (2014).

'Ideas and interests in British economic policy' (Chapter 3) is a much earlier essay. It belongs to the Thatcher period and was first published in 1989 by the Institute of Economic Affairs (IEA) as *IEA Reading* 30, and then republished in *Journal of Contemporary British History* in 1996. It was based on an IEA symposium at St George's House, Windsor Castle, supported by the Liberty Fund, which sought to answer the question under what condition do ideas have a lasting effect on policy. This essay explores the interaction between ideas and interests in understanding the Keynesian and Thatcher eras. It uses three accounts of what is most important in shaping public policy; general doctrines about the nature of society and the role of government, such as Dicey's contrast between individualism and collectivism; economic interests; and historical and institutional contexts. The role of think tanks, expertise, and the competitive democratic process in developing the role of general doctrines and the climate of ideas are discussed, and are contrasted with interest accounts which rely on theoretical insights into the structure of classes or the structure of collective action or the structure of public choice. Both approaches, it is argued, are vulnerable to a critique employing historical methods to reconstruct the actual contexts in which public policy is made.

'Hayek on knowledge, economics and society' (Chapter 4) was written for the *Cambridge Companion to Hayek* in 2006. Hayek is a thinker I first began studying in the 1970s because of his importance to the new 'social market' thinking in the Conservative party, and because of his earlier interventions in British politics when he was a Professor of Economics at the LSE in the 1930s and 1940s. The more I read Hayek, the more interested I became. After he had published *The Road to Serfdom* in 1944 Hayek had become an intellectual outsider. When he won the Nobel Prize for Economics in 1974 many economists were surprised, because he had not published any new economic research since the 1940s. Many liberals derided his account of liberalism in *The Constitution of Liberty* (1960) as going back to the nineteenth century. He was widely regarded as an ideologue pushing an outdated version of nineteenth-century economic liberalism. I came to think of him very differently. The ideology was certainly there, but so too was an innovative account of the nature of knowledge which had huge implications for all the social sciences. This became the argument of my book 'Hayek: the iron cage of liberty' published in 1996. This essay takes the argument further in seeking to reconstruct that aspect of Hayek's work. It examines Hayek's theory of knowledge, and the role which it plays in his writings on economics and society. Hayek argues that the knowledge which members of modern societies possess is imperfect and incomplete, because knowledge is fragmented and dispersed among millions of individuals, because the limits of human reason make many things unknown and unknowable, and because modern societies are as a result complex evolving organisms which cannot be understood or controlled by the normal methods of science. Acting on the assumption that human beings do have the knowledge to control society leads to serious harm. Hayek was critical of all social theories that pretended to such knowledge, including much of mainstream economics. His political pessimism derived from his epistemological pessimism, but the essay argues that he remained trapped in the rationalism he was so keen to reject and failed to apply his pessimism to the interaction of market economies with the natural world.

Theme 2: Socialism and social democracy

The second theme represents some of my writing on Marxism, socialism and social democracy. My engagement with Marxism was extensive, particularly in the 1970s. My way into political theory and also political economy was originally through a close and extensive reading of Marx. One central focus of my work on ideas and ideologies has been to analyse the main doctrines of political economy and their relationship to the ideologies of the modern era. My early interest in political theory was in Marx and his legacy, and this has never gone away, even if later it had to compete with my interest in Hayek. Gavin Kelly, who became a close friend and collaborator, has often spoken of when he started as a research student at PERC in 1993 and noticed with some surprise that my office had a poster of Marx on one wall and a poster of Hayek on the other. My continuing interest in Marx is represented in this collection by 'Marxism after communism' (Chapter 5), published in the *Review of International Studies* in 1999. This article assesses what is living and what is dead in Marxism after the collapse of the Soviet Union in 1991 and the proclamation by Francis Fukuyama and others of a second end of history and the ideological triumph of capitalism. Some of the themes of this essay are picked up and developed in 'The western ideology' (Chapter 1) and also in the essay on G.D.H. Cole (Chapter 6). This essay discusses the importance of the Soviet Union for Marxists and socialists as a living demonstration, however flawed, of the possibility of an alternative to capitalism. It argues that a future for Marxism as an intellectual tradition depends on its ability to transcend the historicism and realism which characterised Marxism–Leninism and return to its classical roots as a critique of political economy which analyses the forces that engender social injustice and inequality. The continuing insight of Marxist analyses, it suggests, can be seen in recent work on the state, accumulation, regulation, hegemony, globalisation and social reproduction.

The second essay under this theme is 'G.D.H. Cole and the history of socialist thought' (Chapter 6). This was the Introduction to a new edition of Cole's famous five-volume history published by Palgrave-Macmillan in 2002. Cole's history covers not only socialist thought between 1789 and 1939 but also, in the later volumes, a history of socialist movements after 1848. Cole was a distinctive contributor to socialist thought himself, because of his opposition to what he called the two centralist creeds of Marxism–Leninism and social democracy. He was a leading socialist intellectual for over forty years and, although forced to make his peace with Marxism–Leninism and social democracy which had squeezed out all alternatives, he was a strong critic both of Soviet Communism and of parliamentary socialism, and his real commitment remained with the decentralised forms of socialism such as guild socialism which he had championed when he was young. He died in 1959, so did not live to see the great revival of interest in these older forms of socialism after his death.

The final two essays under this theme are both focused on social democracy. 'Social Democracy in a global world' (Chapter 7) was written for a *Policy Network* collection edited by Olaf Cramme and Patrick Diamond and published by Polity Press in 2009. It argues that, after being internationalist in the nineteenth century, social democracy became predominantly national in character after the First World War, reinforced by the breakdown of the liberal world order in the 1930s following the Great Crash. It examines how the nation–state acquired a new legitimacy during post-war reconstruction after 1945 within a new liberal international order under the leadership of the United States and with policies of full employment and economic redistribution, and how the era of national protectionism gradually became outmoded because of the push to greater globalisation in the 1980s and 1990s, which restricted the autonomy of national governments. Following the 2008 financial crash, the dilemmas of social democratic governments in balancing the need for global engagement with maintaining national support have become acute.

'The quest for a great Labour Party' (Chapter 8), a piece written for David Marquand's festschrift in 2018, is about some of the ideas and debates over strategy within the British Labour party. It reflects on the party's political strategy and ruling ideas through an assessment of David Marquand's biography of Ramsay MacDonald, which was first published in 1979 and republished with a new postscript in 1997, and Marquand's analysis of the progressive dilemma which MacDonald's life illustrates. MacDonald sought to create a Great Labour Party modelled on the Great Liberal Party of the nineteenth century. This was a party which had a national and a cross-class appeal, uniting many sections of society behind a progressive alternative. He was opposed by those, including many of his former colleagues in the Independent Labour Party, who argued that class interest and class struggle should be the basis of Labour politics. MacDonald started a profound debate over the purpose and strategy of Labour which has recurred in every period of the party's history.

Theme 3: Oakeshott and conservatism

The third theme contains two papers on Michael Oakeshott. As mentioned in the Introduction, I developed an early interest in Michael Oakeshott's work when studying at the University of Durham under David Manning, and I have been intellectually engaged with it intermittently ever since. Oakeshott is much less well known than many other important twentieth-century thinkers such as Hayek, particularly outside England. But he has been an important intellectual presence within the Conservative party, generally recognised as the leading Conservative political philosopher of the twentieth century. Two essays are included in this collection. The first is 'Oakeshott's ideological politics' (Chapter 9), which was written for the *Cambridge Companion to Oakeshott*, published by Cambridge University Press in 2012. It asks whether Oakeshott should be considered as a liberal or as a conservative thinker. It examines the nature of ideology and Oakeshott's insistence that his own positions and writing were not ideological. The essay demonstrates that there are considerable ideological elements in some of Oakeshott's writings, particularly in his essays on the post-war Labour Government as well as some of his later writings, including *Rationalism in Politics* and *On Human Conduct*. The essay concludes that while Oakeshott may be considered a liberal in many of his attitudes, in politics his positions are clearly conservative. His standing as a Conservative thinker is not misplaced.

The second essay, 'Oakeshott and totalitarianism' (Chapter 10), was a contribution to a collection edited by Terry Nardin, *Oakeshott's Cold War Liberalism*, which was published by Palgrave Macmillan in 2015. This essay explores Oakeshott's view of totalitarianism through some of his earlier writings, including an early essay which was published posthumously, 'The politics of faith and the politics of scepticism'. Oakeshott saw the roots of totalitarianism as lying not in the fascist and communist movements of the twentieth century but much further back, in a disposition towards politics which he called the politics of faith. It arose in the early modern era, associated with thinkers such as Francis Bacon. The counter disposition was the politics of scepticism. Oakeshott favoured the politics of scepticism as an antidote to the politics of faith, but he recognised that without the politics of faith the modern world as we experience it could not have come about.

Theme 4: Politics and fate

The final essay in this book stands alone. 'The drifter's escape' (Chapter 11) is an attempt to trace the concept of the political in Bob Dylan's song lyrics. It was first published in a collection edited by David Boucher and Gary Browning, *The Political Art of Bob Dylan*, published by Imprint Academic in 2004. This project arose from a panel organised at the Political Studies Association Conference in 2000 at the LSE by Lawrence Wilde. I attended the panel, foolishly made some comments and was invited to contribute to the book. I have rarely enjoyed writing anything so much. It is included here as a reflection on the ideas and the sensibility which influenced so many in the generation which grew to political consciousness in the 1960s. Dylan's view of politics and the political world is complex and many-sided but generally bleak, summed up in the lines 'power and greed and corruptible seed seem to be all that there is'. The many references to politics which appear in his songs reveal some persistent themes, particularly alienation, and his view that the political world is an alienated world. This is explored through Dylan's sense of a coming apocalypse (particularly in his religious period), his imagining of the political world as a prison, a graveyard, and an Insanity Factory, and his sense that the only way to survive is to become an outlaw. Dylan reminds us of how politics is experienced by most people around the world, and he has not grown any more optimistic as he has aged. His 2020 album *Rough and Rowdy Ways* contains a seventeen minute song, 'Murder most foul', about President Kennedy's assassination in 1963, and the slow decay of America that it set in motion. It brings me back to where I began.

1

The Western Ideology[1]

One of the most striking features of our time has been the ascendancy of neo-liberalism as the ruling doctrine of international and national politics, an ascendancy which has been accompanied by the apparent disappearance of serious alternatives. Capitalism may be teetering once again on the edge of a terminal crisis, but there are no gravediggers in sight. This time around not only are there no gravediggers there are no longer any rival economic systems either.

The moment that announced the present era was the opening of the Berlin Wall in 1989 and the subsequent collapse of communist regimes across Eastern and Central Europe and in the Soviet Union itself. These events erupted with a most dramatic suddenness, and very few anticipated them. Leonard Schapiro, acute analyst of Soviet politics though he was, did not foresee it. In his obituary notice on Schapiro for the British Academy written in 1984, Peter Reddaway quoted from one of Schapiro's last analyses written in 1982 just before Brezhnev's death, where he departed from his habitual caution to offer a longer-term prediction about the direction of Soviet politics:

> The experience of the recent past suggest that there is a strong likelihood that the Politburo, after Brezhnev has gone and the dust of the succession struggle has settled, will contain a strong contingent of members who favour conservatism, consensus, stagnation, tolerance of inefficiency and corruption at home, the continued growth of military might, and a policy of maximum expansion abroad, within the limits imposed by the desire to avoid nuclear collision with the Western powers.

Reddaway, writing in the Chernenko era two years after this prediction was made, commented that it seemed amply justified.[2]

The fall of communism led to an outburst of celebration and triumphalism in the West. It vindicated the long struggle and the risks of the cold war, and the victory when it came appeared complete and unequivocal. The surrender of the Soviet Union was an ideological surrender rather than one forced by military defeat, but it was a surrender nonetheless, and marked the eclipse of the most potent challenger to the liberal world order following the defeats earlier in the century of Germany and Japan. It was hardly surprising therefore that these events should have been the occasion for congratulation. Francis Fukuyama captured the moment with his declaration that Hegel had been right all along, if premature, and that history had now definitely ended, by which he meant among other things that the long ideological civil war in the West was over, and that liberalism had won. There was now no alternative to liberal capitalism and democracy, and no serious challenger left.[3] History, as the authors of *1066 and All That* once put it, had come to a full stop.[4]

The ascendancy of neo-liberalism, however, did not begin in 1989. Its roots go much further back, to the revival of the western economy under US leadership after the Second World War. Already in the 1960s Hayek had proclaimed, 'It is high time for us to cry from the house tops that the intellectual foundations of socialism have all collapsed',[5] and had announced that the socialist century, which had begun with the failed revolutions of 1848, had ended in 1948. The 1950s had witnessed its own end of ideology, hailed by many as the reconciliation between capitalism and socialism. The conservatives, it was said, had accepted the welfare state, and the socialists had accepted that further extension of state power carried too many risks to individual freedom.[6] This compromise was denounced by Hayek as conceding far too much to socialism, and indeed it proved to be premature when hostilities were resumed in the 1970s. The end of communism in Europe, however, had a finality which was hard to dispute, marking the end of an ideological, political and economic schism which had lasted seventy years, and with consequences not just for the struggle between capitalism and communism, but for the deeper struggle between socialism and liberalism.[7] Democratic government and free market capitalism, said Fukuyama, had been universalised.[8]

Neo-liberalism as a term has been most often used by its enemies rather than by its friends, but it has gradually come to be more widely adopted, not least because there is no more satisfactory term, especially given the associations which the term liberal has acquired in the

United States, and also in Britain.[9] Neo-liberalism stands out among contemporary western ideologies in seemingly being untouched by the swirl of relativism, scepticism and postmodernist doubt which has been such a marked feature of recent political thought. It breathes the confidence and optimism of an older style of western thinking in its attachment to universal values, and sports an uncomplicated belief in truth, objectivity and progress. In this it shows its attachment to the West. But it is also western in another way. It celebrates the liberal global order which has grown up under western, and specifically US, leadership, regarding these political and economic institutions of the United States as models which the rest of the world should embrace, and which it will have to embrace if it wishes to emulate the United States.

Neo-conservatives have taken this argument further. Although there is a connection between the two doctrines, there are also crucial differences. Neo-liberals see their project as a confident restatement of the classic foundations and values of liberal civilisation in the contemporary era. These values are universal in their reach and in their scope, and express truths about modernity which may have been obscured or lost in the recent past, but are now being recovered. Neo-conservatives, in contrast, are steeped in politics and stress the primacy of politics over everything else including economics. Neo-conservatives celebrate the triumph of neo-liberalism and the triumph of the West, but they also see it specifically as a triumph for the AngloSaxondom which Nietzsche so disliked, and for its leading state, the United States. So closely did the West and the project of the West become identified with the US during the cold war, that the accelerating trends towards globalisation which neo-liberalism celebrated have been depicted by some neo-conservatives as well as opponents of neo-liberalism as 'Anglobalisation', the projection of Anglo–American values, policies, institutions, model of capitalism, and military interventions around the world.[10] For many critics neo-liberalism expresses the values not of a universal civilisation but of US or Anglo–American civilisation.[11] It is indissolubly wedded to the power and interests of the world's leading state, the United States.

The critics of neo-liberalism sometimes do not move beyond this characterisation, so neo-liberalism is used as an all-purpose term of abuse. But neo-liberalism is more than just an ideological cloak for the interests of the powerful. Its ascendancy also accurately reflects in important respects the way in which the modern world is ordered. Most political arguments are now conducted within a framework set by it. This does not mean that there is a uniformity of opinion or a uniformity of policy in the western world, still less elsewhere. It is obvious that there remains a great deal of difference and diversity. If we are all neo-liberals now, then at least we must concede that neo-liberalism has many faces, among them neo-conservatism, and various forms of social and Christian democracy, not to mention the illiberal democracies and authoritarian systems which have emerged in parts of Europe and around the world.

Neo-liberalism, however, is not just one standpoint among many in the political marketplace, but in part reflects and justifies the fundamental structures which underpin and circumscribe that marketplace. If neo-liberalism were just another doctrine it would be easier to dismiss it, but it also reflects something much more fundamental in the political economy of modernity – the recognition that there are certain characteristics of modern society, such as the extended division of labour, individual property rights, competition and free exchange, which have to be accepted as givens rather than choices. In this sense the main dispute in political economy in the modern era has been settled, and settled substantially in favour of neo-liberalism, with some important qualifications.[12] Many of the critics of neo-liberalism continue to dispute this, but while there certainly remain important choices between alternatives within this neo-liberal framework, few any longer make the argument that there are realistic choices between alternative frameworks.

The significance of neo-liberalism appears more clearly if it is placed in a larger context, that of the western ideology and liberal modernity. By the western ideology I mean the set of doctrines which have legitimated and promoted the institutions of liberal modernity in the last two hundred years. Since the fall of Rome, ideas of the West became strongly associated with Christianity in its different forms, and Christianity remains a major shaper and signifier of the western ideology, but in the modern era liberalism became its main expression. That did not have to be so. The western ideology from the start has been contested, and there have been fierce disputes over who has the right to define it. These disputes have ultimately been settled by who has come out on top. In this sense the neo-conservatives are right. The meaning of both the western ideology and the West itself has been that defined by the leading states of the West. Neo-liberalism is the latest variant of the western ideology in a double sense. It is the inheritor of key parts of the liberal tradition and enunciates its truths as universal truths, and at the same time it is a key expression of the world view of the world's only remaining superpower, the United States.

Modernity and the West

To understand the western ideology we need to understand the idea of the West, and the role which this idea still plays in our politics. This has never been a simple concept. Its meaning has constantly evolved and been contested, and its geographical location has shifted. At the heart of every conception of the West has been the notion of an East, an opponent or rival, which gives the West its unity and identity. The West was always defined against an East of some kind, whether the original Greek distinction between the West of the Greeks and the East of the barbarians, or the distinction between the western and eastern Roman empire, and the Western Church and Eastern Church, or after the fall of Constantinople the contest between the Christian West and the Ottoman East.

As Europe became dominant in world affairs, so the notion of a western civilisation with a unique mission and status in human history took shape. As the first modern nations, the Europeans claimed innate racial superiority over all other peoples. But within Europe there was no political unity and constant struggles between the leading nations for position and power. There was dispute too over where the true centre of western civilisation lay, and which nation could lay claim to be the true representative both of the historical West and of the contemporary West and its future. Which of the European nations best understood the nature of modernity, and the new forces which it had unleashed? There was constant conflict over the meaning of the West and which country was at the heart of it.

Christianity powerfully shaped the West and the character of western modernity. But the Christian civilisation of the West in the thousand years after the fall of Rome was in world terms a relatively backward civilisation. What transformed it into the leading civilisation of the contemporary era, borrowing extensively from the more advanced civilisations of the East,[13] was the coming of modernity, shaped by the West but profoundly altering the meaning of the West, although in ways which only evolved slowly.[14] Modernity is the combined result of three slow unfolding revolutions – in political economy, in knowledge, and in politics. It is the intersection of these three revolutions, which gave rise to capitalism, science and democracy in their modern forms, which have reshaped the world and ushered in a third and the latest stage of human development.[15] In important respects we are still living in the transitional phase of this great transformation, which has been so uneven in its effects across the planet, making it hard to understand its true character and prospects. It is only now, for example, in 2007 and 2008 that for the first time in human history a majority of humans live in cities rather than on the land.[16] By 2030 it is expected to be 60 per cent. China, which currently still has 60 per cent of its population on the land, is expected to reduce that percentage to 25 per cent in the next twenty years.

The United States drew on all the different national experiences of Europe, combining them, and ultimately transcending them. It outdid all the European nations in its pursuit of liberty, equality, and rationality – all touchstones, along with property and Christian faith, of the American creed.[17] Because the United States became the embodiment of modernity in the twentieth century, alternative versions of the West and of the western ideology were displaced, sometimes only after a prolonged struggle. Many of them, even when they had originated within the heart of the West and the western ideology of modernity, were deemed anti-western. The United States in particular was strongly opposed from its very beginnings to the *anciens régimes* of Europe, and to the values of hierarchy, tradition, authority, and inequality which they embodied. But it came to be equally opposed to new ideologies such as socialism and communism which sought to go beyond liberal versions of the western ideology of modernity, as well as those ideologies such as Nazism and fascism which rejected some of its core values. During the twentieth century the US was twice drawn into a global war and fought against German and Japanese militarism, Nazism and communism, in the course of which it was obliged to set out and defend its own conception of a liberal and democratic world order, and seek to realise it through the establishment of international bodies, first and falteringly with the League of Nations, and then after 1945 with the United Nations and the new agencies of multilateral governance.[18] By the middle of the twentieth century every power in western Europe that might have been a rival to the United States and an alternative centre for the West had either been defeated or subordinated to the United States. By the end of the twentieth century the collapse of communism meant that for the time being there was also no power outside Europe that could contest the dominance of the US.

The various historical Wests of the past sometimes made universal claims but had limited capacity and global reach to enforce those claims. What changes with modernity is the development of new capacities to spread and impose western ideas, western institutions, western practices and western values across the whole world. The West's encounter with the rest of the world has been deeply ambiguous in the modern period, and this made attitudes to it deeply ambivalent. On the one hand the West has been associated with universal doctrines promising freedom, equality and prosperity and human rights, and the end of discrimination whether based on gender, class or race. On the other hand it has been associated with the exercise of power, often legitimised by doctrines of racial and cultural superiority, and therefore with empire, colonialism, and many other forms of intervention and domination. Throughout the modern period the West has been a source of both attraction and repulsion for the rest of the world.

One of the key contingencies in modern history has been the outcome of the competitive struggles between the leading nations of the West. These have determined the particular pattern of modernity which has come to hold sway, and in particular the form of the western ideology that justifies it. There was nothing inevitable in this, but the shape of this historical pattern, at least from our vantage point at the beginning of the twenty-first century, is clear enough. It is a history of the building of a particular kind of liberal order, under the hegemony first of Britain and later, much more comprehensively and purposively, under the hegemony of the United States.[19] The original architects of this order were Britain and France, and they remained the key players throughout the nineteenth century. But France lost its primacy to Britain after the defeat of Napoleon and after Britain's emergence as the first industrial nation. This ensured that the type of global order which would be built would be a commercial one as well as an imperial one. The nation of shopkeepers had triumphed. Relations between Britain and its former colonies in the United States were to remain cool for a century, but ultimately the United States was drawn into the commercial order which Britain did so much to construct, and came to see the preservation of this order and its defence against those nations that sought to overturn it as its paramount national interest. The Anglo–American understanding that developed in the early part of the twentieth century reached its zenith during the Second World War, and the assumption by the United States of the leadership role it had up to then mostly spurned.[20]

Britain was never the leader of a united West as the United States was to become after 1945. It had neither the inclination, nor the ideological resources for such a task. It was preoccupied with its territorial empire as much as with its commercial empire, and its universalism was muted. The United States, drawing on its own political tradition suffused not only with English institutions and constitutional principles but also with the Enlightenment language of French universalism, adopted from the start a very different ideological position in relation to world politics. It proclaimed freedom, universal human rights, the right of self-determination, the end of empire. In the face of the Soviet refusal to join the liberal order which the United States was constructing, the United States organised an Atlantic alliance to defend the values of the West. The willingness of almost all European states outside the Soviet sphere of influence to accept US leadership meant that for forty years the West possessed an exceptional coherence and unity, one which it had never previously had, but one which began to fracture quite rapidly once the cold war ended.[21]

It is in this context that the emergence of neo-liberalism as the latest variant of the western ideology should be understood. It is inseparably connected with the continued dominance of the United States in world affairs. The meaning of the western ideology in any era has always been a question of power as well as ideology, and as already noted, the ascendancy of the liberal version of the western ideology has been far from assured. It was also subject to severe challenges in the form of states that disputed the ascendancy of first Britain and then the United States as the leading states of modernity. It was subject to ferocious internal critiques, from conservatives, nationalists, nihilists, socialists, communists, and radicals of all kinds. The liberals themselves have hardly been united. The western ideology accordingly has covered a wide spectrum of ideas and beliefs, and at times has seemed quite incoherent as a result. But despite many vicissitudes western liberalism has proved remarkably resilient as an intellectual as well as a political project, and has now reemerged to define once again the core of the western ideology.

Liberal political economy

From this perspective what marks out the liberal variant of the western ideology is its political economy on the one hand and its association predominantly with the English-speaking states on the other. In terms of political economy what is most significant is the commitment to an open rather than a closed economic system. Globalisation on this account is not a new perspective, it is not a new discourse, and it does not represent a new stage in the development of the global economy. There are particular features about contemporary globalisation which are different,[22] but the promotion of openness has always been a central concern of liberal political economy, and the adoption of this perspective first by Britain and later by the United States was crucial to its success. It means that after the three titanic struggles of the twentieth century, the major challenges to this liberal order have been defeated, and its unity preserved and extended. Many fought to prevent this happening, but they did not prevail.

The consequences for how we think about the western ideology run deep. Rejecting the triumphalism of the end of history John Gray has argued that the ascendancy of neo-liberalism, far from being the liberation from totalitarianism that it itself proclaims, is in fact only the latest example of a rationalist, interventionist, monist creed, the latest Enlightenment project which is doing every bit as much damage as Marxism did, because it seeks to impose one truth, one universal model, rather than recognising the irredeemable incommensurability and incompatibility of values expressed in different cultures and political communities. For Gray it is in the nature of any Enlightenment project that it leads to its attempted imposition by force. 'Post-Christian cults' like Marxism and neo-liberalism present a false hope of unity and harmony when we should be limiting our hopes and learning to live with conflict.[23]

Gray has been much criticised for his view of the Enlightenment, on the grounds that it was never the kind of uniform 'project' that he suggests.[24] Many Enlightenment thinkers were highly sceptical about the capacity of reason to reorder the world, doubtful about the prospects for human progress, and emphasised other values, such as tolerance and consent. But what certainly did emerge during that passage in European thinking that has become known as the Enlightenment was an idea of the future as being different from the past, and a new awareness of the economy as a factor in politics. This last insight became one of the seminal ideas for the thinkers of the nineteenth century, because it addressed one of the central aspects of modernity, the consequences of the trends towards global division of labour for all territorial jurisdictions, including multi-national empires and nation-states.

Liberals have always concerned themselves with a wide range of questions other than economic ones, and many have deliberately set their face against reducing everything to economics, most famously perhaps when John Stuart Mill (temporarily) found to his consternation that utilitarianism, the foundation of modern economics and a vital part of his intellectual formation, no longer had any value for him.[25] But the dominant forms of liberalism have still been profoundly shaped by the conception of economic life which the new study of political economy put forward, and this has affected the trajectory of liberalism ever since. Isaiah Berlin's influential restatement of negative liberty as the essential meaning that liberals attached to liberty, and his rejection of positive liberty as a path which led towards totalitarianism, restated the classic liberal view of Paley and Sidgwick among others[26] that freedom had to be understood first and foremost as the protection of a private sphere of free action and non-interference. Crucial to such a sphere are private property rights, and in this way the separation of private and public, and the acceptance of the sphere of private exchange as the main source of dynamism, innovation and creativity in modern society became established. The understanding of politics through political economy is one of the most essential features of the western ideology. It has been severely contested by rival theories, but in practical terms it has always survived, and has become inseparable from how modernity is experienced and understood.

Critiques of the western ideology

The liberal version of the western ideology has also been subjected to numerous critiques. The thinkers loosely grouped under the heading of the Counter-Enlightenment questioned the faith in reason and progress, and emphasised the intense attachments of national identity and culture against desiccated cosmopolitanism and abstract universalism. The Romantic revolt which played such an important part in the development of modern national consciousness and the construction of modern nationalisms was in part nostalgia for what was being lost in the transition to a modern society and in part a defiant resistance to the dominance of the liberal doctrines of free trade, universal rights and progress in defining the new society which was coming into being. The German distinction between Kultur and Civilisation contrasted the shallow universalism of the French and the narrow-minded utilitarianism of the English on the one hand, and the deep spiritual inner engagement of the Germans on the other.

The Counter-Enlightenment also gave rise to conservative defences of the various *anciens régimes* of Europe, including the British state, which delayed, in some cases for decades, the progress of liberalism and secularism, and the adoption of liberal institutions. The majority of the *anciens régimes* that survived or were restored after the French Revolution were still in existence at the outbreak of the Great War in 1914. For Lord Salisbury and many other Conservatives delay was life, the task of the Conservative being to provide shelter in our time.[27] Such a modest ambition never satisfied nationalists, who wanted not just to delay the progress of liberalism but also to subvert it altogether and to establish a quite different meaning of the West. Conservatives wanted to apply the brake on liberal progress, but nationalists wanted a different direction, one centred upon the nation. Both nationalism and Conservatism became central influences on modern politics, but the

Conservatives could not reverse liberal modernity and the nationalists in the end could not subvert it.

Socialism represents a different case. It too launched a major critique of liberal modernity, often incorporating elements of Romantic and even conservative thinking. But the key aim of socialism, and in particular its more radical Marxist variant, was not to halt or destroy liberal modernity but to complete it. Liberal modernity fell short of its own ideals of liberty and equality and lacked the capacity to achieve them, because of its reliance on institutions such as private property which were the cause of inequality. Socialism offered a different version of modernity, one which went beyond liberalism and fulfilled its promise. Socialists accepted the liberal belief in progress but thought that there was a stage beyond the political and economic forms which liberalism promoted. Liberal modernity was the first step towards a much more complete emancipation of the human species.

These dreams of a society beyond capitalism, based on a socialist political economy, and on a political community beyond the liberal representative state, offering a much more intense form of participation, gave socialism in all its forms its hold on the political imagination through two centuries. The disillusion which has accompanied the failure of the practical attempts to move beyond liberal modernity, both in the form of the various communist regimes and in the abandonment of transformative politics by the established social democratic parties of the west, has seemingly left no alternative to liberal modernity.[28] The position of liberals and socialists on progress has been reversed. Socialists fear it, neo-liberals celebrate it.

A final critique of liberal modernity is not associated with particular political movements or political alternatives to liberalism, but with an intellectual stance, that of postmodernism, which questions the ground on which liberals claim authority for their beliefs. The rejection of ideas of truth and objectivity, and of the existence of universal values and universal truths, of any validity in the ideas of progress, has been a strong current in western thinking in the modern era. Nietzsche's critique of the foundations of western thinking shaped all later accounts, with its emphasis on the dependence of truth upon perspective.[29] The consequences of such an approach within the western tradition have been profound, and have contributed to the rise of value pluralism, postmodernism, and relativism. So immersed in scepticism about everything have the contemporary western academy and culture become, and so addicted to pluralism, that it is a shock to hear again the strident certainties of the western ideology being set out by the advocates of neo-liberalism, seemingly impervious to postmodern strictures. Whatever the cultural and academic fashions of the moment the western ideology articulates something that is reproduced daily in the lives of everyone living in this global economy and the forms of rule and knowledge which sustain it. Postmodernism in its different forms is an important cultural critique of modernity in the West,[30] but for the great majority of people living on this planet, the idea of postmodernity, as a stage of human development beyond modernity, seems premature. Far from having transcended the stage of modernity, most human societies are still in transition to full modernity.[31]

The future of the western ideology

This does not mean we should seek refuge once again in questionable philosophies of history which supply historicist or determinist readings of the past which few find convincing any more. It is rather that we cannot easily dispense with narratives of historical development. We need such a narrative if we are to make sense of where we have come from and where we might be going. Without such narratives, politics in the way in which it has been understood in the modern era becomes impossible. Historical development is not predetermined, its meaning has been continually contested, and has been shaped by many contingencies and choices and unintended consequences, the cumulative effect of which has been to produce the particular pattern of institutions and relationships which characterise the modern era. We need to come to grips with the elusive concept of modernity, and enquire how it has been promoted, and by whom, whether there are many modernities or only one, whether modernity is inescapably western, and what implications that has for other cultures and states outside the West, whether liberalism, particularly in the form of neo-liberalism supplies the horizon of possibility of our current political imagination, and whether the only conceivable version of this western ideology is the one that finds favour with the dominant power in the contemporary world, the United States.

Part of the disquiet with neo-liberalism is that it seems such a narrowing of the potential of western civilisation. This extraordinarily diverse tradition can surely not be summed up by a single doctrine. The extinguishing of alternatives to neo-liberalism has created a generalised mood of despair among its critics. This has led some to denote all regimes whether left or right, democratic or authoritarian as neo-liberal, since all have to operate within the constraints which neo-liberalism prescribes. In Europe, for example, this means that not only the regimes headed by Blair, Schroeder and Chirac, and now by

Brown, Merkel, and Sarkozy are indistinguishable, but also those of China, Japan, Brazil, and South Africa. There are no real differences between models of capitalism, only one uniform capitalist policy which is a neo-liberal policy and laid down through the key international agencies, such as the IMF, the World Bank and the WTO, reflecting US priorities.

A contrasting view is that the days of the western ideology are themselves limited. The extraordinary unity which was achieved under US leadership during the cold war can no longer be preserved. The US has become increasingly impatient with many of its allies, and its policy more unilateralist, now that its position as the sole superpower is unchallenged. Since the end of the cold war, and particularly during the presidency of George W. Bush, doctrines of US primacy replaced multilateralist doctrines. In many areas the US appeared unwilling any longer to act as a hegemonic power within a system of international rules and agreements.[32] If the unity of the West can no longer be preserved, the western ideology will appear more and more an instrument legitimising the role of the United States and its allies, rather than as a set of universalist prescriptions independent of any state.

Critics of the western ideology and the role of the US point out that the capacity of the United States to remake the world in its own image is declining, and that the world is characterised by increasing differentiation of cultures and political systems. There is no necessary convergence on US capitalism and US democracy.[33] The 1990s on this view may have been the highpoint for liberalism. From now on the fragility of the foundations of liberalism will be exposed, and the challenges to liberal order will grow. Rising powers such as China and India will increasingly develop their own perspectives and their own modernities, based on their own civilisations and their own values. They will not feel obliged to copy the West, and they will no longer be forced to do so.

A third view is that the western ideology has narrowed to an unacceptable extent, but that it can still be rescued, by releasing it from its moorings in an exclusively western tradition, and too close an association with the United States. This is the view of cosmopolitan liberals of various kinds, who wish to revive and continue key aspects of Enlightenment thinking, in particular Kant's programme for perpetual peace, the gradual translation of moral norms into legal norms, and the juridification of relationships between states, to cover not just security relationships, but economic, and environmental relationships as well.[34] A great deal of effort has gone into elaborating the arguments for global justice on cosmopolitan principles, and in analysing the potential for new forms of governance, such as the European Union.[35]

Cosmopolitanism has many detractors, as it always has done since Kant first enunciated some of its key principles. There are powerful realist, nationalist and conservative objections to its feasibility and its desirability. It also has the big problem of whether it is simply offering a new version of the western ideology, one that, since it does not change the underlying liberal political economy, amounts to little more than a more humane variant of the western ideology rather than any kind of replacement for it.

There is, however, at least the possibility that cosmopolitanism may be more than just another version of the western ideology. The objections to it have considerable practical force, but decreasing intellectual force. That is because cosmopolitan arguments do address the key problem of our time, the mismatch between the challenges thrown up by the increasing global economic and ecological interdependence of the planet, and the political capacities of our governance arrangements including the international state system. These challenges are not imaginary, and the scale of them is clearly growing. Two of them, nuclear weapons and global warming, pose fundamental threats to the existence of the human species.[36] Others include nuclear proliferation, environmental change, new technologies such as nanotechnology, new diseases, genetic modification of the human species, and global poverty and inequality.[37] All these problems are transnational rather than national in their scope and require transnational solutions, and therefore a huge increase in the collective ability of the human species to reach agreements to tackle these problems.

None of these problems are a product of liberal modernity. It is the particular intersection of capitalism, science and democracy which has given rise to an ever-expanding global market, an ever-increasing rate of technological change, and an ever-rising demand for universal rights as liberalism has promised but never delivered, particularly in respect of gender and race. The solutions cannot be simply technical or market solutions, they have first to be political solutions. To solve them would require at the very least new global public spaces for deliberation, new transnational agencies, acceptance of new international laws binding national governments, and a new global public realm where differences could be accommodated and the basis for consensus and legitimacy for transnational action could be created.

Kant rejected the case for a single world government, wisely it might be thought in view of the history of the last two hundred years. A world government still appears a utopian prospect. Kant favoured instead the building of a league of nation-states, composed of republican states able to trust one another and committed to a set of universal principles which would allow the gradual subjection of international relations to the rule of law. He anticipated the later realist argument derived from Hobbes that for any such project to work it would first be necessary to remove the security fears each nation entertained about its neighbours. Once nations no longer feared they might be attacked, they might be prepared to cooperate on other issues.

Some progress has been made towards a Kantian international order, particularly in the last sixty years, but not very much, and certainly not enough in relation to the dangers which the world now faces. Modernity is only just getting into full stride with the entry of India and China into the global economy fully for the first time. The implications of this change and the additional strain that will be placed on all support systems of the planet will be intense. The idea that these problems can be wished away, or that somehow the vast inequalities and imbalances of the planet which liberal modernity has created can be solved either by US leadership alone, by reliance on the global market, or by retreat into national enclaves or regional blocs is fanciful.

It may also be fanciful to think that they can be addressed by adopting cosmopolitan principles. But notwithstanding the difficulties it would seem our best hope, perhaps our only hope. A realistic cosmopolitanism accepts the continued existence of nation-states as the fundamental source of political legitimacy and identity, but seeks to supplement them with a range of new institutions and public spaces at regional, and global levels. It also seeks a fundamental renegotiation of the terms of the western ideology, to create the basis for a dialogue between all cultures and all civilisations. The way forward is not to impose a version of the western ideology on everybody else and oblige everyone to become western. What is needed is to distinguish between the genuinely universal aspects of the western ideology, those which need to be accepted as the common basis for all societies which make the transition to modernity, and those aspects which are related to particular historical features of European societies. Different cultures have no problem in discussing basic human values and in agreeing what are the most important ones. Such a universalist perspective has been explicit in the UN Charter from the beginning. What is proving much harder is moving to the next stage.

Gareth Stedman Jones, contributing to a symposium on the end of history, listed the problems that remained unsolved, such as global poverty, fundamentalist religion, atavistic nationalism and looming environmental catastrophe, and concluded: 'Any good Hegelian must fervently hope that the World Spirit will take another step forward as quickly as possible.'[38]

In 1914 Leonard Schapiro aged six was on a train journey from Glasgow to Riga, during which a German official entered the carriage and, seeing the nanny trying to warm the boy's feet, exclaimed: 'Cold feet, cold feet! Soon all Englishmen will have cold feet!'[39] The world war soon to erupt was a war between great powers for domination but also a war of ideas, German Kultur against English Civilisation, and the liberal ideas associated with it. One hundred years later that liberal idea is still supreme, although once again assailed on all sides. It is not just Englishmen today who risk getting cold feet.

2

Neo-liberalism and the Tax State[1]

The present period is one of economic turbulence but ideological stability. Despite the scale of the 2008 financial crash, there has not so far been much sign of the kind of shift in the ideas governing economic policy which followed the economic upheaval of the 1930s and the smaller upheaval of the 1970s. The 1930s gave birth to Keynesianism and social democracy while the 1970s gave birth to monetarism and neo-liberalism. But, although challenged by recent events, for the moment neo-liberalism appears to be retaining its ascendancy. How should we understand this resilience? And how should we understand neo-liberalism? These are the questions with which this essay is concerned. It makes three main claims. First, neo-liberalism is more than simply a contingent reaction to Keynesianism and social democracy. Part of its resilience as a set of ideas is that it draws upon perennial themes of classical liberal political economy, particularly concerning the nature of commercial society and the role of the state in a market economy. Second, neo-liberalism is not a unified doctrine, but has several distinct strands, which can be contradictory. Third, one of the most striking contradictions is over neo-liberal attitudes to fiscal conservatism.

One influential way of understanding neo-liberalism draws on Karl Polanyi's account of ideological development in the capitalist era. He suggested that the liberal market economy was created through deliberate policy and state action in the nineteenth century, which destroyed traditional forms of economy and society, and brought, as a reaction, the rise of collectivist and nationalist movements aiming to reimpose political control over the free market and reestablish community and security for citizens.[2] This double movement was played out over many decades and reflected the social and political struggles which defined the modern world. Some recent analyses inspired by Polanyi have suggested that neo-liberalism can be understood as the first phase of a new double movement, with neo-liberalism emerging initially in the 1970s as a reaction to the excesses of the welfare state and Keynesianism. Through the application of its ideas in the 1980s, a new era of free market dominance was enabled. But this would in turn, it was suggested, be followed by a further reaction to curb its excesses and reimpose political controls over the market.[3] On this reading, the financial crash of 2008 potentially signalled the beginning of that reaction.

Another influential placing of neo-liberalism in historical context is present in Peter Hall's argument that paradigm shifts in economic policy, involving major changes in the basic assumptions as well as the settings and instruments of economic policy, are quite rare.[4] The two clear-cut cases of transition from one dominant paradigm to another required a long and painful period of political, economic and ideological conflict and restructuring first in the 1930s, and then in the 1970s. The paradigm of classical liberalism, with its emphasis on sound money, free trade and laissez-faire which was ascendant in Britain, the United States and many European countries before 1931 broke down following the 1929 crash and the subsequent Great Depression. It was eventually replaced by a new Keynesian paradigm which made possible the Keynesian welfare state and different varieties of social democracy and Christian democracy in Europe after 1945. This was the era of embedded liberalism. Different national domestic policies reflecting national preferences and values to secure domestic legitimacy were combined with a liberal international economic order recreated under US leadership after 1945. The Keynesian paradigm was then itself challenged in the 1970s by monetarism, one of the key doctrines of what became neo-liberalism, at a time of renewed trouble for the international economy.

During the 1980s and 1990s 'neo-liberalism' came to be seen as a new dominant orthodoxy, a powerful discourse or set of discourses deployed at many levels making theoretical and commonsense claims about how the economy worked, and increasingly dominating debate on public policy.[5] The crash in 2008, and the profound nature of the dislocation which has ensued, has raised speculation that these events might herald the end of the neo-liberal era and the transition to a new paradigm for public policy. The credibility of neo-liberalism appeared dented for a time after the crash, and there was speculation about a return to Keynes,[6] and the possibility of political and ideological challenges to the intellectual orthodoxies which had dominated since the 1980s. But four years after the crash neo-liberalism appears remarkably resilient, and there are few signs of such a shift taking place. No major alternative to neo-liberal economic policy has emerged, and familiar neo-liberal ideas still supply the everyday commonsense that dominates discourses about economic policy in the media and the political class, and provide the organising assumptions shaping the formulation of policy. Many neo-liberals have been content in this crisis to defend the existing order of things and look for ways to return to business as usual. More radical ideas have come from movements like the Tea Party in the United States who want to use the opportunity of the crisis to down-size the state.

The failure so far of neo-liberalism to make way for a new paradigm has led Colin Crouch to argue that we are living through 'the strange non-death of neo-liberalism'.[7] There is certainly no clear evidence as yet of a new Polanyian double movement, the emergence of a challenger to the assumptions of neo-liberalism. Francis Fukuyama suggested in 1989 that we should not expect there to be a new wave, since neo-liberalism is the synthesis which has resolved all the contradictions of capitalist modernity, and provides a framework which cannot be transcended.[8] There are no serious alternatives left. If there is one day a new Polanyian double movement, it may be years, or even decades away. In the short run the political response to the present crisis may lead to the further deepening of the present paradigm rather than to its overthrow. On this view, which is popular among hedge fund managers, the wave of neo-liberalism is far from spent. The crisis of 1929 helped produce a radical project to create an extended state, one expression of which was the post-1945 social democratic Keynesian welfare states of western Europe. This extended state was challenged ideologically and politically in the 1970s with the emergence of the neo-liberal project to contract and reorder this state. But the neo-liberal project only met with limited success, which is why some of the most influential accounts of the 2008 crash are neo-liberal accounts, blaming the crash on the persistence of the Keynesian welfare state rather than on neo-liberal policies which deregulated finance. On this view, neo-liberalism is resilient because it remains the radical project with most traction in this crisis. The radical wing of neo-liberalism think this crisis is a good opportunity to push further the project to contract the state, not to retreat. The next swing of the pendulum is therefore not automatically away from neo-liberalism. A more radical neo-liberalism is one possible outcome from this crisis.

This essay explores one aspect of this apparent resilience of neo-liberalism by tracing its ideological roots in earlier forms of liberalism. One of the difficulties in considering neo-liberalism is to pin down exactly what the term covers. It is easy to exaggerate its unity and coherence, and lump together a diverse set of ideas and policies, which have many internal tensions. Rather than accept a monolithic account of neo-liberalism as an all-embracing and all-conquering single ideological force, its diversity needs to be acknowledged.[9] It is this diversity that explains in part its resilience. The genesis of neo-liberalism can be traced to a much older set of discourses about the market economy, the household economy and the tax state. It is partly because neo-liberalism draws on these much older ideas that it is so hard to dislodge; it expresses certain perennial truths about the political economy which we all inhabit, and it is this which often gives its ideas the edge. But it does not exhaust the truths about this political economy, and it is not all-conquering (despite the overblown rhetoric at times which has accompanied it) because like its rivals it does not have final or uncontested solutions to the dilemmas of our modern political economy.

Strands of neo-liberalism

Neo-liberalism is commonly used, although not very often by neo-liberals themselves, as a general term which denotes the revival of free market doctrines in the second half of the twentieth century, and particularly since the 1970s. There are a number of strands of neo-liberalism, of which the most important are Ordo-liberalism, the Austrian School, economic libertarianism, the Virginia School, the Chicago School, and supply-side economics. Many of them were already represented at the Mont Pelerin Society, convened by Hayek in 1947, and which has been meeting ever since. This revival of economic doctrines celebrating the free market and seeking to limit the role of government was regarded by some of its early critics as a misguided attempt to revive earlier formulations of liberalism which had been superseded and were no longer relevant to the political and economic conditions of the twentieth century. But in the last three decades of the twentieth century, neo-liberalism furnished a powerful set of doctrines which became influential in many countries, in particular the United States and Britain, but also in many others, including Chile and several other Latin American states, Australia and New Zealand, as well as many countries in Eastern Europe following the opening of the Berlin Wall and the collapse of the Soviet Union.

Many international as well as domestic policies were shaped by these doctrines, in particular over finance and trade and the idea of what constituted good economic practice and good governance. In this way most economies in the international economy were influenced by the new free market doctrines.

Ordo-liberalism was the first form of neo-liberalism. The German Ordo-liberals, such as Alexander Rüstow and Wilhelm Röpke in the 1930s and 1940s, were strong critics of Nazism both economically and politically. They understood by neo-liberalism a political order which combined a free economy with a strong state, and which was subject to the rule of law. The economy should be as free and decentralised as possible, but the state had to be strong and legitimate in order to break interest groups and cartels which formed to prevent markets from working.[10] The Ordo-liberals were not opposed to the state, but they wanted it to be confined to its proper sphere, which was protecting the key institutions which made a decentralised market economy possible. These 'neo-liberal' ideas combined with social democratic ideas of welfare and industrial partnership to shape the moderate and pragmatic policies of the social market economy which characterised the West German Bundesrepublik in the 1950s and 1960s.[11]

The Austrian School and its two most important twentieth-century representatives – Ludwig von Mises and Friedrich Hayek – were implacable opponents of all forms of collectivism and socialism, and warned of the dangers of creeping state intervention.[12] Like the Ordo-liberals, Hayek emphasised the need for strict fiscal rules to keep government limited and to avoid inflation. He developed a distinctive economic theory which treated markets as inherently imperfect because of the fragmented and dispersed character of knowledge, but also as the only possible foundation of a free society. He accepted that a strong state was necessary to safeguard the market order, but he was suspicious of democracy because it allowed temporary majorities to interfere with the principles of a liberal order.[13]

Economic libertarianism is mainly associated with the United States. It includes supporters of the minimal state, such as Robert Nozick,[14] and those who want no state at all – the anarcho-capitalists, such as Murray Rothbard.[15] Economic libertarians argue that individual rights are inherent, absolute and pre-social. They are opposed to the state because it involves coercion of individuals, for example through taxation. They favour the dismantling of most or all of the programmes associated with the modern state, including, in the case of anarcho-capitalists, the military and the police. If individuals require protection from risks of any kind they need to pay for it. Economic libertarians are critical of classical liberals like Hayek for supporting spending to provide an economic baseline below which no citizen should fall.

The Virginia School applied economic analysis to the public sector, arguing that agents in the public sector have the same motivations as those in the private sector, but lack the discipline imposed by markets and competition. This leads to continuous pressure for expansion of the scale and scope of government, and places increasing burdens upon the private sector. The public sector is held to be inherently inefficient and wealth consuming rather than wealth creating. The conundrum of public choice economics is that any policy to curb the public sector requires altruistic behaviour on the part of policy-makers, but the basic assumptions of public choice economics deny that policy-makers can be expected to act altruistically. To solve this problem, public choice liberals advocate the adoption of constitutional rules,[16] such as a balanced budget rule, which prevent governments from running deficits, and which make unconstitutional certain policies, such as wealth taxes, even if voted for by a popular majority. Public choice economics has been influential in the development of the new public management which has reshaped the delivery of public services in the last two decades.

The Chicago School has been one of the most influential parts of the mainstream of modern economics. It views the economy from the standpoint of money and finance, rather than as a system of production or as a political economy. Milton Friedman, one of the pioneers of this approach, developed the monetarist critique of Keynesianism,[17] and more recent exponents have included Robert Lucas, with his theory of rational expectations. The economy is modelled mathematically as though it were a set of financial markets abstracted from any political, social, cultural or psychological conditions, with assumptions of perfect competition, rational expectations and no significant externalities. Policy solutions which promote the greatest possible freedom of market agents are assumed to be inherently superior. In contrast to the Austrian School this strand of economic theory assumes that markets are perfectible, as in the efficient market hypothesis, which holds that markets are rational, making use of all available information and accurately pricing risk. Some of these mathematical models informed the investment decisions of banks in the financial boom which ended in 2008.

Supply-side economics became popular initially in the 1980s. It argues that growth in a capitalist economy is best promoted by cutting taxes, particularly on upper income groups, and freeing business activity from regulation. By boosting growth and making high earners more willing to pay taxes, tax cuts boost tax revenues and therefore balance the budget but at a higher level of output. Spending cuts to balance the budget have a lower priority. These policies were adopted by the Reagan administration and also by the administration of George W. Bush, leading to a rapid increase in US debt, because taxes were cut while spending, particularly on defence, greatly increased. The same prescription is at the heart of the Romney/Ryan programme in 2012, as leading fiscal conservatives in the US have pointed out. Supply-siders have been very influential in neo-liberalism, but they have been at odds with Ordo-liberals, the Austrian School and the Virginia School, who tend to be fiscal conservatives, believing that the first priority of governments is to balance the books.

In the immediate post-war period neo-liberalism, in its Ordo-liberal form, was mainly influential in Germany and some other European countries. From the 1970s onwards, however, new strands of free market thinking began to emerge and neo-liberalism, particularly in Anglosphere countries, began to be identified with the clutch of doctrines opposed to welfare states and mixed economies, and bent on uprooting social democratic aspects of the post-war political economy, which tolerated a wide variety of domestic policies. The growing fiscal burden of the state was highlighted, and linked to the dependency culture fostered by welfare programmes. The political consensus that had lasted since the 1940s in many countries about the proper role of government in a market economy came increasingly under intellectual and political attack. A decisive moment was the endorsement of key neo-liberal doctrines by Margaret Thatcher and by Ronald Reagan, who came into office in 1979 and 1980, particularly monetarism and elements of classical liberalism in Thatcher's case, and supply-side economics in Reagan's. The understanding that formed between these two political leaders suggested that there was now a coherent neo-liberal doctrine which defined the new economic policies spreading from the United States and the United Kingdom.[18]

Neo-liberalism and classical liberalism

Neo-liberalism can be understood in Polanyian terms as a paradigm shift, contrasting the Keynesian era with the monetarist era which followed, the rebellion against the social democratic state, or in Foucauldian terms as a new form of governmentality.[19] But a different way of thinking about neo-liberalism is to understand it as the latest manifestation of much older discourses in political economy, the eighteenth-century idea of commercial society, and the early twentieth-century idea of the tax state. This perspective emphasises the continuities in thought between different eras, rather than sharp historical breaks. The idea of commercial society, for example, which came to preoccupy so many eighteenth-century political thinkers and which has profoundly shaped the political thinking of the modern world, is an essential part of our understanding of what makes this world modern. Istvan Hont has memorably evoked its key themes in *Jealousy of Trade*.[20] He argues that many of the ideas that were developed in the eighteenth century still define the nature of the problems that confront contemporary states. Many of the circumstances and contexts may have altered but the paradigm of commercial society has not been transcended. It is still the intellectual horizon of our world as far as political economy is concerned. He argues, for example, that the debate on globalisation which dominated the 1990s lacks conceptual novelty because it rehearsed themes and explored dilemmas which had first been aired more than two hundred years before.

At the root of this conception of political economy are the peculiar character of the modern market economy and the modern state and the lack of congruence between them. Both have practical and imaginative foundations,[21] but they are different. Markets are founded on exchange between independent owners, the stimulation and satisfaction of wants, the calculation of costs and benefits, the division of labour, the ownership of capital, the maximisation of profit, and the drive for accumulation. They have expanded to connect the whole world and render it interdependent. There are always many markets but imaginatively the market is not complete until it is a world market and equivalence reigns. States by contrast are multiple. Each state claims a particular jurisdiction and relates to a particular national community. Its practical foundations are securing internal order and external defence, raising taxes and promoting the prosperity and welfare of its citizens. Its imaginative foundations derive from its unitary form as a fictitious person, and its indirect representation – its claim to represent its people as a community of fate.

Markets and states become locked together because the benefits of trade are such that no state can forego them. No state can afford to put itself outside the international trading system, but the consequence of remaining within is a ceaseless struggle to compete with other states and to emulate the most successful. This constrains what states can do, but if they are successful it also opens great opportunities to them and to their citizens. It provides states with the capacities and resources which they need to defend their national territory from attack, and to expand it when the opportunity arises. As states became more dependent on one another this did not necessarily mean they became more peaceable. It could also mean they became more capable and more willing to wage war. During the nineteenth century Britain, as the leading industrial and commercial state, broke new ground by moving to complete free trade, making itself dependent upon the international economy by abandoning self-sufficiency in food and later many other things as well. Britain maintained its free trade policy right up to and even into the First World War, despite its leading rivals imposing large tariffs against British goods. For most of the nineteenth century, Britain became the country to emulate – as Marx explained to his German readers, English development was not something they could ignore. They would be obliged to follow and compete. Jealousy of trade was at the foundation of modern conceptions of development, encouraging poor and less developed countries to catch up with rich ones, and become developed.

As the country that had to be emulated Britain was in a position to set the rules of the international economy, and duly did so, from the gold standard and its associated monetary and fiscal rules, to rules on accounting, shipping, insurance, finance and contracts. Britain's espousal of liberal free trade rules were proclaimed as universal rules, but also had the advantage of benefiting Britain's particular interests, a fact which was not lost on critics. Friedrich List accepted the intellectual case for free trade, opposed its adoption when there was such disparity between states in terms of their economic development. In such circumstances, free trade only served the interests of the strongest and most developed states.[22]

By the middle of the nineteenth century, liberal political economy had been fashioned into a powerful set of arguments and policy prescriptions. Political economy and economic analysis may since have parted company, but writing, argument and discourse within the paradigm established in the eighteenth century have continued up to the present, because much more than economic analysis this paradigm still captures the essential features of the political and economic context in which economic policies are formulated and debated. Neo-liberalism can be understood as the latest manifestation of the liberal political economy favoured in nineteenth-century Britain. At that time it was distilled into a set of principles which included free trade, sound money, and laissez-faire, and which became the organising assumptions of British financial and economic policy, and through Britain's example became the organising assumptions of many other states as well.

Three types of household

Since its origins political economy has always been predominantly *liberal* political economy, sometimes with national and socialist variants and critiques. It has always been embedded within the institutional matrix of household, market and state. The distinction with which we are most familiar is that between the market economy and the state, but this ignores the original meaning of economy, the economy of the household. Three important meanings of household need to be distinguished – the family or individual household, the corporate household, and the public household. These forms of household are distinct from the concept of the market economy, or catallaxy as Hayek preferred to call it. Hayek invented the term catallaxy, from the Greek verb *katallattein*, meaning to exchange.[23] He did so because he was critical of the term economy, with its roots in Aristotle's concept of *oikonomia*, the management of the household. Such an economy meant an enterprise with a single purpose, directed from the centre by a single will, involving sharing, planning, allocation, and distribution. Hayek did not dispute that there were households in this sense, but he did not accept that this was an adequate way to capture what was essential about the market order. Its basic principle was that it did not have a single purpose, but served many purposes, and therefore could not have a single directing will in control of it. The point of a catallaxy was precisely that it was coordinated through a set of general rules, which did not prescribe behaviour, but left economic agents free to engage in whatever activities and contracts they liked. The catallaxy might still be made up of a multitude of households, but it was organised on a quite different principle from them, and if this principle was infringed then the benefits that came from trade were put at risk. For Hayek and many other economic liberals the great problem of the modern political economy which Britain had pioneered was that the secret of its success was not fully understood, and that governments would seek to intervene to manage it as though it were a household, with a single purpose, and in doing so would kill the springs of prosperity and enterprise.

One of the reasons for this was the continuing hold of the classical conception of the household. Managing a household meant planning, allocating and distributing resources. It implied a central directing will, and the direct consideration of fairness and welfare in decision-making. The traditional household was also associated with notions of economising and therefore being economical, two terms still very much in daily use. To economise means to cut costs, to stop doing things, or to do the same with less. Managing a household is associated also with balancing expenditure against income, and a particular set of virtues – prudence, sobriety, accuracy, thrift, frugality. Households like these are the rock on which sound finance and productive enterprise are to be built in the liberal imagination. Hayek would not deny this. Ideas of fairness and justice may have their place in the family household, since it is potentially an arena of sharing, of altruism, of friendship and love, of personal relationships (which can also be despotic and exploitative). The contrast is with the catallaxy, characterised by impersonality, decentralisation, the observance of general rules, coordination through prices, connections over vast distances. In this way a utilitarian sociability is established, which becomes a positive sum game for all the participants.

The family household remains a very important part of contemporary political economy, although not as important as it once was, because most economic production in developed economies is no longer sited in families. But families are still essential in nurturing and supporting family members, through unpaid domestic labour, enabling their members to be participants in labour markets, and supporting those who are not able to be. They are also a key site for consumption, not least of financial services. But two other types of household have become increasingly significant in contemporary liberal political economy.

The first are corporations. In the eighteenth century these were confined to state-created bodies such as the East India Company, which were granted a particular trading monopoly. In other cases of corporate enterprise liability was unlimited, which kept corporations small and fragile. All the leading political economists of the eighteenth century, including Adam Smith, strongly supported unlimited liability as a way of keeping entrepreneurs honest and accountable. During the nineteenth century as the scale of industrial enterprise increased, so this restriction increasingly hampered major investment projects such as the railways. There was strong pressure for legislation to allow limited liability, and eventually this was passed in the 1860s.[24] It was one of the most significant reforms of property rights in modern capitalism, was widely copied, and led directly to the rise of the corporate economy, and the dominance of the international economy by the great corporate giants of the modern era.

The modern corporation has become a key and much neglected third party in the relationship between states and markets.[25] Companies themselves are not catallaxies, despite a number of attempts by economists to theorise them as such.[26] Rather they are run as economies, as households, subject to a single purpose and directing will, and with their own internal mechanisms of distribution and allocation and planning. They are strategic actors operating within the market catallaxy and within national states, and seeking to shape both to their advantage. States, if they wish to build up their capacity and increase their competitive advantage, must support their leading companies and enable their expansion, while at the same time seeking to attract foreign companies to set up production facilities and distribution networks within their jurisdiction. Tax regimes, regulatory regimes, financial regimes must all be adjusted to ensure that a country is 'open for business'. In this way, jealousy of trade has also become jealousy of investment.

The tax state

A third type of household which is important in understanding contemporary political economy is the public household. This is an old way of thinking about the state, but one which has also been neglected, until Daniel Bell revived the term in an article in *The Public Interest*, subsequently reprinted in his book *The Cultural Contradictions of Capitalism*.[27] He distinguishes between the economy of the domestic household, in which production and exchange are regulated by a shared conception of the common good, and resources are distributed according to some conception of need, and the economy of the market, in which production and exchange are regulated by price, and ends are not common but individual. Wants replace needs as the criteria for determining how resources are allocated, and there is rational and precise calculation of the costs and benefits of different options, and the return on investment. These distinctions are also embedded in the idea that needs are satiable and therefore limited, while wants are insatiable and unlimited. This is one of the sources of hostility to modern markets and to the idea of catallaxy, captured in Aristotle's notion of chrematistics – acquisition that is unlimited and directed to selfish material gain, contrasted with the sober, prudent management of household finances. Chrematistics came to be associated with finance, with usury, the charging of interest, the making of money from money, inspiring a horror and distaste which recurs among all the cultural critics of capitalism on both left and right, and reappears in contemporary politics in concerns with bankers' bonuses and the reckless behaviour of the investment banks.

Bell sees the public household as arising originally to perform certain functions for the new commercial society. There were some common needs which only a public body could discharge. These public goods included defence against external attack, enforcement of law, protection of property rights, and guaranteeing stable money. Different states added other functions at different stages. For the United States Bell argues that the public household was enlarged by three key developments in the course of the twentieth century. These were: first, the adoption of a normative economic policy from the 1930s onwards, which involved the US federal government becoming involved in the direction of the economy and developing plans for allocation, redistribution, stabilisation and growth; second, commitment to substantial investment in science and technology, spurred in part by defence needs and the strategic competition with the Soviet Union, but also to enable US corporations to retain their industrial and commercial leadership, and to permit new sectors to emerge; and third, the normative social policy which appeared in the 1960s and is devoted to the redress of social and economic inequalities. This has encouraged the development of new welfare programmes, a focus on human capital, and the emergence of an entitlement culture associated with human rights.

Bell argues that the modern state was always a public household, different from the market economy, and organised on different principles. What has happened more recently is that it has expanded far beyond the very limited functions which were expected in the past. The modern expanded state he observed in the 1980s threatened to absorb both the private family household and the corporate households through the increasing scope of its regulation and the increasing enlargement of its capacities, including its capacity to tax. In this way it becomes an arena for the satisfaction of private wants, which, since they are insatiable, threatens the basis of commercial society and its separation from the state.

Together with the idea of commercial society it is the idea of the tax state which has been most important in shaping neo-liberalism. One of the earliest analyses of the tax state and its implications was made by Joseph Schumpeter at the end of the First World War. It became a common theme in much neo-liberal, libertarian and conservative argument from the 1970s up to the present, and underpins arguments for lower taxes and lower spending. As the state expands under pressure from private households, both individual and corporate, to take their interests and needs into account, so it intrudes more and more on commercial society and risks restricting the freedom of the catallaxy, by making discretionary interventions rather than relying on general rules. In his article published in 1918, 'The crisis of the tax state', Schumpeter addressed the problem of fiscal policy in the wake of the financial, industrial and economic collapse of Austria–Hungary at the end of the First World War.[28] He argued that, 'the public finances are one of the best starting points for an investigation of society, especially though not exclusively of its political life.' He quoted the socialist economist, Rudolph Goldscheid, that, 'the budget is the skeleton of the state stripped of all misleading ideologies.'[29] Schumpeter argued that the tax state had been very important in the development of commercial society but had now acquired its own momentum.[30] Once the state existed as a social institution becoming staffed by people who identified their interests with the state, and once it had become recognised as essential by citizens for the services it provided, then the state can no longer be understood just from the fiscal standpoint. Taxes created the modern state, but once formed the state begins to extend its tentacles into 'the flesh of the private economy'. It is this intrusion into the private economy which Schumpeter sees as a particular modern problem, which has to be dealt with if the tax state is not to collapse, bringing down with it commercial society and the capitalist entrepreneur. The balance between the two had to be restored, but in the circumstances of 1918 it looked extremely difficult. For Schumpeter the problem was the general loss of faith in capitalism, the undermining of its legitimacy, which made its survival doubtful. But he also saw clearly that the tax state and commercial society were irrevocably intertwined.[31] The problem for the tax state was that the people would come to demand ever higher public expenditures and that the tax state would lose its connection with the real economy and the self-interest of individual economic agents. The productive base would start to shrink, exacerbating the problems of balancing the budget. The difficult of keeping the tax state anchored in economic reality would grow.

The tax state and commercial society, Schumpeter's 'public economy' and 'private economy' did survive, but he anticipated the later concern that would be voiced about the capacity of the public economy to enlarge itself continually at the expense of the private economy, to invade its sphere, and ultimately to destroy it. The implication from Schumpeter's analysis is that the tax state can only survive if it nurtures rather than supplants the private economy from which it draws its strength. This has been a central concern of liberal political economy in the last hundred years: how to give the state sufficient strength to provide the legal and institutional framework and the wider support which commercial society needs to prosper, without allowing an unchecked expansion of state power and public programmes. It becomes a preoccupation of Ludwig von Mises and his strand of the Austrian School, and particularly of Hayek.[32] If both the private economy and public economy are seen as 'economies', as households, citizens may be persuaded that the private economy is too anarchic, too wasteful, too inefficient, and that the rational bureaucratic planning of the public economy is inherently superior. The private economy has to be understood as a catallaxy which is the foundation of the public economy and not subordinate to it, making one of the prime tasks of the state the safeguarding of the character of the private economy as a catallaxy in the face of bureaucratic and democratic encroachments upon it.

Fiscal conservatism and economic crisis

The growth in the size of the public household in commercial societies in the last hundred years (in the case of the UK from below 10 per cent to above 40 per cent of GDP) fundamentally altered the politics of the crises which periodically interrupt economic progress. The response to crisis had always been governed by fiscal conservatism, the liberal principles of sound money and balanced budgets which were at the heart of British fiscal policy in the nineteenth century, and were widely regarded as the reason for the remarkable record of fiscal stability and continuity which the British state had secured. Where other states had run up huge debts and had had to default, British credit was unmatched. Although its national debt had been 250 per cent of GDP because of the costs of financing victory in the Napoleonic Wars and remained above 100 per cent throughout the nineteenth century, Britain had no trouble financing its debt, and reducing it gradually through the Sinking Fund. The debt rose again as a result of the costs of the First World War, but the British state responded in the 1920s by very severe spending cuts, the 'Geddes axe', proportionately much deeper cuts than anything contemplated today. The return to the gold standard in 1925 at the pre-war parity of $4.86 was denounced by Keynes because it required a further massive deflation of British costs, a lowering of British wages in order to make British goods competitive in international markets. It was the immediate cause of the miners' strike and then the General Strike. The adjustment needed to restore the gold standard was loaded on to private households. Following the crash on Wall Street in October 1929, the minority Labour Government in Britain had to grapple with the rising tide of unemployment and financial collapse across Europe. The Chancellor of the Exchequer, Philip Snowden, was a socialist but a Gladstonian Liberal when it came to public finance. Socialism he kept insisting had to be paid for, and the health of the private economy came before any schemes of redistribution. His policies to balance the budget brought down the minority Labour Government and forced Britain off the gold standard.

A similar denouement occurred in the United States. Following the Great Crash, the US Treasury under Andrew Mellon followed a policy which was the orthodox solution for dealing with a financial crisis. The basic problem was seen as the misallocation of resources which had occurred during the boom of the 1920s. The fictitious values which it had created needed to be destroyed, and as quickly as possible, through a sharp deflation to ensure a rapid and soundly based recovery. If governments intervened and tried to prevent the market destroying the inflated values which had been created in the boom, they could only do so by distorting economic activity and risking inflation, paving the way for a further and more damaging collapse in the future. For Mellon the good thing about a recession was that assets returned to their rightful owners. His advice to Herbert Hoover as the slump deepened was to liquidate labour, liquidate stocks, liquidate the farms, liquidate real estate, and purge the rottenness out of the system. This liquidationist approach was to be held responsible by both Keynesians and by monetarists for turning the slump into a depression. It led to governments taking a very different response to major financial collapse.

The solution to the crisis of the laissez-faire state led to the abandonment or at least relaxation of the rules of fiscal conservatism. The extension of the state took many forms, but one of the most familiar was the Keynesian welfare state. The important contribution of Keynesianism was less the specific rules for the conduct of fiscal policy which it introduced, as the political assumption that the state had a responsibility to manage the economy to produce economic growth, full employment, and stable prices, and to provide for the social and economic security and well-being of its citizens. These organising assumptions established a presumption in favour of increasing state powers and state funding to solve social and economic problems. With rapid post-war economic growth, the new balance between state and market appeared to be both manageable and superior to what had gone before, and the new model was much celebrated.[33] But by the end of the 1960s economic growth was beginning to falter, and both unemployment and inflation began rising. This gave neo-liberalism its chance.

The policy message of neo-liberalism appeared clear. There should be a return to the principles of fiscal conservatism in order to curb the growth of the state and check inflation. Hayek and Friedman could agree about the goal even if they disagreed about the means. Neo-liberals also insisted that domestic policy should be subordinated to the requirements of the international market. This meant focusing on adjusting and adapting domestic institutions to improve competitiveness and efficiency. A policy package of monetary targets and supply-side reforms, including tax cuts, flexible labour markets, privatisation, and light touch regulation became the standard neo-liberal prescription for countries wishing to prosper in the international economy and receive aid and credit. The discourses around these policies became entrenched not just in national governments but also in international agencies and organisations, including the World Bank and the IMF, the OECD, and the European Union. Austerity packages to eliminate deficits and bring down debts, and structural reforms to increase productivity and growth have become standard, and they have remained the default policy options after the crash, although tempered by the need to indulge in extraordinary measures to keep the banks afloat.

The 2008 crash occurred with neo-liberalism in the ascendancy, and most government operating, in some cases reluctantly, within a neo-liberal framework. It provided an opportunity for governments to endorse the principles of fiscal conservatism and rein back the state. Despite much rhetoric to this effect, however, governments have been slow to move in this direction. They have been more concerned not to make the mistakes that were made after 1929. Keynes and Hayek had clashed then over the best policy to deal with a crisis in the tax state and in the market economy. Hayek remained convinced by the experience of the response to 1931 that the only way to preserve the catallaxy was to return again to rules which could not be set aside by governments. In the 1970s, the era of stagflation in the world economy and the second great economic crisis since 1929, it was often argued that Keynesianism had been discredited, and that the rise of monetarism and the doctrines of neo-liberalism represented a repudiation of the enlargement of the public household which had occurred since the 1930s. But the paradox of neo-liberalism is that while it has restructured the state since the 1980s, nowhere has it significantly reduced it. Many neo-liberal governments have raised rather than lowered public spending. The distribution of benefits may be different, but the tax state is alive and well under neo-liberalism and continuing to advance.

It was appropriate therefore that many of the responses in 2008 should have had a distinctly Keynesian flavour. Many American conservatives were strongly opposed to the bailouts and the fiscal stimulus announced by Hank Paulson and George W. Bush, and continued by Barack Obama. Many of them, particularly in the Tea Party, are intent on rehabilitating Andrew Mellon, arguing that his supply-side approach to taxation in the 1920s and his balanced budget approach to fiscal policy were correct, and that it is the New Deal which is responsible for America's current difficulties and ever-expanding debt by making possible the growth of big government and the culture of entitlement and dependency. But so far no government has been elected in a western democracy prepared to balance the budget by drastically reducing the size of the state. Too many people have too many entitlements which cannot be touched.

Although many of the principles of the old 'sound money' policies have been abandoned much of the rhetoric of the older conception of the public household remains in the new politics of austerity which has established itself almost everywhere. One of the most familiar arguments is the analogy repeatedly drawn between the finances of the public household and the finances of the private household. After 1931 it was discredited by Keynesian arguments. However, these have never been easy to communicate to citizens, compared to the simple idea that the state should balance its budget just like the individual household must balance its budget, cutting expenditure to match income, living within its means, paying down its credit card. A recent idea which has the same lineage is the notion that the public household should be treated as a cost centre, its revenues and its spending ring-fenced and made to balance. What such images wish to deny is that the state is a household very different from the private household because it has the ability to borrow, to tax and to print money. It is these powers which the old liberal political economy sought to bottle up, and it is these powers which Keynesian political economy is accused of unleashing. It accounts for some of the deep hostility to Keynesianism, treated by some of its critics as speculative public finance which substituted judgement and discretion for firm rules.

Yet despite this, Keynesian pragmatism and discretion are still alive and well in Britain and the United States. George Osborne, the UK Chancellor after 2010, did not reverse the major stimulus and the bailouts which rescued the British financial system in 2008. Barack Obama went further in adding to the stimulus, although not by enough to satisfy Keynesian critics like Paul Krugman.[34] In the UK, the Coalition Government used the discourse of austerity and moral proprieties of fiscal conservatism to great effect,[35] but never attempted to match the rhetoric of fiscal conservatism with policies which might deliver it. Radical alternatives were disarmed, because while these governments had many fiscal critics on their right, who rehearsed radical economic libertarian arguments of their own, there were many fewer voices providing a positive case for the public household. The resilience of neo-liberalism reflected a widespread appreciation among citizens that something must be done about debts and deficits in the public household, on the understanding that core entitlements were not seriously threatened.

It was rather different in the eurozone, where a much more Hayekian or Ordo-liberal policy was followed. The fiscal compact which had been agreed between the members of the eurozone and was designed to save the monetary union imposed very tight fiscal rules on permitted deficits which if implemented implied a deeply deflationary policy of austerity, forcing all members of the eurozone to cut their spending and reduce their costs in order to stay abreast of the most productive economy, Germany. Although the eurozone (like the EU) is a polity, it is not a state and has no demos, which made securing legitimacy for this policy of austerity seem insuperable to most observers. The eurozone needs a public household of the Keynesian kind if it is to be acceptable to all the members, but the only public household which Germany seems prepared to tolerate is firmly Ordo-liberal. Despite their desire to emulate Germany and maintain competitiveness, the strains on many of the individual states to live within these rules are too great. Either the attempt to create this technocratic economic government will be given up, or a much more far-reaching integration will be necessary, which will also transform the nature of the European Union, involving a much larger EU budget (currently it is only 1 per cent of GDP compared to approximately 20 per cent for the federal government in the United States). If this is not done, European states will seek to protect their own private economies – including private and corporate households – by deploying the resources and capacities within their separate public households. This is where states remain very important. If the crisis is extreme enough they can choose to reorganise and restructure all their household economies – private, corporate and public – in order to remain competitive within the wider international catallaxy. The politics of crisis lays bare once more the essential lineaments of our modern political economy and the perennial dilemmas it poses for states.

Fiscal conservatism can therefore be seen as a way of holding the line, of trying to restore the balance between the market economy and the public household which existed before the crisis, and loading the costs on to the private households. Neo-liberalism appears resilient because fiscal conservatism is the default position to which states return at times of crisis. The congruence between markets and states has to be restored in ways which allow growth to resume. But in order to make sure that occurs, neo-liberalism can sanction far-reaching intervention by the state to restructure individual, corporate and public households. For an older liberal political economy and for the Hayekian strand of neo-liberalism fiscal conservatism is not a tactic, but an unbreachable set of rules. For many contemporary neo-liberals, however, from Ben Bernanke to Mervyn King, the reverse is true. Tim Geithner and George Osborne alike have been urging the eurozone to reduce austerity and promote quantitative easing through the issuing of eurobonds. It is one of the many paradoxes of this crisis that the EU, in this respect at least, should appear more Hayekian than Anglo-America in its response to the crisis.

The resilience of neo-liberalism lies in the fact that it is more than a doctrine of macro-economic management which can, when circumstances change, be discredited. Neo-liberalism is rooted in an understanding of the twin imperatives – the commercial society and the tax state – which continue to define our political economy. The central tension in neo-liberalism is that, while it arose as a critique of the extended social democratic tax state which had grown up in that era, it has not yet found ways to reduce significantly the size of the tax state.[36] One of the results has been the explosion of credit and debt, which led inexorably to the financial crash. Fiscal stimulus and fiscal austerity have been variously employed to contain the problems created by the crash, but they do not offer lasting solutions. Governments simply hope that growth will return at some stage, as it always has. But the longer it is delayed the more the resilience of neo-liberalism will be tested, by political movements on both the left and on the right. This is already beginning to happen in Europe, but still only in a modest way. What is also possible is that neo-liberalism itself may take a radical turn and generate programmes which seek through the adoption of flat taxes, for example, and major reductions in state spending to redraw radically the lines between the market and the state. Despite the rhetoric of the 1980s this has not really been attempted so far in the neo-liberal era. Neo-liberals in practice love the extended state, or at least certain parts of it. That is why supply-side doctrines advocating tax cuts without spending cuts are so beguiling. Neo-liberals think of themselves as fiscal conservatives, but many of them in practice are far from that. This ambivalence makes neo-liberalism very flexible and helps explain its resilience. It has many tunes to play. But it also points to its limits.

3

Ideas and Interests in British Economic Policy[1]

The relative importance of ideas and interests in shaping economic policy has been much debated. One influential position, associated with Dicey, argues that public policy in each age is shaped by general doctrines about the nature of a society and the role of government. Individualism, which dominated the nineteenth century, was supplanted by collectivism in the twentieth, only for collectivism in its turn to be challenged by the revival of doctrines of economic liberalism in the 1970s and 1980s. An alternative tradition, represented by both public choice and Marxism, rejects this account of the formation and the development of public policy, emphasising instead the role of interests and explaining how policy evolves, rejecting ideological and idealist accounts. A third tradition criticises the other two for being reductionist, which prevents them from analysing the complexity of the historical and institutional contexts in which economic policy emerges.

The dispute about the relative importance of ideas and interests in the shaping of policy and events is among the oldest in political science. Since we can only know the world through concepts, the real opposition is not between ideas and interests but between two kinds of ideas. Interests do not exist in some substratum of human experience which is devoid of concepts. What individuals desire, intend, value and need are what constitute their interests.[2]

The problem in political science has always lain in determining exactly what is involved in the different dimensions of interest, and how these are related to doctrines and other forms of intellectual knowledge which arise from systematic reflection on human experience. Doctrines in this sense are contrasted with the practical knowledge which is the basis of interests and of social life.

If all intellectual knowledge remained reflective it would be removed from practical experience and would have no influence on events. But intellectual knowledge, particularly if not exclusively in modern times, continually overflows its boundaries and has become an instrument of considerable power in the realisation of interests. This is most apparent in the case of the applications of scientific knowledge, but modern rationalism also extends to the design and evaluation of social and political institutions.

In the study of society, however, there has never been the kind of intellectual consensus that some of the physical sciences have enjoyed. As a consequence the evolution of economic policy, for example, is sometimes presented not as the interplay of individual and group interests, but as a struggle between rival doctrines or even *Weltanschauungen* ('world views').

Rationalist modes of discourse are now so deeply embedded in our culture that most discussions of policy assume their validity. The dispute between ideas and interests can seem one-sided as a result. Doctrines are privileged in rationalist thought as belonging to a higher order of rationality than interests. Interests are conceived as private and either individual or sectional, whereas doctrines are taken to be universal, partly because they offer more complete and objective explanations than any account founded upon interests, and partly because they claim to represent the interests of all, the public interest. For that reason they claim to offer a guide to the choices policy-makers face which has more moral legitimacy and practical efficacy.

Political economy and public policy

Two kinds of doctrines are relevant to the argument of this essay. Joseph Schumpeter and Lionel Robbins both distinguish political economy from the science of economics.[3] Robbins defines political economy as the principles of public policy in the field of economics, concerned more with prescription than with description, and devoted to the search for solutions to the problems of policy. Like Schumpeter, he sees economic analysis as the province of value-free generalisations, providing objective knowledge of how economies work. The economist is a technician called in because of his expert knowledge.

Most economists in this century have shared this view of their role and their discipline. Keynes looked forward to the day when economists would be regarded like dentists, while Milton Friedman defended his decision to give advice to the Chilean military government in these terms:

In spite of my profound disagreement with the authoritarian political system of Chile, I do not consider it as evil for an economist to render technical economic advice to the Chilean Government, any more than I would regard it as evil for a physician to give technical advice to the Chilean Government to help end a medical plague.[4]

The realm of normative prescription is reserved for political economy. The distinguishing feature of political economy according to Schumpeter is:

an exposition of a comprehensive set of economic policies that its author advocates on the strength of certain unifying normative principles, such as the principles of economic liberalism, or socialism.[5]

My purpose here is not to inquire whether this distinction is valid, but merely to note that this separation between normative doctrines and value-free science is one of the cornerstones on which the economics profession has been founded. The basis of the distinction, however, is certainly not that only political economists are concerned with policy. Economists are just as much involved. Although they cannot advise on final goals, they can advise on the practicality of achieving particular goals.

This might be fairly straightforward if there really did exist an 'economic consensus'. But although mainstream professional economics contains a core of ideas to which most practising economists subscribe, there remain quite distinct models as to how the economy works which have widely divergent implications for policy. The gulf between economics and dentistry remains rather large at present.

The advantage which economic doctrines enjoy in the policy arena is the status that being a form of expert knowledge confers. It is the ability of economics to present itself as a science that is crucial here. The use of a scientific mode of investigation guarantees the objectivity of the results and the value of these results for policy. As McCulloch put it:

a new science has been discovered ... a knowledge of its laws must henceforward be indispensable to legislators. One of the main hopes of human improvement is the diffusion of a wide knowledge of its principles.[6]

In the literature on the forces that have shaped the development of economic policy the influence of doctrines, both the doctrines of political economy and the doctrines of economic science, looms large. These doctrines claim to be concerned with the public interest and to offer a better view of the economic problems confronting governments than do perspectives based on interests which are said to be partial and devoted to the realisation of the aims of minorities.

In this essay I consider two accounts of the dominant perspective – first, Dicey's view of the eclipse of individualist political economy by collectivist political economy; and, second, the view that British economic policy was radically transformed by the Keynesian revolution, a revolution in the views of the economics profession as to how the economy worked. I will then examine two critiques of these approaches, first, the theoretical challenge contained in interest models of politics as developed in different ways by both public choice theory and classical Marxism; and, second, the public policy critique, which concentrates on the role of institutions and circumstances. Some conclusions are then attempted.

Individualism and collectivism

Dicey's lectures on the relation between law and public opinion in England during the nineteenth century, first published in 1905, remain one of the most influential accounts of the evolution of public policy in Britain. Dicey argued that the opinion of the governed is the real foundation of all government:

> the existence and the alteration of human institutions must ... always and everywhere depend upon the beliefs or feelings, or, in other words, upon the opinion of the society in which such institutions flourish.[7]

In support of this view he quoted Hume's famous paradox of government:

> As force is always on the side of the governed, the governors have nothing to support them but opinion. It is, therefore, on opinion only that government is founded; and this maxim extends to the most despotic and most military of governments, as well as to the most free and most popular. The Soldan of Egypt, or the Emperor of Rome, might drive his harmless subjects, like brute beasts, against their

sentiments and inclination; but he must, at least, have led his mamelukes, or praetorian bands, like men, by their opinion.[8]

In the modern era, with the advance of democracy and popular sovereignty, Dicey thought that public opinion was increasingly ruled by general doctrines. He detected a major shift in the course of the nineteenth century from individualism to collectivism as the doctrine underlying most legislation passing through Parliament. The destruction of the old public policy consensus around the ideas and prescriptions of liberal political economy Dicey regarded as a development with enormous significance for the future. He saw the rise of collectivism as inexorable, even though he remained personally committed to individualism.

The basic distinction for Dicey between individualism and collectivism lay in the different attitudes of the two doctrines to the state and to the proper limits of its authority and responsibilities. The contrast he drew between a declining individualism and a rising collectivism was shared by many other social scientists in the twentieth century, including Joseph Schumpeter and Samuel Beer.[9] Collectivism was often presented as the ascendant idea, the doctrine that was supplanting individualism by correcting its shortcomings. Samuel Beer in his book *Modern British Politics,* published in 1965, spoke of the 'era of collectivism' in the twentieth century, which had given rise not just to a socialist collectivism but to a liberal and a conservative collectivism as well. Collectivist doctrines had become the foundation of all political discourse, and individualist and libertarian doctrines of both right and left had been relegated to the sidelines.

Many different reasons were identified for the triumph of collectivism, but chief among them was the pressure of democratic electorates for government programmes that involved higher government spending and taxation; the growing complexity of industrial societies; and the apparent failure of the old liberal political economy to provide policy solutions to problems like unemployment and poverty.

Rise of collectivism reversed?

Dicey seems to have regarded the advance of collectivism as irreversible, but this view is no longer widely held. The revival of liberal political economy and the ideas of classical liberalism in the last forty years suggest that a new Dicey surveying the scene in 2005 might take as his theme the decline of collectivism and the rise of individualism.

All such accounts portray the development of society as essentially a contest between general doctrines about the nature of society and the role of government within it. The dominance of these general doctrines is ascribed partly to the role of intellectuals and partly to the politics of democracy. Intellectuals have a key role to play in the formulation and dissemination of these general doctrines. The Fabians have become the prototype for all such groups, exercising an influence far beyond their numbers or their institutional positions of power. But they were by no means the first, or the last. The political economists and the utilitarians were notable forerunners. The Institute of Economic Affairs is a notable successor.

One of the characteristics which these groups share as organisations is a concern with propagating their particular doctrine as widely as possible, seeking to influence a broad spectrum of political opinion in order to establish consensus for their ideas. Many of the intellectuals involved in these groups dislike the restrictions of partisan attachments and prefer to remain free-floating. What they remain bound to is a particular view of the world, a particular way of analysing its problems, and a preference for a particular kind of solution. The Fabians believed that no reasonable person who knew the facts could fail to become a socialist. Keynes, similarly, regarded economic policy-making as a rational intellectual exercise, because economic problems were basically intellectual problems and as such capable of rational solution.

The process of mass democracy

Belief in the possibility of a rational social order is closely linked to a second factor in the ubiquity of general doctrines, the political process of mass democracy. Once a competitive democratic process becomes established, there has been pressure for the emergence of mass parties. These are catch-all parties which thrive by aggregating as many interests and groups as possible behind a single platform and organisation. In order to establish the widest possible appeal such parties typically become national parties. To justify their claims to administer the affairs of the whole nation they require the aid of general doctrines to show they are not the prisoners of sectional interests.

One consequence of this process is that sectional interests find it difficult to present themselves as such in the public arena. Instead they seek to show that their sectional interest in a particular programme of policy is in fact a universal interest. General doctrines are important in contemporary politics precisely because they can offer that kind of legitimation. Interests that either are unwilling or unable to present their demands in the form of universal demands can be seriously disadvantaged.

Another important source of legitimation comes from the other kind of doctrine discussed above – the knowledge of the technical expert. In economic policy the role of the technical expert is usually linked to the Keynesian revolution. The argument for a Keynesian revolution is succinctly expressed by Susan Howson and Donald Winch:

> the economic consensus which formed around Keynes's ideas in the late 1930s and during the Second World War was largely responsible for increasing the usefulness of economics and economists to governments.[10]

Howson and Winch argue that the real Keynesian revolution was not a revolution in the policy measures which the economics profession advocated. As is well known, many orthodox economists supported similar policy measures to relieve unemployment. If there was a pre-Keynesian orthodoxy its strongholds were among business leaders, politicians, civil servants and bankers. The real change lay, first, in the way the bulk of economists came to approach policy questions, and, second, in the legitimacy which these approaches gradually acquired in government during and after the Second World War.

The claims made for Keynesianism in the 1950s and 1960s can be seen in retrospect to be exaggerated. There was no final technical solution to the economic problems that had plagued capitalism in the 1930s. But the use of economic expertise in government has become much more systematic, and this is unlikely to alter. What has happened in recent years is that policy-makers have become aware that there is more than one source of economic advice and economic expertise, and they have begun to choose accordingly. All governments now routinely seek to legitimate their economic policies through economic expertise. In this way economics has become an important component of general doctrines of political economy.

The value of economic expertise for this purpose lies in the autonomy of economics as an intellectual discipline.[11] This autonomy is a guarantee that the advice of economists does not simply reflect the view of dominant interest groups or the nature of immediate problems. The discipline generates its own research agenda, its own questions and its own solutions, at a distance from the formation and implementation of policy.

The knowledge which economics supplies appears disinterested and objective. It therefore appears also non-partisan and universal. It can provide valuable reinforcement to the general doctrines that compete for the allegiance of public opinion by increasing their credibility as statements of the public interest.

Doctrines in the marketplace of ideas

What underlies the accounts of Dicey, Beer, and many others is a pluralist account of the development of policy, in which the climate of ideas that becomes established in any period is the crucial determinant. In the marketplace of ideas, doctrines confront one another and battle for supremacy. The ousting of individualism by collectivism determines the character of politics and of legislation for a large part of the twentieth century.

Economic policy is divided up into eras according to which fundamental doctrine was dominant. The pre-collectivist or individualist era is succeeded by the collectivist era, which now in turn is giving way to a post-collectivist era. In similar fashion, the twentieth century can be divided up into a pre-Keynesian era lasting up to 1940, a Keynesian era from 1940 to 1975, and a post-Keynesian era since 1975.

The implication of this kind of periodisation is that fundamental policy change follows changes in the climate of ideas. Those seeking fundamental change must first create a new ideological consensus. Winning the battle of ideas makes possible new initiatives in policy. Collectivism was successful because its advocates were able to convince enough people that it offered both a superior version of the public interest and policies that would work. Keynesianism helped provide the latter, although it should be noted that it was not alone. Neo-classical economics, with its concentration on models of perfect competition and its notion of market failure, had provided theoretical justifications for state intervention. Keynes, however, identified market failure not simply at the margins but at the heart of the market order, and therefore appeared to sanction a much more permanent role for government intervention in the economy than had previously existed.

The interest critique

We have become so used to thinking in terms of the great battles of ideas – individualism against collectivism, socialism against capitalism, Keynesianism against monetarism – that other perspectives are often ignored. But there are powerful objections against the ideological perspective as an adequate explanation of the reasons for change in British economic policy.

One critique comes from those arguments that place much more weight on interests than on doctrines. They do not dispute that general doctrines exist and play a role in policy formulation and development, but they regard their function to be primarily as instruments that serve particular interests. It is interests that drive policy, not general doctrines.

There is no agreement on the definition of 'interest'. As already stated, interests can be defined in terms of desires, intentions, values and needs, and very different accounts can be given according to which dimension is stressed. One of the key points of controversy is over whether interests should be regarded as revealed preferences or whether some objective assessment independent of an individual's own valuation is possible.

One of the most influential accounts of the importance of interests has come from Mancur Olson. His argument, which is set out in detail in his book *The Rise and Decline of Nations,* is that the growth of government intervention and the impairment of the working of market economies during the twentieth century can be traced not to the influence of collectivist ideas but to certain characteristics of the structure of collective action and the political process in democratic states. The opportunity to form groups and associations to express common interests and concerns leads to a dense network of special interests, each one of which depends for its survival on excluding other individuals from membership while offering its actual members selective incentives for staying in the organisation. The most effective selective incentives are those that provide benefits for members that are not available to non-members, while the cost is spread over members and non-members alike.[12]

For Olson the proliferation of special interests supplies the momentum behind the growth of government programmes and agencies which cumulatively disrupt the delicate workings of the market order. The effects are felt through a weakening of economic performance, and a slower rate of growth of output and productivity.

Dominance of special interests in policy goals

Olson suggests that the longer a state has experienced democratic politics, the more unbroken the continuity of its institutions, the more special interests it will have acquired and the more sclerotic will be its economy. The marketplace of ideas may result in a consensus on the goals of public policy, but the marketplace of interests is more important in determining actual policy outcomes. The long-term effect of the free play of group interests in a democratic polity is a gradual reduction in the flexibility of the market order and a growing apparatus of restrictions and controls which favour particular interests and are fiercely defended by them.

It is not hard to see how Olson's analysis might be applied to British economic policy. Britain has experienced exceptional continuity in its political institutions, and has suffered no major rupture from external invasion or internal revolution, which have transformed so many other states in the twentieth century. Democratic politics as it has emerged since 1885 has not suffered any significant interruption and has therefore in Olson's terms provided fertile ground for the development of special interests. The growth of trade associations, trade unions, and lobbies of all kinds pressing for particular state programmes has been a noted feature of British politics during this century.

These developments have often been portrayed extremely favourably. British political institutions have been praised for reconciling opposing interests and allowing a process of compromise and consensus to be established which has maintained social peace and the gradual evolution of British society.[13] Olson does not dispute this, but argues that there was a hidden cost. Britain's 'middle way', eventually accepted by all parties, was an ideological consensus founded on the granting of extensive privileges to particular special interests. Sometimes these special interests were particular organisations such as trade unions and trade associations. But they could also be particular blocs of voters, such as the recipients of mortgage tax relief.

By the 1970s the makers of British economic policy seemed to be drowning in a sea of problems, and faced mounting concern at the relative decline of the British economy and the overload of British government. From Olson's perspective there is no easy remedy. Changing the climate of ideas only changes the way in which the special interests are forced to justify their activities as well as the relative advantages which different groups enjoy in pursuing their aims. So long as the facts of collective action are as he describes them there is no way in which a general interest can arise from the competition of sectional interests.

The same problem can be considered from a Marxist standpoint. Classical Marxism, like public choice theory, is another major tradition which emphasises interests rather than ideas. Its interests are class interests, and ideologies are often presented in Marxist literature as instruments which serve class interests. In this way the use of general doctrines to proclaim a universal interest conceals the pursuit of a sectional interest, the interest of the ruling or dominant class.

Marxist model of class interests

Pushed to its extreme the Marxist model suggests that, whatever their proclaimed goals, the real purpose of state policies is to serve particular class interests. The battle of ideas between individualism and collectivism does not alter the class basis of social and economic organisation, and is therefore concerned only with different strategies for maintaining the dominance of capital.

A classical Marxist account of British politics, like that of Ralph Miliband, provides a critique of traditional pluralist analysis.[14] Miliband criticises pluralism for assuming that the state in a capitalist society can be a neutral instrument representing the public interest. In public choice theory it is the nature of collective action and the inevitability of special interests in a democratic polity which prevent this happening. In Marxist theory it is the structure of class relationships and the irreconcilable nature of class interests.

The explanation for the growth of the state in a classical Marxist account is deeply ambivalent. Marx argued that conflicts between labour and capital and divisions of interest within the ruling class of property owners could produce measures like the Ten Hours Bill, which placed a limit on capital and strengthened the position of the working class. But Marxists have always been divided over whether a gradualist transfer of power from the capitalist class to the working class was possible. Many have argued that the growth of state intervention in the twentieth century has successfully averted the threat of any internal challenge from the working class to the institutions of capitalism and has therefore made capital more secure. Questions of economic policy therefore become different means of managing a capitalist economy, and do not involve any fundamental changes in the way in which the society is organised. The oscillations between attempting to maintain control over labour through wage controls and through unemployment are seen as alternative strategies of control within a framework that protects capitalist interests.[15]

An interest model of policy formulation and implementation has undeniable strengths, as the insights of both Marxist and public choice literature show. Pluralism can be highly normative, deducing the existence of a public interest from its desirability. Marxism and public choice theory at their best offer a realistic account of the political process which cuts through the ideological justifications which are given for particular policies. They ask the classic political science question: 'Who gets what, when, how?'

Nevertheless, interest models do have severe limitations. One is the vice of reductionism. It becomes all too easy, armed with a structural theory of class or group interest, to interpret all policy decisions as expressions of a hidden or private interest. The great strength of pluralism has always been its sensitivity to a range of factors that may be relevant in understanding policy issues.

This defect in interest models of the policy process can be traced to their definition of interest as revealed preferences, and to their concentration upon specific agents, whether groups or classes, as the bearers of interests. This defect is, however, overcome if interest models are used to derive a notion of the public interest.

Public choice theory and public goods

In public choice theory, for example, the market order, its rules and institutions, have been recognised as public goods, which will not arise spontaneously from market exchanges of individuals, because it is in no one person's interest to provide them. They can only be provided politically, through collective action. The question for public choice theory is whether there are circumstances under which collective action can provide support for public goods and not merely private goods.

The argument turns on whether there are genuine public goods or whether all public functions could be provided through markets. If the former do exist it suggests that political processes are less malign than they are sometimes represented in the public choice literature. Political agents may well be striving, if imperfectly, to define and realise a public interest which is more than simply a cloak for providing privileges to special interests. Their success in doing so will depend on the nature of the coalitions they attempt to assemble and on their attitude towards the constitutional limits on government power. The broader and more encompassing the coalition the greater will be the possibility that the party represents a general rather than a specific interest. But that may count for little once a party is elected unless there are strict rules or conventions setting limits to what governments may or may not do. This might seem a slender prospect as far as Britain is concerned, but from a public choice perspective it is the only hope of lasting reforms that deliver greater economic freedom and more limited government. Only if the public interest in the existence of a market order receives political support and becomes embedded in the institutions and procedures of the public realm, will the attempt to reverse the onward march of collectivism be possible.

From the Marxist perspective, also, a notion of public interest can be derived. There is already explicit in Marxism the idea of a genuine public interest which will emerge once classes have been abolished. Its bearer is the working class. But many Marxists have also drawn attention to the existence of a public interest generated within capitalist society.[16] It arises because an interest in maintaining and reproducing the conditions that permit the system of capitalist production to survive is not one that is necessarily held by any individual capitalist.

The existence of what Marx called capital in general indicates the need for institutions and procedures that allow the general interests of capital to be defined and protected. Such a sphere has to be independent of the specific interests of individual capitalists, which makes it open also to influence by a variety of other groups and interests. Policy formation has come to be analysed by many modern Marxists as a sphere that is not reducible to individual class interests and that involves the construction of coalitions of interests which can provide specific benefits to particular groups as well as a credible definition of the public interest which can unite quite disparate groups and interests.[17]

Both interest models discussed here can therefore provide a much less one-sided analysis of the policy process through a grasp of the permanent tension that exists between private and public interests in the political arena. The balance is not always easy to sustain, however. The maintenance of a public interest is constantly undermined by the pursuit of private interests. The temptation then is to revert to fundamentalist solutions, to abolish politics, or to abolish markets, in order to ensure the identity of private and public interest.

The public policy critique

The interest theories oppose a theoretical model to a theoretical model. But there is another very influential perspective which criticises both theoretical models, on the ground that whatever their refinements they remain gross oversimplifications of the very varied circumstances that determine how policies emerge, how they are implemented, and what their outcomes are.

From this standpoint most of the terms in which British economic policy is habitually discussed are misguided. Collectivism, individualism, and corporatism are meaningless abstractions, the Keynesian revolution did not exist, and monetarism does not describe even a coherent doctrine, still less a coherent policy.

What the student of British economic policy should examine are the institutions which determine how policy agendas are framed, how problems are defined, and how solutions to these problems are approached. The explanation of new policy measures is not to be found in the spirit of the age, or in the sway of general doctrines over public opinion, or in the power of interest groups, but in the way in which policy-makers defined the situation confronting them. Such definitions occur within limits which are set by administrative procedures, available knowledge, individual personalities and particular pressures. Ideas and interests may play a part, but it is a part within a context which is already structured by the past, by previous events and decisions. The scope for change, certainly for radical change, is accordingly small.

Political pressures, not 'meaningless abstractions', the key?

The historical method applied in this way can be the great debunker. Dicey made great play of the 1911 National Insurance Act, passed by the Liberal Government, as an expression of the rise of collectivism. Jose Harris's careful historical study of the circumstances surrounding the passage of that act disputes his interpretation. Her conclusion is unequivocal:

> In tracing the evolution of a national unemployment policy it is difficult to point to the decisive influence of any single set of reforming ideas or to discover any logical sequence of institutional change.[18]

She points out the extremely tentative and incoherent character of the reforms. The measures were primarily pragmatic in motivation and aims. They resulted partly from the fear by Liberal ministers that they might be politically outmanoeuvred on the issue. They sought to avoid either of the other two principal solutions to the unemployment problem, the right-to-work ideas of the socialists, or the tariff reform proposals of the Conservatives. A second reason was recognition of the practical inadequacy of existing forms of unemployment relief.

Harris's study is interesting for another reason. She shows that the legislation had unintended consequences. Undertaken for reasons of short-term political expediency, it did help to shape later policy developments and in particular the administrative form of such developments. The framers of the legislation were determined to preserve the market order by ensuring labour mobility and working-class independence; at the same time, the act established an administrative machinery which was capable of greatly extending the control of government over economic affairs. The sanctions which were given to the state authorities to enforce compliance and the degree of information private individuals were required to make available to the state provided important precedents for later developments.

The other principle that was established was the use of policy to promote political consensus. The Insurance Act helped to broaden both the state's tax base and its political support. Harris quotes Winston Churchill:

> the idea is to increase the stability of our institutions by giving the mass of industrial workers a direct interest in maintaining them. With a 'stake in the country' in the form of insurances against evil days these workers will pay no attention to the vague promises of revolutionary socialism.[19]

Although historical accounts of public policy tend to play down the role of ideological principles and interests in initiating policy changes, these examples show that they do nevertheless have a role. But they are generally subordinate to considerations that stem from political calculation and administrative procedure. There is always a particular political context in which their contribution has to be understood. The preference of most historians is to grasp the complexity of each unique situation as it unfolds. This complexity cannot be reduced to doctrines or interests as the prime mover of events.

Incremental solutions to policy problems

The historical method does allot a much smaller role to ideologies, parties and groups, and a much larger one to established trends and cycles, to inertia and inherited practices, and to the practical judgements and actions of politicians. In this view the policy process is largely incremental, there are few dramatic changes, and few breaks in sequence. What is hailed as a major new departure turns out on examination to be a minor adaptation of a policy that already existed.

If this approach is applied to British economic policy in the twentieth century, a very different periodisation would ensue from that discussed earlier. The major breaks are provided by the two world wars, and by changes in the organisation of the world economy, not by revolutions either in the climate of ideas or in economic doctrines. The extension of government responsibility is regarded primarily as a series of ad hoc responses to particular problems, rather than as a blueprint for radical social change.[20]

The attachment to free trade, the gold standard and the principles of sound finance in the first part of the century were natural expressions of the particular institutional form which relationships between the state and the market had come to assume in Britain, and reflected the specific character of British capitalism, its commercial and financial orientation, and the role it had come to occupy in the world economy. Tariff reform was resisted in part for ideological reasons but mainly because it was not judged to be a practical policy. The gold standard was eventually abandoned not because people had ceased to believe in its importance but because it had become impossible to sustain any longer.

On this view it is always the pressure to find workable solutions to those problems which are defined as needing solutions that is most relevant in the development of policy. Doctrines and interests may have most impact in helping to change perceptions of what are to count as problems, but only rarely will they also dictate what the solution is to be. Keynesianism is a good example of this. Keynes certainly helped in getting unemployment defined as a problem in need of political remedy, although the altered political context of the war was also crucial. But as is now well documented, the 1944 White Paper on Employment Policy was a carefully constructed compromise between the views of Keynes and Treasury civil servants.[21]

What became known as Keynesianism after 1945 bore little relation to Keynes's ideas and prescriptions, although his name provided legitimacy for all the various interventions in the economy which governments carried out, usually for severely pragmatic and immediate reasons. Keynesianism acquired the legitimacy it did because it was associated with the exceptional prosperity of the 1950s and 1960s. It then acquired the obloquy it did because it became associated with the inflation and stagnation of the 1970s.

Many historians and some economists would argue that both praise and blame are undeserved.[22] Full employment was created and sustained by forces that were independent of Keynesian demand management, and the shift from Keynesianism to monetarism came about not through intellectual conviction, but out of pragmatic necessity, because of the shift from fixed to floating exchange rates, and the weakening of the possibility of national economic management.

No final victory?

The historical critique is extremely powerful and hard to refute. Casual generalisations and empty theorising are exposed by painstaking examination of the circumstances surrounding the making of economic decisions. A picture is built up which stresses the complexity of any actual historical situation and the multiple factors that are involved in it. Historical inquiry never furnishes the clear-cut historical examples that would be needed to test the theories of historical development.

Detail and complexity are the strengths of historical argument. But there can also be weaknesses. The examination of detail can be pushed to the point where the meaning of what is studied is lost. Dicey's formulation of a shift from individualism to collectivism may at points oversimplify what took place. But did his formulation not capture something which corresponded to a widespread perception and experience of the direction of social change? Is there not a similar perception and experience in existence today?

The belief that such broad shifts are meaningful and can be identified is the basis of W.H. Greenleaf's recent work on the British political tradition.[23] Greenleaf sees himself as engaged in a similar inquiry to that of Dicey. But there are some major differences. Greenleaf does not present collectivism as the successor to individualism, or libertarianism as he prefers to call it. Instead he treats collectivism and libertarianism as the two poles of the British political tradition. They are always present, they cut across all party allegiances, they form the basis from which ideas and policies emerge.

In Greenleaf's concept of a political tradition no voices are ever completely silenced. However dominant one part of the tradition may be for a time, it will not be dominant for ever. The resources of the tradition will in time permit the emergence of counter-arguments. Greenleaf's approach is deeply disconcerting to those who long for final victory in the battle of ideas. It suggests that the climate of ideas may follow a cyclical pattern. Greenleaf is a meticulous historian and is only concerned to investigate the resources and recesses of his political tradition. But he writes in the knowledge that the libertarian strands of the tradition which appeared to Dicey to be likely to suffer a total eclipse have recently been reviving strongly. It is collectivism and collectivist arguments that are on the wane.

Greenleaf offers no explanation for why different ideas should be dominant at different times. But his account is quite compatible with Albert Hirschman's argument in *Shifting Involvements*.[24] Hirschman argues that the relative popularity of individualist and collectivist ideas is subject to a cycle which arises from the fact that both market and state solutions arouse expectations which they cannot satisfy. The goods and services which they deliver inevitably disappoint. As the disappointments accumulate so the attractions of an alternative untried and novel mode of delivery increase. Eventually a major shift in policy is engineered. But the new mode is bound to disappoint in its turn. Hirschman argues that frustration and disappointment, and consequently the desire for novelty and change, are inescapable features of human experience.

The idea of progress in human affairs is no longer as fashionable as it was. The fatalism associated with theories of cycles has become much more prevalent, certainly on the left. If the modern world is an iron cage, not very much can be done to improve or alter it. The optimism that was associated with Keynesianism has disappeared. Few now regard Keynesianism as an irreversible step forward in economic knowledge. The idea of economics as a cumulative science in the manner of some of the physical sciences has been dented.

Some of the supporters of the revival in classical liberalism and of the new conservatism by contrast continue to proclaim faith in the possibility of radical social change which will significantly improve society. They have inherited the faith and the confidence of the early Fabians. Will it prove to be as equally misplaced? The problem with both Fabian collectivism and New Right individualism is that both seem to demand a moral consensus which is unobtainable in modern society. This has led some critics, like Noel O'Sullivan, to suggest that what is required is a return to the ideal of civil association and limited politics, and the abandonment of the attempt to pursue what he terms 'social politics'.[25] Limited politics is concerned with procedures and general rules rather than with substantive policy. Social politics is always concerned with implementing a particular vision of the good life. O'Sullivan argues that many on the New Right are pursuing their own version of social politics.

The rediscovery of civil association

The issue that arises in the light of Hirschman's ideas is whether it would be possible to return to the conception of politics as a civil association, or whether the conditions of modern society make all politics predominantly social politics, or enterprise politics, to use Oakeshott's term. The difficulty with the concept of a civil association is that it is hard to separate procedures from substantive issues of policy. Yet there is no doubt that there has been a very strong revival of interest in constitutional and procedural questions in politics. The rediscovery by many socialists and social democrats of the idea of civil society and civil association and the politics that would be required to sustain them is one of the more intriguing developments of recent years.[26]

It may indicate the need to reassess the political ideas of socialists like Philip Snowden, who was opposed to key aspects of Fabian collectivism. He favoured free trade rather than tariffs, because tariffs were inefficient and increased the cost of food. He believed that socialism must not involve government extravagance. He thought the government should aim for a budget surplus in order to pay off the national debt. High interest payments merely redistributed income from workers to rentiers. In fiscal policy he favoured a progressive income tax and death duties to finance new social services, but proposed to abolish all indirect taxes on food. He opposed spending public money on public works unless they were sound investments. He believed the key to reducing unemployment was to reduce costs. In 1924 he called for a sound and healthy deflation, and he thought the gold standard part of the fixed order of the economy. He considered that it was as much the elementary duty of civilised government to maintain the value of money as to run a police force to check theft.[27]

Snowden has always been dismissed as a Neanderthal representative of the pre-Keynesian Treasury orthodoxy which Keynes destroyed forever. Some of his views seem rather contemporary. Whatever their merits, however, the important point here is that they derived from an orientation towards politics that saw the state as enabling rather than as all-powerful, and which regarded the public interest socialists sought to promote as inseparable from the procedures and rules a socialist government operated within. An emphasis on procedures and general rules makes the key political task the establishment of those conditions, such as the existence of autonomous intermediate institutions, which help promote a vigorous civil society.

British economic policy in the twentieth century is rich in failed experiments. It provides fewer clues as to how a public-interest politics can be generated which does not collapse into social politics on the one hand or into domination by sectional interests on the other. Yet since politics cannot be abolished, any more than markets, the search for the conditions for such a politics is bound to continue.

Postscript 1996

Watersheds and turning points are always hard to identify, and always invite controversy. The radicalism of the changes that took place in

Britain in the 1970s and 1980s has been much disputed. But looking back from the 1990s it does appear that something substantial has altered – in all three aspects discussed in this article, the climate of ideas, the balance of interests, and the contexts within which politicians have to work. Controversy will continue as to whether one of these was most important in triggering the changes in the others, and controversy will also persist as to whether the changes will last or whether there will be a swing back towards a more interventionist state. The legacy of the Thatcherite decade is a troubled one with several prominent supporters of the Thatcherite policies now arguing that the neo-liberal project has become destructive and corrosive of the institutions that are necessary for a free society.[28] On the other side are those who argue that the Thatcherite revolution was incomplete and that a new radical programme is required to take it forward.[29] Despite some success in reducing the share of the state in GDP from 44 per cent in 1983 to 39 per cent in 1990, in recent years the share has climbed back to 42 per cent, and the tax burden is higher than it was in 1979.[30] Productivity has increased, and despite the renewed surge at the end of the 1980s inflation has been brought under control. But levels of investment, training, and research and development in the British economy remain low by international standards.

A change in the global political economy, particularly a sudden increase in environmental danger, might in the future force a new interventionist agenda on all national governments, and new forms of planning. But for the moment the agenda of the 1970s and 1980s looks securely embedded, and although there will be some changes, and periods of greater state activism, there is unlikely to be a return to the kind of collectivist and corporatist programmes which used to prevail. In this sense there is some truth in Milton Friedman's rather grandiose periodisation of the last 200 years into an Age of Adam Smith, an Age of Fabianism, and now an Age of Hayek, one great wave after another.[31] This conception again gives priority to ideas in the manner of Dicey. It captures the movement away from top-down state solutions to problems of economic management. Hayek has been a key figure in this change, both because he stood out against the collectivist orthodoxies when they were so fashionable, but also because some of his writings assisted in the revival of interest in the institutional conditions for economic and social co-ordination that do not depend on rational foresight and centralised knowledge.[32]

The political debates on economic policy are often presented in a polarised form as a preference for either state or market, for regulation or deregulation, for intervention or laissez-faire. But this opposition was always in practice an unreal one, since states and markets are in practice interdependent and cannot exist in isolation. A programme emphasising only one and excluding the other produces the kind of policy failures which Hirschman describes. Future debates on policy are unlikely to repeat the old divisions in the same way. What may instead emerge is a deeper appreciation of the value and the limits of both states and markets as different kinds of institutions for coordinating contemporary economies. Whether this will lead to more successful economic policies remains to be seen.

4

Hayek on Knowledge, Economics and Society[1]

Hayek's theory of knowledge is his most distinctive contribution both to economics and to social science. Its foundation is 'our irremediable ignorance',[2] both as social actors and as social theorists. 'The dispersion and imperfection of all knowledge are two of the basic facts from which the social sciences have to start.'[3] The knowledge which members of modern societies possess is *necessarily* imperfect and incomplete, and can never be perfected. This is so for several reasons which are all interlinked; first, because in any modern society knowledge is fragmented and dispersed among millions of individuals; second, because the limits of human reason mean that many things remain unknown and unknowable to individual members of society, whether in their roles as social actors or social theorists; and third, because the unintended consequences of human action and the tacit nature of so much of the knowledge that individuals do possess mean that modern societies have to be understood as organisms evolving through time, representing extremely complex phenomena which defy the normal methods of science either to explain or to control.

Understanding these characteristics of knowledge in society was for Hayek the principal task of all social and economic theory, and although reason had a key role to play in reforming institutions and guiding policy, it was an extremely limited one and had to be exercised with caution. 'To act on the belief that we possess the knowledge and the power which enable us to shape the processes of society entirely to our liking, knowledge which in fact we do *not* possess, is likely to make us do much harm.'[4] His theory of knowledge provides a thread which runs through almost all his work, the organising idea which he spent fifty years exploring through a variety of intellectual projects, and to which he returned again in his final work, *The Fatal Conceit*. No other idea is as important for understanding Hayek, his intellectual system and his mental world. Much of his work is an extended meditation on the problem of knowledge. Hayek's originality has never been properly appreciated beyond a relatively small circle, partly because Hayek continues to be read through ideological spectacles, and partly too perhaps because were his theory taken seriously much of the approach to the study of society in general and economics in particular would be turned upside down. Hayek was a true radical, an uncomfortable thinker for orthodoxies everywhere, including some of those to which he himself subscribed.

Hayek had an ambivalent relationship with economics. Although he spent the first half of his career as a professional economist, he came to adopt positions which were sharply critical of the way the mainstream in economics had developed.[5] Hayek wanted to set economics flowing in quite a different direction. Few economists agreed with him, or seem to have understood him. Many, like Milton Friedman, praised Hayek as a champion of liberal values but were not persuaded by his approach to economics.[6] When he was awarded the Nobel Prize for Economics in 1974 many economists greeted the news with incredulity, since he was widely seen as an economist who, sidelined during the Keynesian ascendancy, had turned away from technical economics to immerse himself in social and political philosophy. His 1930s works on economic theory were little studied. Many assumed he had been honoured for being one of the leading ideological champions of economic liberalism.

His work has always been controversial, and many different interpretations of it emerged, focused around a number of apparent inconsistencies in his thought, hardly surprising in work that breaks new ground and sees problems in new ways. Just as there is an Adam Smith problem and a Karl Marx problem, so there is a Hayek problem.[7] One of its first formulations was given by Terence Hutchison, when he detected a significant shift in Hayek's methodological stance, involving the discarding of Mises in favour of Popper.[8] At the heart of every Hayek problem is his theory of knowledge, which became the pivot of his thought.

The division of knowledge

Hayek first set out his distinctive theory of knowledge in his seminal 1937 article in *Economica*, 'Economics and knowledge'.[9] The catalyst was his edited volume, *Collectivist Economic Planning*,[10] designed to bring to an English-speaking readership some of the key texts and discussions on the feasibility of centrally planned economies from the socialist calculation debate. With the prestige of Soviet central planning rising in the mid-1930s, Hayek thought it opportune to revive some of the key Austrian School arguments against central planning. It reawakened his interest in some of the broader questions of economic liberalism and the institutional basis of a free economy and free society, and came together with a number of other influences, which included his attempts to theorise how prices changed in the business cycle, the pioneering work of Frank Knight on risk and uncertainty,[11] and the classical political economists, particularly Carl Menger, Adam Smith and David Hume.

In 'Economics and knowledge', Hayek addressed his fellow economists about the way in which knowledge was understood and treated in economics. He set out two questions: first, what role did assumptions and propositions about the knowledge possessed by the different members of society play in economic analysis, and second, how much knowledge did formal economic analysis provide about what happens in the real world.[12] His answer to both questions was – very little. This was because economists wrongly treated the 'data' to be explained as the 'objective real facts as the observing economist is supposed to know them'. But Hayek argued that the true definition of data had to be subjective: 'things known to the persons whose behaviour we are trying to explain'.[13] The 'data' of economics for Hayek were the facts that are present in the mind of the acting person, not the facts present in the mind of the observing economist.

Economics was a science only to the extent that its theoretical propositions referred to things defined in terms of human attitudes towards them.[14] In doing this, economists had grasped an essential truth about the ordering of human societies, namely the role played by the knowledge possessed by each member of the society. Economics had come closer than any other social science to addressing the central question of all social science:

> How can the combination of fragments of knowledge existing in different minds, bring about results which, if they were to be brought about deliberately, would require a knowledge on the part of the directing mind which no single person can possess?[15]

This was the issue that had arisen in the course of the socialist calculation debate, and which Hayek now believed was the key to understanding the difference between rival economic systems, and the superiority of market institutions over any other for coordinating modern societies.

Yet instead of concentrating on how knowledge was acquired and utilised by the members of a society, economists spent most of their energies on developing formal models with assumptions about the knowledge of members of society which were remote from the real world. Hayek did not dispute that the pure logic of choice was a powerful analytical tool, but he was concerned about the ways it was being used, for example in pure equilibrium analysis to construct a set of tautological propositions, remote from any real explanation of social relations.[16] The original intent of equilibrium analysis as developed by Walras and Pareto he felt had been lost.[17] They had both emphasised that their models were not a substitute for reality, since there were so many detailed facts that could not be known. Correct foresight of all future events was not a precondition of equilibrium, but the defining characteristic of the concept. This meant that if there was a tendency towards equilibrium in the economy the knowledge and intentions of the members of the society were converging. To explain why that might be so, however, would need careful empirical examination of the processes by which individuals acquired the necessary knowledge. If this were not done, but simply assumed, the value of the models was sharply reduced.

Hayek argued that the modern market economy was founded on a *division of knowledge* every bit as important as the division of labour which had been emphasised by Adam Smith. In subsequent essays, articles and books he began to develop and deepen this insight. He was still refining and restating it when he died. Knowledge was very different depending on how it arose and where it arose, it could not be assumed that because knowledge existed at one level it could be transferred to another. Specifically Hayek argued that the knowledge which was characteristic of a modern market economy was local, dispersed and fragmented, and much of it was tacit – it could not be articulated. It was acquired and utilised by independent individual agents, but it remained for the most part particular to them. It could not be gathered up and transferred to a central planning board, because it only existed for individuals in particular circumstances, particular places and particular times. But although this knowledge was dispersed and fragmented, it provided the essential means by which a modern economy consisting of a myriad of individual producers and sellers, who were necessarily strangers to one another, could be coordinated to bring about a tolerable, although always imperfect, order and stability. To make that possible, the right institutions had to emerge, and crucially individuals had to be willing to abandon their instincts and follow abstract rules of conduct, which they had not designed and did not know explicitly.[18] Hayek thought that the system of moral rules, next to language, was the most important example of a spontaneous order, an 'undesigned growth, a set of rules which govern our lives but of which we can say neither why they are what they are nor what they do to us'.[19]

This theory of knowledge gave Hayek a new way of stating the case for economic liberalism, as well as a methodology for studying society. By focusing on the way in which knowledge was acquired and communicated in a market economy he was able to mount a critique of central planning as an alternative way of organising an economy, and direct attention to the very different ways in which the two systems used knowledge. The case for economic liberalism had been distilled into a set of dogmas over the course of the nineteenth century, as befitted the dominant commonsense of the age, but by the 1930s it was under increasing attack from various collectivist doctrines, and the older moral arguments for individualism carried less weight. Hayek proclaimed the values of classical liberalism and the case for a free society in a series of polemical works, most famously *The Road to Serfdom*.[20] But the reputation he acquired sometimes overshadowed his more fundamental intellectual contribution – restating the classical liberal case by focusing on how individuals acquire and utilise knowledge in a market economy.

Hayek used this focus on knowledge to remind economists that what was important in the workings of an economy was not the knowledge of the economist but the knowledge of the individual agent. Economists should not make assumptions about what that knowledge was, or imagine that they could ever possess it. All they could (and should) do was start from the concepts which guided individuals in their actions rather than from the results of theorising about their actions.[21] Grasping why individuals hold certain views would allow an understanding of 'the unintended and often uncomprehended results of the separate and yet interrelated actions of men in society'.[22] Such an injunction went against the trend of modern rationalist and scientific thought, which believed that the knowledge of the observer and the scientist was potentially much more comprehensive and complete than the knowledge of the actor. The scientist needed to draw on the knowledge of agents but only with a view to propounding a theory which would incorporate and transcend the particular information which the agent possessed. Ideas such as this had long fuelled the rationalist belief, the fatal conceit as Hayek called it, that human beings could become masters of their fate, acquiring control over both their physical surroundings and their societies. Knowledge could be centralised and put to the service of the whole community to improve every aspect of people's lives. The centralisation of knowledge through the practice of science made possible a planned economy and a planned society. Such attitudes had come to permeate most ideologies and most academic disciplines, including economics.

The knowledge of other minds

In rejecting this rationalist conception of knowledge, was Hayek making an empirical claim or a methodological claim? Many philosophers and economists have preferred to treat it as an empirical claim,[23] the proposition that modern economies could not centralise knowledge in the way proposed by advocates of central planning without producing results far inferior to those achieved through decentralised institutions of markets and competition. Only an economy organised on the basis of free, competitive markets and private property could sustain the standards of living and population of modern societies. Ludwig von Mises in the 1920s had argued that a socialist economy based on central planning was impossible because without decentralised markets and prices there could be no rational calculation of prices.[24] Hayek had accepted the general thrust of Mises' argument but appeared to shift the debate away from Mises' a priori argument that socialism was impossible by definition to the empirical claim that it was the different way knowledge was used in the two systems that made a decentralised market economy superior to a centrally planned economy. If knowledge could not be aggregated or centralised then the only way a modern economy could be coordinated was through institutions that took account of the dispersed and fragmented character of knowledge, and which therefore recognised that a modern economy was so complex that most of the knowledge contained within it could never be known to a single mind. What a single mind could grasp was the outcome of the system, the way in which decentralised exchange based on fragmented and dispersed knowledge could produce a coordinated, stable and predictable social order, capable of sustaining and reproducing itself.

But although there are passages where Hayek presents his theory of knowledge as a Popperian hypothesis about the nature of society, there are many others where he continues to make a priori claims about the nature of knowledge. For Hayek it was never just an empirical question, even assuming an adequate test for it could be devised. There were 'constitutional' not just empirical limits to human knowledge, which formed 'a permanent barrier to the possibility of a rational construction of the whole of society'.[25] The limitations on existing knowledge could only be overcome through the way knowledge was utilised, and not through getting more of it. Knowledge was limited because the human mind was limited, and nowhere more so than in analysing the complex phenomenon of society.

Popper thought that the difference between social science and natural science was a question of degree and that the scope for generating useful knowledge in the social sciences to inform what he called 'piecemeal social engineering' was high. Hayek agreed with Popper that the complex nature of the phenomena that social scientists studied meant that what they could learn about society was extremely limited, and that it was theoretically impossible for the social sciences to aspire to the same kind of control over society as the natural scientists claimed over nature. Hayek was firmly opposed to a positivist (or as he termed it, constructivist) conception of social science on two main grounds: first, because it misunderstood the nature of the phenomena social scientists were trying to explain, and second, because it relied on a false conception of reason.[26]

In his epistemology Hayek's general drift throughout his career is towards Popper and Hume, and away from Mises and Kant, but there remains an a priori cast to many of his ideas, particularly his conception of knowledge. Hayek came to his conception that knowledge was limited, not through an empirical enquiry, but because of his a priori stance on the nature of the human mind and of human nature. 'Man is not born wise, rational and good, but has to be taught to become so.'[27] Human knowledge is limited, and will necessarily remain so, and understanding of societies and economies will always therefore be incomplete. This epistemological pessimism is a fundamental trait of Hayek's thought, though curiously never extended to natural science and the consequences of human domination of the natural world, and contributes to his growing reverence for tradition and his warnings against any kind of interference by governments in the choices that individuals make.

As a methodological postulate it entails that economists and other social scientists should recognise from the outset that they are studying highly complex phenomena which they can never fully know. Knowledge is limited for Hayek in this double sense. The individual agent has limited knowledge of his circumstances (although greater knowledge than anyone else could possess) and limited power to control them,[28] as well as limited knowledge of the knowledge that other actors have, while the economist has limited knowledge of what individual agents know. Although in other contexts Hayek advocated the use of simplifying models, in this instance he argued that introducing an assumption into economic models that agents have 'perfect information' is wrong on two counts. First, agents could never have perfect information – the world they face is one of 'radical uncertainty'; their knowledge is always fragmentary and incomplete. Second, economists have no way of second-guessing agents. Attributing perfect information to them, even for the purposes of creating a model, assumes that it might in principle be possible for agents to approach having perfect information. Hayek denies that this is possible, and regards it as setting up a series of false trails for economists. Most seriously it leads economists to imagine that there might be a way of remedying the information deficiencies observed within actual markets which cause markets to malfunction, so improving economic efficiency. Hayek attributed this false conception of knowledge in social science to the rationalist bias which inclined economists and social scientists constantly to recommend ways of intervening in market economies to improve outcomes.

Hayek's epistemological pessimism is rooted partly in the Kantian view that human minds cannot know the world as it is but only through the categories which the mind itself furnishes, but mainly in the Humean view that human reason is a frail and limited instrument, and the knowledge it produces is always imperfect and incomplete. From the Kantian perspective, mediated through the work of the Austrian School, Hayek took the argument that all knowledge has presuppositions, that theory always precedes experience, and that therefore all knowledge is informed by theory and predicated upon theory. The social world represents itself to our mind as a series of complex phenomena because these phenomena are not natural phenomena but social phenomena – they are made up of many minds like our own, all of which are limited and imperfect, but all of which have their own capacity to interpret, to value and to reason. The result is to introduce a potentially unlimited number of variables and details, the totality of which can never be known to a single mind: 'No mind can take account of all the particular facts which are known to some men.'[29]

One conclusion might be that if social phenomena are really like this, then social science is an impossible project and should be abandoned. Hayek, however, believes that the complexity of the social world makes it a difficult object to study but not an impossible one, so long as its special character is properly understood. The fragmentation of knowledge between many individual minds might seem an insuperable barrier, but Hayek gets across it by suggesting that human minds although independent and separate have enough in common that by knowing our own mind we can know the minds of others. This hermeneutic argument in Hayek, which privileges *verstehen* (understanding) rather than *erklaren* (explanation), leads to the uniform minds hypothesis – the claim that the human mind can understand from the inside the way in which another mind reasons. Some philosophers have disputed that minds are uniform in this way,[30] but Hayek, although he gave some ground to the criticisms,[31] always maintained that there were enough common elements to sustain the idea. As he put it in his essay 'Rules, perception and intelligibility': 'the intelligibility of human action presupposes a certain likeness between the actor and the interpreter of his actions.'[32] Without this idea Hayek would lose one of the major foundations of his theory of knowledge. Since he is committed to the proposition that the data of social science is the subjective knowledge of individuals, which is always limited and fragmented, and that there are many things that can only ever be known to each individual mind, he is committed to a strong version of methodological individualism.[33] It would be a short step for him to claim that all knowledge is individual knowledge. But since he also thinks that all knowledge is fragmented and dispersed, social science is only feasible if there are enough common and collective elements present in all individuals' minds to make the products of other minds capable of being understood.[34]

This aspect of Hayek's theory of knowledge is one of its key elements, and draws heavily upon the tradition of subjectivism in the Austrian School. As he put in his essay, 'The facts of the social sciences': 'We can derive from the knowledge of our own mind in an a priori deductive fashion an exhaustive classification of all the possible forms of intelligible behaviour.'[35] Knowledge of the categories of the human mind allowed the principles governing human action to be discerned, and from that came the distinctive Austrian understanding of the nature of value, prices and costs. Value and costs are to be understood subjectively, the product of the attitudes and preference which individuals have towards objects. As Hayek explains in 'The facts of the social sciences', none of the phenomena which the social sciences study (he cites as examples tools, food, medicine, weapons, words, sentences, communications) can be defined in physical terms. They are all 'teleological concepts' in the sense that their meaning depends on the attitude which some person holds towards them. This meaning can only be understood by entering into the minds of others, and since this is impossible, it can only be done by reconstructing the meaning through the knowledge of our own mind. Social scientists use the analogy of their own mind in order to understand social phenomena: 'We all constantly act on the assumption that we can interpret other people's actions on the analogy of our own mind.'[36]

Hayek maintains that understanding human action is quite unlike understanding natural processes, since for human actions it is impossible to enumerate the physical attributes which would allow the actions to be classified in an objective manner without any resort to the attitudes and intentions of the agent. Hayek was a firm opponent of behaviourism and all forms of positive social science which tried to develop what he regarded as a false objectivism. The core of social science for him has to be subjectivism, and this stems directly from his conception of human knowledge and human action. It follows that the business of social science is not to engage in prediction, nor seek to explain individual behaviour, nor devise ways of measuring human attitudes as though they were physical phenomena. Rather it is to classify types of individual behaviour, to uncover patterns and principles:

> All that the theory of the social sciences attempts is to provide a technique of reasoning which assists us in connecting individual facts, but which, like logic or mathematics, is not about the facts.[37]

It follows according to Hayek that no social science theory can be verified or refuted by facts. He later modified this position, convinced by Popper's arguments. But in his own practice he found little use for falsifiability:

> While it is certainly desirable to make our theories as falsifiable as possible, we must also push forward into fields where, as we advance, the degree of falsifiability necessarily diminishes.[38]

He did not seek to collect facts about modern societies or to test theories. As a result, his evidence and the conclusions he drew from it, for example on British trade unions, was at times highly questionable.[39] He never developed the insight of his economics of knowledge into a research programme.[40] He regarded himself as a theory builder, and for the kinds of theories he was interested in there were no feasible tests. What he sought was social theory which would develop economic reasoning but would not pretend to knowledge it could not possess.[41]

'Economists', he wrote, 'often forget the limits of their power and give the unjustified impression that their advanced theoretical insight enables them in concrete instances to predict the consequences of given events or measures.'[42]

This emphasis on *verstehen* in Hayek's approach to economics and social science raises the question of why he did not go further and embrace history. But although Hayek is often respectful of history and historians, he is critical of the methods of many historians, in particular their inability to understand the difference between description and theory. Many historians as a result either treat facts quite uncritically, as though they existed in some sense objectively, without any mediation by theory, or impose upon the facts some speculative historicist interpretation, as the German Historical School had done. For Hayek, social theory is indispensable to an understanding of human action, and it does not depend on the accumulation of facts or on the attribution of some objective meaning to history. It depends instead on exploring the logic of human action, to understand, if not the detail, at least the general patterns of social interaction.

Social science is therefore the study of complex phenomena, seeking to discover the abstract patterns which govern them. The difference between simple and complex abstract patterns is a matter of degree. Hayek defines it as 'the minimum number of elements of which an instance of the pattern must consist in order to exhibit all the characteristic attributes of the class of patterns in question'.[43] With simple regularities statistical techniques may be very effective in establishing connections and testing theories. With complex phenomena the task is much more difficult. The danger of statistics, according to Hayek, is that it deals with the problem of large numbers by eliminating complexity, treating all the individual elements uniformly, and misconstruing the complexity of their interrelationship.[44] He even declared that no simple regularities were to be expected in social science.[45]

These strictures would rule out most of what economists (and some other branches of the social sciences) do. Their mistake, according to Hayek, is to apply the methods of those natural sciences, like physics, where a great number of simple relations between a few observables are possible, to society. Instead the social sciences should model themselves on biology or astronomy. What they needed was a cosmology, a theory of the evolution of society, just as astronomy had developed a theory of the evolution of the galaxy:

> The problem of how galaxies or social systems are formed and what is their resulting structure is much more like the

problems which the social sciences have to face than the problems of mechanics.[46]

Hayek greatly admired Darwin's theory of evolution, not because it could or should be imported directly into social science (he strongly condemned social Darwinism and socio-biology),[47] but because it was one of the best examples of pattern prediction in science. It uncovered not laws but a general pattern,[48] the detail of which could never be filled in, but which provided an explanatory principle that gained acceptance from fellow scientists. The theory did not predict specific events, merely described a range of possibilities, its empirical content consisting in what it said could not happen.[49] Hayek argued that this was the standard which economics and the other social sciences which sought to be theoretical had to match. They too were studying organisms which evolved, but in this case the organisms were made up of a vast number of individuals, and the interactions between them and the order that resulted could only be explained by understanding the nature of human action, and how coordination of the plans of myriad individuals depended upon them following abstract rules of conduct which had arisen in a process of group selection, because of the fragmented and limited nature of their knowledge.

Unintended consequences: two kinds of rationalism

Hayek's critique of the assumption of perfect information in models of economic equilibrium and his focus on the 'unintended and uncomprehended' character of knowledge drew him inexorably towards a much larger target, the role of reason in modern culture. In attacking rationalism he was aware that he would be misunderstood, particularly as he at first labelled his approach anti-rationalist. He later discarded this in favour of Popper's term critical rationalism. This was less confusing, since Hayek always thought of himself as a rationalist, a believer in the value of human reason, the importance of science, and of universal truths. He was never an irrationalist or a nihilist. He believed very deeply in the values of western civilisation and many of the values of the Enlightenment were his values. But he argued that there was not one but two kinds of rationalism in the western tradition, and that the form of rationalism which became dominant after the French Revolution was misguided and dangerous, and had eclipsed true rationalism. If unchallenged it would prevent any proper analysis of the nature of western civilisation, its economy and society, and how it might be preserved and strengthened.[50]

Critical rationalism was a tradition that had been lost or submerged, according to Hayek, and for it to be recovered it was necessary to confront what he called variously scientism and constructivism – the beliefs that in the modern era human beings were able to throw off the chains of tradition, superstition, convention and precedent, and design institutions, choose morals, invent values and plan societies as though they were starting from a blank sheet.[51] Rationalism in the form of modern science had come to be associated with the growth of human knowledge and the possibility of subjecting both the physical world and the social world to human purposes and preferences. It was the latter Hayek thought pernicious. For this kind of constructivist rationalism nothing from the past should be preserved just because it was from the past. Everything that had been inherited should be interrogated by reason, and if found inadequate or inappropriate should be abolished.

Hayek did not in principle disagree with this. There were many things that liberals achieved in the nineteenth century of which he approved. He did not favour absolutism in any form, or the monopoly of power by church or state, or slavery. He believed strongly in personal freedom, and in reforms which extended it wherever possible. But like many liberals he became concerned about the threat which was posed to liberty by certain aspects of democracy and the spread of collectivist ideas. The powers of reason were not used just against the *anciens régimes* of Europe, but increasingly against the liberal market order as well, and the ideal of a classless planned society run in the interests of all its members took hold. The ferocity of Hayek's assault upon scientism stemmed from his conviction that it mattered hugely which kind of rationalism, and therefore which concept of knowledge was dominant in western civilisation, because only his kind of rationalism, he believed, was compatible with the further progress of this civilisation. If constructivist rationalism was allowed to reign unchecked then western civilisation would be launched on a road to serfdom which would end with the extinction of human freedom. For Hayek rationalism and freedom were very closely connected, but it was a particular kind of rationalism that was required. Intellectual error was for Hayek as much as for Keynes the source of grave social consequences, so in seeking to remedy that intellectual error Hayek saw himself as performing an essential task in the battle for freedom.

Hayek did not invent an alternative rationalism. Instead he drew on an older tradition, the tradition of Mandeville, Smith, Ferguson and Hume, as well as on Kant, and Humboldt. For Mandeville and the Scottish philosophers a major focus of social enquiry was the unintended consequences of social action, the creation of orders which were the result of human action but not human design.[52] The great importance of Smith, according to Hayek, was that he was the first to see that 'we had stumbled upon methods of ordering human economic cooperation that exceed the limits of our knowledge and perception'.[53] The most important problem requiring explanation was how the activities of so many independent agents in modern societies were coordinated, so that these societies exhibited high degrees of stability and order. Human agents with their limited knowledge could act in ways that could produce a result which none of them individually had aimed at or could imagine or needed to understand. Rules had over time been selected which led individuals to behave in ways that made social life possible.[54] It was a rational process because all agents were acting to obtain the best possible result from their own standpoint, but the order that resulted was not designed or planned or intended by anyone.[55] The modern social order for Hayek was distinctive not just for its complexity, but because the way it had been constituted through the activities of so many minds over so many generations made it in important respects unknowable. The knowledge that was most important for the survival of this civilisation was the tacit knowledge encoded in the traditions, conventions and rules which had been inherited, and were the fruit of human action over millennia, rather than human design in one generation. He was fond of quoting A.N. Whitehead: 'Civilisation advances by extending the number of important operations which we can perform without thinking about them.'[56]

Hayek's reformulation of the nature of knowledge in human societies using the insights of economic theory gave him a new way to understand and formulate the insights of classical liberalism. If knowledge was dispersed and fragmented in the Great Society, the society of strangers, it followed that this was a necessary condition for the creation of order in such a society. The market order was imperfect but 'the only way so many activities depending on dispersed knowledge can be integrated into a single order'.[57] Social scientists and economists should concern themselves with understanding how this order had evolved, what its institutional underpinnings were, and how it might be sustained. Society had to be understood as an organism rather than as a machine. Abstract rules of conduct – such as several property, honesty, contract, exchange, trade, competition, privacy[58] – had furnished a new morality which helped human beings to choose among or avoid their instinctual drives. They were the product of a long history of experiments, of trial and error, which embodied a wisdom which could not be arrived at in any other way. Adam Smith's metaphor of the invisible hand, or as Hayek rephrased it less poetically 'the unsurveyable pattern',[59] expressed this characteristic of modern societies. The alternative to the invisible hand was the visible hand of human reason, taking control of human societies and remodelling them according to rational blueprints, which however lacked the all important sanction of evolutionary experience, and therefore risked claiming a knowledge which human beings could not possess.

Hayek is sometimes thought to be so pessimistic about the possibilities of human knowledge that he discounts the importance of human reason. But that is a misreading. With Hume he stresses the limited capacity of human reason, but with Kant he acknowledges that recognition of the limits of knowledge also creates the possibility of knowledge. Hayek nowhere suggests that knowledge is impossible, that human reason is unimportant, or that human beings should not seek to act rationally. What he opposes is a conception of human reason which attributes to it powers which it cannot possess. The belief that it can leads to many mistakes, because it means that instead of society, rationality and action being understood from below, as a spontaneous and unplanned process that can produce order, they are understood from above. The observer and the scientist claim a higher rationality, superior to the rationality of the individual member of society.

Economics and policy

If this approach were consistently followed it would pose a major challenge to the dominant forms of understanding knowledge and the role of science in the modern world, with far-reaching implications for economics and social science and for policy. It suggests that the problem we face is always too little knowledge rather than too much, and that the limits of our understanding should therefore impose caution on how much we interfere with the delicate organism which is society. Economists and social theorists have to engage in policy discussion and policy advice, but they should be humble about the limits of their knowledge, and cautious about their prescriptions. The failure of economists to have more impact upon policy was because they tried to imitate the procedures of the physical sciences and treated as important only what was accessible to measurement.[60]

Hayek once wrote how Austrian colleagues used to joke that they were better theorists than their German counterparts because they had so little influence on practical affairs.[61] Hayek spent his life as a theorist and only had an indirect influence on public affairs, but he had a clear idea of the role of the theorist in public policy, echoing

Keynes' view that the key task for social and economic theory was to distinguish between the agenda and non-agenda of government.[62] Only a social theory which understood the limits of reason in human affairs, the imperfections of human nature, and the character of human knowledge could succeed in doing this. Since the economist would never know all the relevant circumstances 'the economist should refrain from recommending isolated acts of interference even in conditions in which the theory tells him that may sometimes be beneficial'.[63] What such an understanding ruled out was any attempt to refashion a whole society according to the dictates of reason, because human beings could never know enough to do this. The only possible course was to try to understand the civilisation which had evolved, while always recognising that there were many aspects of it which would remain unknowable and some of which might appear irrational and incapable of justification. Hayek's advice was to respect the higher wisdom embodied in the rules and institutions which have been bequeathed to us: 'If life is to proceed, we must, in practice accept much which we cannot justify, and resign ourselves to the fact that reason cannot always be the ultimate judge in human affairs.'[64]

Such a stance can seem both fatalist and extremely conservative, and is at odds with Hayek's own practice. *Law, Legislation and Liberty* contains the outline of a utopian scheme to reform political institutions and remove the defects of democracy. His writings are full of other ideas for redesigning particular institutions and improving the workings of competition, as for example in his proposal for removing the state monopoly on money.[65] This is because Hayek did not oppose planning or rational design or reform as such. Indeed he once declared that the social scientist had the right 'critically to examine and even to judge every single value of our society'.[66] The issue, he always maintained, was not whether planning should be done or not, but whether it should be done centrally or divided among many individuals.[67] There are many passages in his writings where he explicitly defends planning, for example to promote competition.[68] He was opposed to laissez-faire, which he regarded as a rationalist doctrine taken from the same mould as socialism,[69] and argued instead for a theory which could define the proper functions of the state as well as the limits of state action.[70] He thought it entirely legitimate that any particular rule inherited from the past could be examined and if necessary abandoned or modified. Without that there could be no progress of any kind. If all rules emanating from the past had to be accepted, then modern societies would still be holding slaves and burning witches. What Hayek rejects is any wholesale junking of rules of conduct and morality, and their replacement by a new rational design. Yet attempts at wholesale revolution of the kind Hayek fears are extremely rare. The difficulty for his account of the relationship between theory and practice is that piecemeal, incremental reform is far more common, and here Hayek is a much less certain guide to what we should accept and reject.[71]

Hayek believed that only those who had studied and fully appreciated the complexity of the organism of modern societies could be trusted with making suggestions for changes to inherited rules. The only way it could be effectively improved was by improving the abstract rules which guide the individuals.[72] His own suggestions for institutional reform were put forward in that spirit, as proposals that might find favour and be adopted or which might not. No single person had the authority to prescribe how society should in future evolve. Yet despite Hayek's readiness to turn his hand to institutional design, his lasting message is one of caution. By comparison, German neo-liberals like Walter Eucken, whom Hayek admired,[73] believed more strongly than he did in the principle of a strong and active state to promote the market order.[74] Hayek, like Hume, recognised the necessity of politics but thought that little good could come from it, and sought ways to minimise the harm it could do.[75] His epistemological pessimism about the nature of knowledge was matched by a political pessimism about the possibilities of reform. He was much more struck by the likelihood of human beings unwittingly destroying the basis of the civilisation they had created by ill-considered rationalist planning than by their capacity to strengthen the institutions of the market order: '... until we have learnt to recognise the proper limits of reason in the arrangement of social affairs, there is great danger that in trying to force on society what we think is a rational pattern we may smother that freedom which is the main condition for gradual improvement.'[76] This is why he counselled that we must often accept what appears irrational and unjustifiable and contrary to our sense of justice and desert: 'The individual has to be prepared to adjust himself to changes and to submit to conventions which are not the result of intelligent design, whose justification in the particular instance may not be recognisable, and which to him will often appear unintelligible and irrational.'[77]

The way in which Hayek approaches the social world is paralleled in the way in which many environmentalists approach the natural world. Both are conceived as extremely delicate, living organisms which have evolved in particular ways and whose operations are imperfectly understood. Human interventions that alter the balance risk destroying the forces that create and sustain the order on which all human life depends. Hayek treats the market order similarly as a social ecosystem which we interfere with at our peril. What he does not address directly is whether the market order is compatible with the natural ecosystem. A liberal market order of the kind Hayek advocates permits constant interference in the natural ecosystem through the ways in which natural resources are acquired and utilised to sustain modern industry and urban lifestyles. Can a liberal market system generate spontaneously in time the innovations, new rules and changes in behaviour necessary to prevent the fatal undermining of the ecosphere on which all human activity ultimately depends?

Hayek saw most environmentalist arguments as new pretexts for intervening in the market order. He was sensitive to environmental problems, but he thought it morally objectionable for rich countries to tell poor ones that they must restrict the growth of either their population or their economy to save the planet.[78] He argued that most environmental problems are best left to the capacity of the social ecosystem to adapt and experiment. The imposition of controls by the state on the growth of population or on the use of natural resources does more harm than good.[79] Controls will be ineffective and will hinder the emergence of possible solutions. Hayek might have recognised the problem of climate change, but would have rejected recent calls for drastic action by governments to avert potentially irreversible damage to the planet. He fought a long and ultimately broadly successful campaign against the idea that detailed management of the economy by government was necessary to ensure growth, prosperity and high employment. The contemporary global economy based on neo-liberal rules is a success for Hayekian principles. But whether Hayekian principles can preserve the ecosystem poses a new and sterner test, because he never extended to natural science and technology his critique of constructivist rationalism in social science. Although rationalism has retreated in the social sphere, it still has few restraints in its quest to master and control the natural world, posing increasingly serious questions for the civilisation that Hayek so valued.

There is a further paradox. Hayek's critique of rationalism is derived from his understanding of the way in which modern societies had evolved and were coordinated, and has major implications for the methodology and practice of economics and social science. Hayek's lasting achievement was to focus attention on the limited and fragmented nature of knowledge in modern societies and the need for social and economic theorists to make that the cornerstone of their thinking. Yet in some ways he remained trapped in the rationalism he was so keen to reject. If our reason is so feeble, and if knowledge is necessarily imperfect and dispersed, how do we know this to be true? To make that claim Hayek has to take up the privileged status of observer that he is so critical of in constructivist rationalism. If he were not prepared to do so, he could not justify his project of social and economic theory at all. Despite his denunciation of the ills of scientism and constructivism Hayek is closer to the rationalism he criticises than he might like.

5

Marxism After Communism[1]

Marx always predicted that the development of capitalism as a social system would be punctuated by major crises, which would become progressively deeper and broader until the system itself was swept away. What he could not have foreseen was that the development of Marxism as a theory would also be marked by crises, both of belief and of method, which have periodically threatened its survival. In this respect at least Marxism has achieved a unity of theory and practice. No crisis has been so profound for Marxism, however, as the crisis brought about by the collapse of communism in Europe after 1989.[2] With the disappearance after seventy years of the Soviet Union, the first workers' state and the first state to proclaim Marxism as its official ideology, Marxism as a critical theory of society suddenly seemed rudderless, no longer relevant to understanding the present or providing a guide as to how society might be changed for the better. Marx at last was to be returned to the nineteenth century, where many suspected he had always belonged.

At first sight the collapse of belief among Marxist intellectuals is surprising. After all, Marxism as a distinct theoretical perspective, a particular approach in the social sciences, and an independent critical theory had long been separate from Marxism-Leninism, the official and ossified state doctrine of the Soviet Union. The various strands of Western Marxism[3] in particular had sought to keep alive Marxism as critical theory, and had frequently turned those weapons of criticism on the Soviet Union itself. 'Neither Washington nor Moscow' was a favourite slogan of the independent Marxist left. Indeed, what defined the so-called New Left, which emerged in the wake of the events of 1968, was not just its critique of western capitalism but its equally strong opposition to Stalinism in Eastern Europe and the former USSR.

But in spite of this attempt to break free from old intellectual shackles, Marxism in general could not entirely escape its association with actually existing socialism and remained deeply marked by the historical accident of being linked in the twentieth century so inextricably with the fortunes of one particular state: the Soviet Union. This association was fanned by the opponents of Marxism, who labelled all Marxists (and most social democrats) as communists and totalitarians, notwithstanding their protestations to the contrary.[4] But the association did have some basis in fact and was reflected most obviously in the ambivalence which the left continued to display or feel towards the USSR. Even those Marxists most critical of the Soviet Union could not ignore its historical significance and the fact that it appeared to represent some alternative to capitalism, however flawed in its implementation, and therefore a stage of society and history beyond capitalism. Furthermore, in the stand-off between the superpowers after 1945, the very existence of the Soviet Union limited the reach of the United States and created a space for resistance movements and alternative regimes in the Third World. Many Marxists, in fact, supported the USSR not because they admired the Soviet system, but simply because they were opposed to the United States, and because on occasion the USSR did lend support to revolutions, for example in Cuba and Vietnam.[5] Many also gave reluctant support to the USSR because at times it appeared to represent less of a threat to peace than did the United States. During the most intense moments of the Cold War – especially in the early 1980s – many on the Marxist left tended to be less critical of the Soviet Union than the United States for fanning the arms race.

The link which developed after 1917 between Marxism and the interests of a specific nation-state had another major effect: the rise of a rival form of realism in international relations in the shape of official Marxism-Leninism. This offered an assessment of the international system based upon an instrumentalist account of the relationship between state policy on the one hand and the interests of national capital on the other. The struggle to seize markets, resources and territory was regarded as the essence of the imperialist era, which Lenin predicted would be the last stage of capitalism. This brand of realism differed from mainstream realist theory in at least three ways: in being more openly materialist, in seeing a close connection between the action of states and their internal character, and in offering a broader view of the determinants of state action than just the calculation by elites of their security interests. In the theory of imperialism, in particular, what states did abroad very clearly reflected the interests of the dominant sections of their national capital and not just something as vague and ill-defined as the national interest. Nonetheless, Marxism-Leninism still viewed the international system in terms of conflict and states, and of competing national economies, rather than the global economy or the world system.[6]

It would be wrong therefore to see Soviet Marxism or Marxism-Leninism as having been theoretically opposed to realism. The opposition between it and mainstream realism as it developed in the cold war era was primarily ideological. The partisans of the two realisms backed different states, but they shared similar assumptions as to how the international system worked, disagreeing only over which state played the more progressive historical role. But what made two realisms possible was what made the post-1917 state system different from the state system of the nineteenth century. There was not just a continuation of great power rivalry, but also a contest between universalist ideologies and social systems. This became magnified after 1945 into a struggle between capitalism and communism, each championed by one of the two superpowers. In this bipolar world the ideological struggle between East and West had a profound impact on domestic politics in all countries, and established a complex network of alliances. Even severe detractors of all great power politics were forced to have an ideological preference for either the United States or the USSR. It was scarcely possible to be even-handed and condemn both equally. And for many, the USSR was not only a key player in the system of states, but the ideological 'other' – one which had a significance and magnetism far beyond its status as another superpower in a two-superpower world.

For this reason the collapse of the USSR had a deep impact not just on the international order but on the ideological arena of world politics as well. Its ignominious implosion appeared to destroy the credentials of the broad Marxist left at a stroke.[7] The triumph of the West and the triumph of capitalism were complete triumphs, and were hailed – and widely recognised – as such. The pulling down of the statues erected to the leaders of Marxism-Leninism was paralleled by the metaphorical pulling down of the theoretical edifices of Marxism in the rest of Europe, as well as in the Third World. For radical intellectuals (however distant they might have been from the Soviet Union) the shock was especially great. Politically they may have had little time for the USSR; however, so long as it survived in whatever state of political degeneration, it provided a point of reference for anti-capitalist opposition in the West. Critics did not have to profess loyalty to the Soviet Union; but the fact that it existed allowed them to be critics of their own society – and its disappearance made it more difficult for them to remain so. How could they when Soviet-style planning had not only failed to deliver the goods but had been openly rejected by the majority of those who had lived under the capitalist alternative for so many years?

In this way the fortunes of the USSR and the fortunes of Marxism became fatally entwined, and this explains why the collapse of the former appeared much more significant than just the collapse of an especially large state. Marxism's critics hailed it as an end of ideology, an end of history. Admittedly, Marxism lived on as the official doctrine of a number of states, Cuba, Vietnam, North Korea and above all China. But in the first three its only purpose seemed to be to justify one-party rule, while China, though clinging to centralised party rule, has clearly abandoned the idea of creating an alternative society or economy. Instead, from the 1980s it developed a state-led strategy which aimed at facilitating China's incorporation into global capitalism.[8]

Crawling from the wreckage

What if anything is left from the wreck and does Marxism have any relevance in the new world order which has emerged in the 1990s? One prominent view is that Marxism is now defunct as a political practice and as an ideological doctrine, and that any insights which still inhere in Marxism as a mode of analysis are best dissociated from the Marxist label and incorporated in new forms of social science.[9] Marx might then be used in a manner similar to Hobbes or Machiavelli or Kant, to reinforce an argument, or to offer a particular perspective on the problems of international politics. What would be abandoned would be the pretensions of Marxism to be a self-contained, overarching theory of the social sciences, an interdisciplinary alternative to mainstream disciplinary approaches, with its own set of concepts, methodology, and special relationship to political practice.

Many defenders of Marxism argue, however, that the collapse of communism, far from being a disaster, is in fact a great opportunity to revive the *discourse* of classical Marxism and abandon the *doctrine* of Marxism-Leninism. It liberates Marxism from a false position, tied by association to a state which had long since ceased to have anything to do with Marxism as a critical theory of society, and which represented not a step forward but a step backwards towards a just society. Marxism is therefore set to regain its vitality and its reputation for critical analysis which it enjoyed before the 1917 revolution. No longer linked to the fortunes of any particular state, it can analyse the forces which are shaping the international state system and the global economy in a dispassionate and objective manner, once again understanding the social relations of capitalism as *global* social relations. The analysis does not start from the nation-state; it starts from the global economy. The state is understood once more as one aspect of the social relations which constitute global capitalist society.[10] Marxism has lost its chains, and can speak in its own authentic accents once more to reignite a revolutionary politics.[11]

If Marxism is to have a future, however, it will not be because there is a return to the world before 1914. The global economy is very different today from what it was then, and forms of political struggle and resistance are very different also. When Marxism first emerged it identified the workers' movement as the agent which would overthrow the capitalist system. Marxism at the end of the twentieth century is a theory in search of an agent.[12] It is still capable of providing a searching and often unequalled account of the nature of the global political economy and the structures which shape its development. But as a political practice it is no longer a serious presence and lacks an effective political strategy. Very few parties of any size or significance now call themselves Marxist parties, or adopt a Marxist ideology. The old unity of theory and practice (often precarious in the past) has finally been sundered.

This may turn out to be an opportunity. The creativity of Marxism has tended to be frozen by realist doctrines such as the theory of imperialism and by instrumentalist accounts of the state, but also by historicist narratives which identified the agent of revolution as the industrial working class, and socialism as the necessary goal of history. To regain its analytical power and its place among other key perspectives with which we try to understand our world, Marxism needs to rediscover what makes it distinctive, its critique of political economy. It does not start from a blank sheet. There is a rich legacy of ideas and approaches within Western Marxism which can be drawn upon. This article will discuss ways in which contemporary Marxist theories, often building on approaches to the international system which developed in the 1970s and 1980s within western Marxism, are developing new ways of thinking about international politics which transcend the historicist and realist biases of the past.

Transcending historicism

Francis Fukuyama's claim in 1989 (before the opening of the Berlin Wall and the collapse of the Soviet Union) that history had ended was roundly criticised, particularly by postmodernists who saw it as yet another meta-narrative of modernity, but perhaps least by Marxists themselves, who recognised the importance of Fukuyama's question, drawn as it was from Alexandre Kojeve's Marxist interpretation of Hegel.[13] The issue Kojeve and Fukuyama raise is whether the great ideological contests unleashed since the French Revolution over the organisation of economic and social life have run their course, with the acknowledgement that the institutions of free market capitalism and liberal democracy are the horizon of modernity.[14] There are no viable alternatives to these forms, no higher stage of human development. Whatever can be achieved in terms of improving the distribution of resources has to be achieved within the limits of these institutions.

These claims strike at the core of Marxism as a political theory of revolution, since the aim of Marx's historical materialism was to demonstrate that there was a stage of human development beyond capitalism which would guarantee the kind of freedoms and opportunities which capitalism had promised but was unable to deliver because of the way it was organised as a class society. Only the abolition of classes and the abolition of the conditions which reproduced class relations in a capitalist society could allow class society with all its inequalities of power and resources to be overcome.

Redressing such social inequalities remains at the core of any Marxist project, but what the debate on the end of history drew attention to was whether Marxists needed to be attached any longer to the particular narrative which for so long had framed its enquiries. This narrative was historicist by adhering to the notion that history had an objective meaning, and was evolving towards an inevitable destination through a series of historical stages. Such historicist guarantees in the past did much to discredit and invalidate Marxist scholarship. The struggle to purge Marxism of this kind of historicism has been a long one; what Fukuyama has succeeded in doing (inadvertently) is reminding his Marxist readers that, for Hegel, the meaning of history was revealed only after a particular phase of history is past. Hegel pronounced history dead after the battle of Jena in 1808, because he recognised in the principles of the French Revolution as carried forward by Napoleon's victorious armies the fully developed principles of modernity. What escapes Fukuyama and many of his critics is that the claim that history has ended can only be a judgement on a particular history, and a particular time. At the very moment of the judgement a new process will be under way. What is valid in Fukuyama is his insight that the end of the 1980s was a decisive turning point. A new world was being made, and this involved the supersession of the terms of the ideological battle of the old. What is invalid is his belief that this new world will not develop its own history.

The fall of communism forced Marxists to acknowledge finally that the confident belief that socialism would involve the replacement of the market by some form of planning, however decentralised or democratically organised, was flawed. This belief was one of the lasting legacies of the 1917 revolution. Although some Marxists always argued that the Soviet Union was not socialist at all but 'something else', many did believe that it contained certain socialist elements, however distorted and corrupted.[15] Those elements were precisely the elements which prevented it from being a market economy and subject to market disciplines. And for most Marxists (though again not all) socialism was always identified with the existence of a non-market economy – and according to most Marxists this type of economy was either superior in character or in transition to something higher.

In the last ten years, this historicism has almost completely disappeared, and there is now little disposition to think about some stage of human development beyond capitalism guaranteed by the evolution of history. But this does not mean that it is not possible within a Marxist framework to raise questions about what an alternative to capitalism might look like, or what ethical principles may be used to criticise the existing organisation of the international order. Two examples of these kinds of writing are the analytical Marxism of John Roemer[16] and the critical theory of Andrew Linklater.[17] Roemer has developed new thinking on the characteristics of a socialist economy. His version of market socialism offers a decentralised model of a socialist economy in which productive assets are publicly owned but in which all economic activity is organised through markets. This is a theoretical exercise, exploring different possibilities in social and economic organisation. It starts from the assumption that a political transfer of all assets from private to public hands has occurred. Roemer is not interested in the mechanism by which such a transfer might take place, and those Marxists from the analytical school who have investigated that question have been pessimistic about the political conditions ever arising within democratic political systems which would create electoral majorities for socialism.[18] Nevertheless, work on organisational forms which do not prejudge the desirability of different modes of governance has begun to make a significant contribution to the imagining of alternatives to dominant capitalist forms.[19]

Andrew Linklater has developed a very different kind of analysis. He has sought to extend the idea of critical theory developed by the

Frankfurt School to issues of international politics.[20] Linklater takes as the most important legacy of Marxism the development of a critical theory which explores the possibility for human emancipation and for creating a universal society, which would include all peoples, which the progress of industrialisation has made possible. He argues that it was this insight which gave Marxism its great moral force and which allows the formulation of ethical principles by which existing arrangements in international politics can be judged.[21]

The rejection of historicism by what remains of the Marxist left – and in particular the belief in the historical inevitability of higher stages beyond capitalism – has not of course meant the abandonment of historical materialism. It has rather aided the return to the fundamental contribution made by Marxism to the analysis of social development and to politics. Marxism's great strength, acknowledged by many of its detractors as well as by its advocates, was its incisive analysis of capitalism as an economic and political system, how that system came into existence, the social relations and institutions which defined it, and how these were reproduced and sustained both temporally and spatially.[22] Such a focus is more interested in capitalism as an existing reality rather than socialism as a distant possibility, and therefore more focused on capitalist reproduction rather than capitalist crisis. The adaptability, resilience, flexibility, inventiveness and dynamism of capitalism as a social and political system take precedence in the analysis over its fragility, vulnerability, sclerosis and imminent demise. The possibility of crisis and the conditions under which it occurs remains a key part of Marxist analysis, but it is no longer considered within the political perspective of immediate political revolution and the transition to socialism, but within the broader context of the conditions of reproduction of capital.[23]

The historicist elements in Marxism previously introduced a strong moralising tone into the discussion of certain institutional characteristics of capitalism, particularly the market, because this was destined to disappear in the higher stage of socialism. With the discarding of historicism Marxists have been freed to develop a theory of the capitalist economy which no longer demonises the market, but treats it instead as one tool through which economies are governed. This has opened the way to analyses of the institutional diversity of capitalism, discarding the assumption of an invariant logic of capital, and investigating the contribution which markets make to the reproduction of capital, how markets are embedded in other institutions, how they are constituted and regulated, and how they can be steered.[24]

Transcending realism

One of the distinctive contributions of a Marxist perspective to international politics is its understanding that capitalism from the beginning was global rather than national in its reach. This insight became clouded during the ascendancy of Marxist theories of imperialism, but in the 1970s it was reborn in new theories of how the economic, social and political institutions of capitalism make up a world system[25] or world order.[26] One of the spurs to this has been the development of the discourse around globalisation. Marxists can rightly claim that Marx and Engels were among the first nineteenth-century theorists who perceived the trends towards globalisation not just of economic activity, but of social arrangements, culture and politics. For Marx, the creation of the world market was one of the outcomes of capital accumulation. The undermining of existing boundaries of territory and concepts of space was one of the main ways in which new sources of profit were located, and the reproduction of capital assured.[27] Marx's famous passage from *The Communist Manifesto* is often cited, but it bears repeating, because it encapsulates so well the extraordinary insight which Marx and Engels had into the dynamism of capitalism and its consequences for the political organisation of the world economy. Their tone, as many commentators have noted, was more adulatory than critical of the achievements of capitalism:[28]

> The bourgeoisie has through its exploitation of the world market given a cosmopolitan character to production and consumption in every country. To the great chagrin of reactionists, it has drawn from under the feet of industry the national ground on which it stood. All old-established national industries have been destroyed or are daily being destroyed. They are dislodged by new industries, whose introduction becomes a life and death question for all civilised nations, by industries that no longer work up indigenous raw material, but raw material drawn from the remotest zones; industries whose products are consumed not only at home but in every quarter of the globe. In place of the old wants, satisfied by the productions of the country, we find new wants, requiring for their satisfaction the products of distant lands and climes. In place of the old local and national seclusion and self-sufficiency, we have intercourse in every direction, universal interdependence of nations.

And as in material, so also in intellectual production. The intellectual creations of individual nations become common property ... The bourgeoisie, by the rapid improvement of all instruments of production, by the immensely facilitated means of communication, draws all, even the most barbarian nations into civilisation. The cheap prices of its commodities are the heavy artillery with which it batters down all Chinese walls ... It compels all nations, on pain of extinction, to adopt the bourgeois mode of production; it compels them to introduce what it calls civilisation into their midst, i.e. to become bourgeois themselves. In one word, it creates a world after its own image.

This passage has been rightly cited as one of the first theories of globalisation,[29] remarkable for the way in which it draws together economic, political and cultural aspects of the impact of capital accumulation and understands capitalism as a global system. But for much of the twentieth century the organisation of capitalism *as a global economy* has not been central to Marxist analysis. Instead, as argued earlier, the organisation of capitalism as *imperialism*, a more narrow political concept, was emphasised instead.[30] One of the consequences of the collapse of the Soviet Union has been the recognition that the global economy has entered a new phase. For the first time since the early years of the century it can be said to be truly unified, or more accurately as Castells puts it, unified for the first time.[31] In the seventy years after the 1917 revolution the global economy did not cease to exist, but its organisation was marked by the strength of national economies, regional blocs, and in policy terms by protectionism and state regulation. All national economies became relatively closed, particularly in the period up to the 1950s. In the 1960s and particularly after 1971 this structure of the global economy began to break down, and the pressures towards greater openness increased. The discourse of globalisation became current, and then dominant in the 1980s. No country or regime appeared able to withstand the pressures for greater openness; the process culminated in the opening of the territories of the former USSR, which followed the previous opening of China (by its communist government). The extent of incorporation of many countries continued to vary, but only a very few countries in the global economy, such as Cuba and North Korea, remained significantly closed at the end of the millennium.

In the nineteenth century the growth of the world market went hand in hand with the strengthening of the most powerful capitalist states, and their political and military reach within this world market. While Marxists shared many of the same assumptions as liberal cosmopolitans like Richard Cobden as to the power of global markets to transform the world and undermine nation-states, they were also sceptical about the prospects for a peaceful world of economic interdependence. On the contrary, they argued that there was a close connection between economic and political power, and that the state would be used to create favourable conditions for capital accumulation.

The relationship between the global economy and the international state system is a central question in international political economy. Marxists have always argued that there is a close connection between economic and political power, although there have been fierce controversies about the degree of autonomy possessed by the state, and whether the state is best understood in terms of the logic of capital or the struggle between classes.[32] But a further controversy, which can only perhaps be fully appreciated now that Marxism–Leninism and the phase of Marxist realism are over, is whether the focus of the Marxist analysis of capitalism should be the national state and the national economy or the international state and the global economy. Are the social relations of capitalism to be grasped as global or national phenomena?[33] Marx recognised the very strong pressures towards the creation of a unified global economy, and at the same time the fragmentation of political power into a multitude of separate authorities, but left relatively few clues as to how he would have theorised the tension between the two.

Imperialism and war

The tension has been resolved in different ways in Marxist writings. The most influential in the twentieth century was the theory of imperialism, and its variants, which offered a Marxist-realist account of international relations focused on individual capitalist nation-states. Theorists of imperialism argued that the most powerful states used their military and financial capacities to seize as much territory and resources as they could to increase the opportunities for successful accumulation by their own capitalists. The rivalry between the leading capitalist powers was therefore endemic in the system of capital accumulation itself. As the world market was extended and its immense possibilities opened up, the absence of any overarching political authority created fierce competition between states – economic, political, and finally military. The link between capitalism and war became one of the firmest postulates of Marxist analysis, expressed in its classic form in Lenin's immensely influential pamphlet *Imperialism*.[34]

The outbreak of the First World War appeared to vindicate this Marxist analysis, and with the establishment of the Soviet state this became one of its central beliefs and *Imperialism* one of its canonical texts. However, there were from the start other ways of analysing the tendencies of the global economy in Marxism, for example those developed by Karl Kautsky, Rudolf Hilferding, or Rosa Luxemburg. These became buried by the rush to canonise Lenin, and the freezing of Marxism-Leninism as a state ideology. The full richness of the Marxist analysis was obscured. Only much later did new theories of the global economy and world order reemerge.

The thesis of imperialism leading to war had been employed to explain the division of the world into regional blocs in the 1930s and the outbreak of the Second World War, but the theory began to work extremely poorly from the 1950s onwards. The main conflict in the international state system was between the United States and the USSR rather than between the leading capitalist powers (Europe against America) and the great colonial empires were dismantled. The concept of discrete national capitals, which underlaid the idea of imperialist powers using economic, political and military means to compete against one another, also began to break down as capital appeared to become more transnational with the emergence of large global companies.

The greater openness of the global economy in the 1990s has echoes of the world before 1917, but with some important differences, not least the absence (so far) of the interimperialist rivalry, the aggressive nationalisms and the drift towards war which so marked international politics at the beginning of the century. The economic and organisational structure of capitalism is also quite different; in the course of the twentieth century it has been transformed by the rise of the public limited company, Fordist production methods, the incorporation of science into the production process, and the expanded role of the state in the reproduction of capital.

The more open global economy of the 1990s also contrasts quite markedly with the interwar years, when Marxists predicted that rivalry between the leading imperialist powers would again plunge the world into war. The contemporary (and highly uneven) development of new regionalisms around the three poles of the global economy – Europe, Japan and the United States – has introduced a new tension but hardly matches the regional blocs of the 1930s.[35] The global economy is by no means free of military conflicts, which continue to involve several of the leading capitalist states, but there have been no signs of military clashes between these states themselves.

Hegemony

One influential explanation for the lack of conflict in the cold war era employed the concept of hegemony. The division of the world between the two superpowers helped to suppress the natural conflicts between different capitalist states, and enabled the leading capitalist powers to be successfully united under American leadership to defeat communism.[36] But some Marxists, like Ernest Mandel, thought that this was an unnatural state of affairs, and predicted that once tension was reduced between the superpowers the old pattern would reassert itself and capitalist states would once again use military power to further the interests of their national capitalists.[37] But although the cold war has now ended and the Soviet Union has been dismantled, there is no sign that the conflicts over trade and investment between the US and Japan, or between the US and the EU, which undoubtedly exist, will be resolved by force.

The concept of hegemony applied to the problems of the more open global economy of the 1970s and 1980s was important in stimulating the development of new approaches which rejected the nation-state as the primary focus, and sought to grasp capitalism once more as a global system of production and exchange.[38] One of the more ambitious attempts to do this was world systems theory.[39] Originating as a critique of modernisation theory, it developed a concept of capitalism as a world system in which there was continual conflict between the centre and the periphery and between the different components of the centre for control of the periphery. The world system develops through cycles in which at any one time one power may be in a position to unify the centre and exercise hegemony over the whole world system due primarily to its economic dominance, which is closely tied to relative economic performance as measured by trade, productivity and foreign investment. In world systems theory, the world moves through periods of relative stability and prosperity followed by periods of relative conflict, disorder and war. The ending of the cold war on this account does not signal the beginning of a new phase of American hegemony, but a phase in which American power will be increasingly challenged as other states assert themselves.

In world systems theory, capitalism is understood primarily as a system of exchange and circulation, rather than as a system of production. The competition between nation-states is conceived still as realists would understand it, but there are many other agents and forces as well which shape the world system. A different approach was developed by Robert Cox. Like world systems theorists, Cox departed considerably from classical Marxism. He treated capitalism as a global system which needed to be understood through specific historical structures (ensembles of ideas, material capabilities and institutions), and at three different levels (social forces, states and world orders). Cox included nation-states, but widened the analysis to production systems and broader forms of governance, and put special emphasis on the power of ideas. He drew on Gramsci's analysis of national social formations to develop a historical political economy which provided a critical account of how world orders are historically constructed. This approach, as it has been developed by Cox and others, has come to be labelled transnational historical materialism.[40] At its centre is a different concept of hegemony. Cox is more struck by the strength of the forces holding the global order together than in its proclivity to self-destruct, and by the way in which transnational elites seek to win consent for their visions of the world. He focuses particularly on how hegemony is constructed in a world economy in which political authority is fragmented, paying special attention to how transnational elites are unified through the creation of networks which share ideas, aggregate interests and facilitate common institutions. These world orders[41] give rise to what the Amsterdam School have called comprehensive concepts of control,[42] such as Keynesianism and neo-liberalism, which are then diffused through national political systems. Monetarism and neo-liberalism were not ideas which arose in particular domestic contexts and were then exported. They were fashioned within the transnational networks of the capitalist class and then adopted and adapted within particular countries. Nation-states remain important in this world but they are not all-important. There are many other agents, in particular transnational companies and international organisations, the 'organic intellectuals' of the new transnational ruling class. The needs of the transnational business elite for order and predictability lead to the creation of global institutions and the co-option of political groups around the world. One implication of these analyses is that a transnational state is gradually emerging in which key domestic elites have become part of a transnational elite, dedicated to maintaining the institutions of the transnational global economy rather than being concerned with purely domestic interests. The decisive locus of power in such conceptions lies with transnational capital itself; it is its interests and agendas which now drive the global economy and global politics. There are of course many frictions and conflicts, both within states and between them, but these have in general been managed and kept subordinate to the wider aims of ensuring that the global order itself is sustained.

Accumulation and regulation

An important alternative tradition to the emphasis on capitalism as a unified global system have been those traditions in western Marxism influenced by Gramsci and later Althusser, which have focused on national paths of development, and national social formations, distinguishing between their economic, political and ideological levels, and analysing the way in which different modes of production are combined. Most influential of these has been the regulation approach.[43] The regulation school developed the concepts of regimes of accumulation and modes of regulation to characterise different national social formations. Regimes of accumulation are interlinked patterns of production and consumption which can be reproduced over a long period; modes of regulation are the rules, norms, conventions, networks, forms of governance, and institutions which organise and sustain regimes of accumulation. With these tools, regulationists have analysed the peculiarities of different national social formations and the types of production system, Fordism and post-Fordism, which characterise them. They show how certain kinds of policies and institutional arrangements protect and insulate societies. In this way the regulation school is part of a broader engagement by Marxists with the historical institutionalists in exploring the specificities of national capitalisms, and whether there are different models of capitalism, which are path dependent and institutionally distinct. The regulation school, although it discusses global trends and global patterns, plays down the significance of either accumulation or the market on a world scale, preferring to analyse capitalism as a set of interlinked national economies, which are structured through political, legal and cultural relationships.[44]

The reproduction of capital

World systems theory, transnational historical materialism and the regulation approach have been criticised by those Marxists who wish to revive the classical Marxist emphasis on capitalism as a system which is defined by the accumulation and reproduction of capital.[45] These approaches all emphasise the need to understand capital as a social relation – the accumulation of capital means simultaneously the reproduction and extension of the social relationships which constitute capital. These are long-term structures which include the economy, the state and the household. Theorists such as Ernest Mandel have analysed the long waves of capitalist development, and their punctuation by social, political and economic crises.[46] This Marxist tradition criticises world systems theory for its reliance on a theory of circulation, markets and exchange in its analysis of power in the global system, the Gramscians for the weight they give to ideology and politics, and the regulationists for their emphasis upon national social formations in the reproduction of capital and the imprecision of concepts like Fordism and post-Fordism. Classical Marxism has in its turn been criticised by representatives of these other schools for determinism and reductionism. But it remains a powerful analytical tool for seeking to understand capitalism as a global system of accumulation. A major contribution to this tradition has recently been made by Robert Brenner, seeking to understand the trajectory of capitalist development in recent decades.[47]

Fundamental to any Marxist analysis is its understanding of the economy, how capital is reproduced, how profitability is maintained, and how crises develop. The Marxist insight that the capitalist economy although fragile and unstable is also hugely productive, adaptable and dynamic directs attention to how capitalism reproduces itself. Reproduction of capital has increasingly been conceived in a much broader manner than was once common, in particular through studies of domestic labour and the organisation of the household.[48] Classical Marxism continues to emphasise that the driving force of capitalism is the search for profits, to make possible the self-valorisation of capital; everything is secondary to this. The driving force is not the creation of a world market; rather the world market is an outcome of the drive for profitability.

One of the issues raised by the classical Marxist analysis of accumulation is how far this is a process outside politics, essentially ungovernable, a stream which can be dammed and sometimes diverted, but only for a time. Sooner or later the remorseless process of capital accumulation bursts through, subverting all the controls devised to tame it. Historical structures such as welfare states – with their employment rights, minimum wages, and social programmes – which have been established in so many advanced capitalist countries, although in different forms,[49] may rest on economic foundations which can swiftly be undermined if those who control capital conclude that higher profits are to be made elsewhere. This idea of a race to the bottom, or immiserisation as Marx and Engels called it, is regarded by classical Marxists as one of the historical tendencies of the process of capital accumulation, however much it may be delayed or diverted for long periods. Capital always seeks out those circumstances in which costs are reduced to the minimum and profits maximised. The ability of capital to do this depends on a number of factors, including the utilisation of new technologies and the speeding up of the pace and intensity of production to increase the exploitation of labour, the transfer of costs to the state (hence to the general taxpayer rather than the individual capitalist), the reorganisation of domestic labour, and the discovery of new markets. Under capitalism no pattern remains fixed for ever. Upheaval, crisis, reorganisation, innovation are the essence of this most unpredictable mode of production.

The continuing power of classical Marxism to inspire major insights into the shape of international politics can be seen in two major recent works by Manuel Castells and Giovanni Arrighi. Capitalism's dynamism always seems at its greatest in periods of great technological innovation, and the period at the end of the twentieth century with the unfolding of the informational revolution is certainly one of those. At such times all forms of employment can be affected, and huge transfers take place between different sectors of the economy and types of occupation. The consequences are profound for individuals but also for national economies. Castells, in the spirit of classical Marxism, charts how a fundamental change in the way the mode of capitalism is organised has implications for all aspects of social life – culture, politics, identity, leisure, consumption, technology, work and households.[50] At the same time, for all the dynamism of capital and its ability to subvert all existing patterns of social life, Giovanni Arrighi has also pointed to the persistence of hierarchical patterns and uneven development in the world economy. The rich economies stay rich. In the course of the twentieth century the rank order of the leading capitalist states changed, but not the identity of those states, with one exception – Japan. Otherwise the list is the same in 2000 as it was in 1900.[51] These two works have profound implications for our understanding of international politics and the global system.

The future of Marxism

Marxism has the resources to detach itself from the ruins of communism if it moves decisively beyond historicism and realism, building on some of the intellectual traditions of western Marxism and developing critical theory,[52] but not forgetting its central insight into the nature of society, the social relationships which define the different modes of production which have existed in human history. Many of the other aspects which have defined historical materialism in the past, in particular the historicism which saw capitalism as a stage of development towards socialism and the realism which analysed imperialism in terms of the strategies of national capital and states, have fallen away. But capitalism as a very present reality has not fallen away, and Marxism still offers a crucial set of concepts for understanding it.

What precisely is the nature of this contribution? The microfoundations of Marxism have not worn well, despite the huge investment of time and ingenuity in preserving them. The labour theory of value can be defended as a historical institutionalist account of the social relationships which define capitalism, and in which markets are embedded, but not as a device which allows precise measurement of prices or the modelling of the way in which markets work.[53] Since prices cannot be derived from labour-time values, the microfoundations of Marxism cannot supply a theory of how resources are allocated in markets. But the microfoundations of mainstream economics do not provide an adequate account of the wider institutional context of markets. This is where Marxism can still make a major contribution. It provides an understanding of the nature of power, how it arises and how it is exercised in different modes of production through its analysis of how capital as a set of social relationships is reproduced. Understanding capital as a set of social relationships which are always capable of being contested politically and ideologically, rather than as a quantity of resources which are simply utilised in production, remains its critical insight.

Marxism is still noted for its concern with the dynamics of social systems.[54] More than any other observer in the nineteenth century Marx had an extraordinary grasp of what made capitalism as a mode of production such a subversive and revolutionary force, although even he cannot have imagined what its full effects would be. His intuition that capital would not rest until it had pulled all societies and all sectors into the world market and until it had expelled living labour from the production process altogether by driving towards automation was remarkable when it was written, since capitalism had at that time penetrated a small part of the world, and only in England and a few parts of Europe had industrial capitalism really taken hold.[55] Marx has always been much praised, even by his critics, for the quality of his foresight.[56]

But while Marx was insightful on questions like this he was blind on other questions, particularly nationalism. This may be because Marxism's peculiar strength is derived from its economism. Western Marxists for seventy years have been seeking to deny this and deflect attention away from it. Vulgar forms of economism, in which all politics and all ideology are simply reduced to crude class interest, and the state becomes a puppet in the hands of the ruling class, are uninteresting and have been rightly criticised. But attempts to prove that Marxism contains no economism at all end by throwing away what is still valuable in Marxism – its insistence on the need to understand how modes of production depend upon the continual reproduction of particular social relations which then have particular outcomes in terms of the distribution of power and resources. Marxism in the end has to stand by the claim that the economic power which accrues to the class which controls productive assets is a crucial determinant of the manner in which political, cultural and ideological power are exercised. Many kinds of sophisticated concepts can be deployed to understand the intricacies of the relationship, but in the end if the primacy of the economic is lost, then Marxism loses its distinctiveness and its value in social theory. There are after all many theories of the social which do not privilege the economic, or assume that modern society is to be understood primarily in terms of the way in which the economy is organised. Marxism does make this claim, and although it has often been made rather badly, it is a serious claim, which like Hobbes' claim about sovereignty is a perspective on history and on society which cannot easily be set aside.

Making the most of Marxism as economism does not therefore mean embracing instrumental theories of class, which imply that class itself is the crucial feature of capitalism, and that the people who own property form the ruling class which controls society and politics. What is important about an economistic reading of Marx is the notion of capital as a social relation. It is the reproduction of this social relation, and its invasion into so many spheres of social life and into so many parts of the globe that is one of the most central features of any conception of modernity. The fragmentation of ownership with the rise of the corporate economy and the disappearance of an easily identifiable ruling class is not an objection to Marxism if what is important for Marxist theory is tracing how capital as a social relation is reproduced, imposing the structures within which all agents have to operate, whether in assisting capital or resisting it.

Marxism often lost its way in the past through claiming to be a total science of society, and moreover the only objective and true one. These claims were never credible and have become even less so in a period of questioning of the foundations and truth claims of all theories. Marxism is incapable of explaining all the trends and phenomena of the contemporary world, but it can offer an account of such matters as globalisation, inequality, the informational revolution, the changing structure of work, and the changing nature of the state. It also has interesting things to say about the boundaries between the public and the private, and the meaning of non-commodified spheres such as welfare and health – public goods which exist outside the sphere of capital and its operations. But it also provides an understanding as to why any such noncapitalist spheres are never inviolable, and may be subject to political attack and invasion.

A contemporary Marxism needs to direct attention to the potentiality and the limits in the continued spread and development of capitalism as a mode of production. The political interest behind this kind of enquiry has undoubtedly shifted. At one time the perspective was the coming social revolution which would remove the capital relation once and for all. Today's Marxists are more likely to be concerned with how forms of governance at different levels of the international system – global, regional, national, subnational and local – may impose or release constraints on the way in which capitalism operates and is embedded in national and regional societies. This approach would not have been strange to Marx. He recognised the importance of reforms in limiting what capital could do in providing sites of resistance in which other social relations and ideas could flourish. The Factory Acts of the 1840s which set limits on the way in which children and women could be employed in factories were one of the examples on which he commented in *Capital*.[57]

Capitalism as a global system has grown both more interdependent and more fragile. It has generated enormous wealth and enormous knowledge in the last two hundred years which now support a population far in excess of any that has existed in previous human history. At the same time the distribution of the wealth capitalism created has remained highly concentrated and unequal, industrial activities have reached the point where they threaten the life support systems of the planet, and the system of accumulation itself is marked by huge instabilities and imbalances which could still implode in a devastating financial crisis with far-reaching political and economic consequences. Marxist analysis therefore points to the urgent need for new systems of multi-level governance in the global economy to identify, manage and steer these problems. Marxists remain divided in their prognoses. Some are pessimistic and fatalistic about the future of capitalism.[58] It sometimes seems like a giant ship which has slipped its moorings and which drifts on to its destruction because no one can find a way to steer it or take control. But others are more hopeful.[59] If acts of resistance multiply, new structures and new institutions can be built. It may not be possible to live in the modern world without capitalism, but capitalism need not be a single fate.

G.D.H. Cole and the History of Socialist Thought[1]

G.D.H. Cole was one of the leading intellectuals of the British Labour movement in the first half of the twentieth century, ranking with Harold Laski and R.H. Tawney. Through his enormous output of books, articles and pamphlets, he became one of the best-known socialists in the world. He wrote *A History of Socialist Thought* in the final years of his life; the first volume appeared in 1953 and the last posthumously in 1960. It had been substantially completed, and was prepared for publication by Cole's wife, Margaret Cole, with the help of Julius Braunthal and Humphrey Cole. The five volumes (two of them double volumes) comprised over 3,000 pages of text, and were a remarkable achievement, which Cole himself never expected to live to complete.[2] He had been in poor health ever since diabetes was diagnosed in 1931 and his condition worsened in the 1950s.

His original intention had been to write simply a history of socialist thought and not a history of the socialist movement, but although this worked well for the first two volumes, which deal with the early socialists and with Marx and Bakunin, Cole found that in the later periods he could not disentangle the two, and expanded the book to include a detailed history of how socialism developed as a political movement through the insurrections of 1848, the founding of the First International, the Paris Commune, the Second International, the Russian Revolution and the struggle against fascism. He concluded his *History* in 1939, although in his final volume he often refers to post-1945 developments.

Cole's *History* covers the period between 1789 and 1939, but the bulk of it is focused on the 'Socialist century' inaugurated by the events of 1848.[3] This was the period when socialism, having been associated with a few isolated thinkers and groups, grew into a worldwide movement which transformed politics and political debate. Cole was an active participant in the later stages of this history, and an original contributor to socialist political thought in his own right, as one of the chief theorists of guild socialism. His *History* is remarkable for its detail and its encyclopaedic knowledge as well as for its lucidity. It is primarily a history of European socialist thought, and in particular of socialist thought within Britain, France, Germany and Russia. But space is also found for many other European countries, as well as for socialist movements in other parts of the world, including the United States, China and Japan. The breadth and depth of his knowledge are astonishing, and these volumes will always be read for the portraits of individual socialist thinkers, and for the huge variety of socialist thought which he includes.

A History of Socialist Thought was written at a particular time and in a particular context. As a result of the Second World War and its aftermath socialism had never been stronger. Isolated and contained within Russia in the 1920s and 1930s, communism had spread across the world and was now installed in Eastern and Central Europe, including part of Germany, as well as China. Powerful communist parties were established in many countries from France to Japan. Social democracy which had been so battered by the rise of fascism had been rebuilt and was back as a major force in western European politics. But for all the apparent advances of socialism, Cole's final volume is tinged with regret, disillusion and foreboding. The heroic days of socialism seemed to be over, and the two main forms of socialism on offer, Soviet Communism and social democracy, seemed unlikely to lead towards socialism. Thirty years after Cole's death, his forebodings were fulfilled. 1989, the bicentenary of the French Revolution and the centenary of the founding of the Second International, saw the wheel come full circle for socialism. The fall of the Berlin Wall signalled the end of communism in Europe, and the failure of the experiment which had been launched by the Russian Revolution in 1917. At the same time the programmes of European social democracy were no longer socialist in Cole's sense, because they no longer aimed at the abolition of wage labour and the elimination of private ownership of the means of production.

Although much of the socialism which Cole explores in these volumes now belongs to the past, his *History* is of lasting value in charting the different forms socialism assumed, and the way in which it was shaped by events, personalities and doctrines, and also in explaining the reasons why socialism ceased to make progress. His *History* will always be read by those who wish to understand the nature of the socialist movements in the period of their greatest scope and influence.

Life

George Douglas Howard Cole was born in 1889 in Cambridge and died in 1959 in London.[4] His father was an estate agent. He was educated at private schools, including St Paul's in London, which had a high academic reputation, and was particularly good at preparing its best students for entry to Oxford and Cambridge. Cole won an exhibition to Balliol College, Oxford, and after graduating with first class honours in Greats, he secured a prize fellowship at Magdalen College. After a spell working full-time in research posts for trade unions and as a working-class adult education tutor he returned to Oxford as Reader in Economics in 1925. In 1944 he was appointed to the Chichele Chair in Social and Political Theory and a Fellow of All Souls.

He first became a socialist at school as a result of reading William Morris. What particularly attracted him in Morris was his utopian vision of a community based on equality and human fellowship. This romantic idea of a new moral world was always at the heart of Cole's socialism. Indeed he described himself as a utopian socialist.[5] But what also inspired him was the Labour movement, its organisations, its beliefs, its culture. His first major book was *The World of Labour,* published in 1913, which analysed the Labour movement in Britain, France and the United States, its organisation and its prospects, and asked what the Labour movement was capable of making of itself. Throughout his life Cole never left this world of labour. It provided him with his benchmarks and his beliefs. He worked assiduously to organise and educate the working class, believing passionately in the independent action of the Labour movement as the instrument through which socialism would be achieved.

Cole joined the Fabian Society at Oxford and quickly became one of its rising stars, but his utopian streak and his strong support for trade union direct action rather than parliamentary action brought him into sharp conflict with Sidney and Beatrice Webb and other leading Fabians. After heated rows Cole resigned from the Fabian Society in 1915 and was not to rejoin until 1928. Cole always believed much more in building socialism from the bottom than in imposing it from the top, and in his early writings was sceptical about the desirability of allowing the Labour movement to become too involved with the state, for fear that it would be compromised. Cole became one of the leading exponents of guild socialism, which saw the future socialist society as a decentralised federation of self-governing guilds, organised on a functional basis. The guild socialists were strongly opposed to centralising power in the state and to the narrowness of representative parliamentary democracy, arguing that this would destroy the freedom, choice and autonomy which were indispensable aspects of a socialist society.

Guild socialism belonged to that strand of socialism before the First World War which favoured direct action over parliamentary action, and wanted socialists to keep their organisations independent of the existing state. The state was not an instrument which could be used to deliver socialism. Cole threw himself wholeheartedly into working for the trade unions, and managed to claim exemption from conscription because of his wartime post with the Engineering Union (the ASE). He became a leading theorist of guild socialism through publications such as *Self-Government in Industry* (1917) and *Guild Socialism Restated* (1920) and developed ever more intricate models of organisation for a future socialist society organised along guild lines without any overarching centralised state.[6]

The appeal of guild socialism, however, was fleeting. The huge changes wrought by the First World War – including the Bolshevik seizure of power in Russia and the proclamation of the first workers' state, along with the collapse of so many of the old empires and *anciens régimes* of Europe and the establishment of mass democracy – transformed politics, and polarised the socialist movement between the advocates of a revolutionary seizure of power, following the Bolshevik example, and the advocates of gradualist parliamentary reform. This schism between communism and social democracy, reform and revolution, was to become one of the great themes of his *History*. But it also contributed to the rapid demise of the guild socialist movement. The tide was moving strongly in favour of state action to establish socialism, with the debate focusing on whether socialists should overthrow the existing state or seize control of it.

In common with the rest of his generation of socialists, Cole had to choose after 1918 whether to throw in his lot with the communists or with the social democrats. The unity of the Second International had been broken in 1914 and was never to be restored. Socialism could no longer pretend to be a united movement. Many of the guild socialists in Britain joined the newly formed Communist party, and it was attractive to Douglas and Margaret Cole at first. But the tight discipline and authority of the Bolsheviks persuaded Cole that this was not for him, and in the decades that followed he emerged as a strong, although always sympathetic, critic of communism. At the same time Cole was also extremely doubtful about parliamentary socialism, but in practice, he found himself increasingly drawn into the politics of the British Labour party. He came to recognise that any strategy for achieving socialism in Britain had to be focused on the Labour party. Influencing this party and the wider Labour movement became the centre of his activity and his life's work.

Cole poured out writings through the 1930s and 1940s aimed at exploring the possibilities of democratic socialist change and seeking to educate and persuade the widest possible audience. He never paid much attention to his academic reputation or to producing the books that might have secured it. Far more important to him was to produce the arguments and the writings which could advance the cause of socialism. *A History of Socialist Thought* is the culmination of his life's work, and the distillation of forty years of selfless work for the Labour movement. At the same time it is an extraordinary work of scholarship. Cole uses hardly any footnotes, and does not provide references or sources for his judgements and conclusions. Nothing was to interrupt the accessibility of the text. But the weight of scholarship and the depth of understanding are apparent on every page.

Cole was greatly helped in his work by his wife, Margaret Cole, whom he met through the Fabians. In the 1930s they helped set up the New Fabian Research Bureau and became active Fabians once again. Cole became the first chairman of the Fabian Society while Margaret served as honorary secretary from 1939 to 1953.[7] She never liked the male atmosphere of Oxford, and lived most of the time in London. Cole divided his time between the two. Throughout his career Cole kept up an extraordinary volume of publication, which extended to detective stories, co-authored with Margaret. Despite his commitment to internationalism he was intensely and passionately English, even parochial, in many of his tastes. He loved Southern England, particularly the Cotswold hills, but disliked mountains, as Hugh Gaitskell reported.[8] He travelled rather little in his life, but he knew France well and was very sympathetic to French culture. The thinker to whom Cole was most drawn, and to whom he returned again and again, was Rousseau. One of the earliest books he wrote was an edited Introduction to *The Social Contract*.[9] He acknowledged the intellectual power of German socialism, but never learnt to read German, and never warmed to German culture or the German intellectual tradition.

Another sign of the influence of Morris and the English Romantic tradition on Cole was his strong aversion to science.[10] Along with some Oxford colleagues he took the lead in 1951 in blocking the proposal to call the new professional association for academic political scientists the Political Science Association, despite the fact that political science was the accepted term for the discipline in the United States, and had also been incorporated in the title of the LSE (the London School of Economics and Political Science). Cole's hostility to the term science stemmed in part from his opposition to Marx's notion of scientific socialism, which he identified with determinism and fatalism. He never accepted the broader German meaning of science as *Wissenschaft*, meaning any disciplined form of knowledge. Cole believed in the study of society as part of an open, democratic activity which was based on principles and evidence, and involved choosing between alternatives. He recoiled from the idea that the social world could be analysed scientifically and predictions made about human behaviour which could then be used to control it.

What is socialism?

The great theme of Cole's *History* is an exploration of the different meanings that have been attached to socialism, the different kinds of activities in which socialists have engaged, and the different visions of alternative societies they have entertained. The basic insight he uses to organise his material emerges very clearly in the first volume, where he speaks of the two conflicting tendencies in socialism which have existed within it more or less from the beginning. The first tendency conceived socialism mainly in terms of state action and politics, while the second conceived it as a form of cooperation, 'aiming at a way of community living that was to come about by the voluntary action of the converted, and not through legislation'.[11] These tendencies were represented among the early socialists by the contrasting approaches of Fourier and Saint-Simon, and according to Cole have been present throughout the history of socialism:[12]

> These two tendencies have persisted, the one leading towards either Anarchist–Communism or Syndicalism or towards the modern form of Co-operation as 'a state within the state', and the other towards either Marxian Communism or the various doctrines of modern 'Democratic Socialism'.

Cole argues that the first tendency gradually got stronger until it virtually ousted the second tendency altogether in the course of the twentieth century. The main reason for this he attributes to the success of Marxism in seizing hold of the social democratic movement in the closing decades of the nineteenth century.

For Cole this development is greatly to be regretted. Even after his head told him that he needed to make his accommodation with democratic socialism if he was to have influence over the course of events, his heart remained with 'Co-operation', and with the early socialists who enunciated it – Fourier and Owen above all, but also the Ricardian socialists, Bray and Thompson, as well as those whom he places outside the socialist tradition, like Sismondi and Proudhon. These last two he sees as important forerunners of socialism because of their willingness to explore alternative forms of economic organisation to competition and the free market. Proudhon's emphasis on mutualism, and his desire to make new forms of communal solidarity the foundation of social order greatly appealed to Cole.

The decisive criterion which determines whether a thinker is socialist or not for Cole is the question of private property. Wishing to get rid of competition between individuals or to reestablish a form of communal solidarity was he notes quite common among a range of thinkers, many of them looking back nostalgically to some imagined feudal past. What distinguished the early socialists as socialists was their identification of private ownership of property as the main obstacle to creating a different kind of society and eradicating the evils of capitalism. Proudhon and Sismondi are not socialists by this criterion, even if their formulation of the social problem makes them influential on later socialist thought.

The importance of the principle of cooperation as enunciated by Robert Owen and some of the other early socialists was that here for the first time was an alternative to capitalism which proposed a way of abolishing both competition and the state. Many of the early socialists like Thompson and Bray were strongly opposed to the state. Thompson, for example, saw government as the protector and defender of the private monopoly of the means of production, and advocated strong independent trade unions as the means by which the working class could emancipate itself and establish a new kind of society.[13]

There is a direct line here between the arguments of Owen, Bray and Thompson and the arguments of the guild socialists in the first two decades of the twentieth century. Cole believed passionately that the working class needed to remain independent and self-reliant, and that the new society which socialists sought had to be organised separately from the existing society – a state within a state. Labour had to construct its own world and seek its own salvation. One of the reasons for Cole's attachment to this approach was his commitment to pluralism.[14] He believed that there was not a single path to socialism but many paths. The circumstances of each national society were different and each needed to work out its own path to socialism,[15] while within each national society there was room for different experiments and choices. He always rejected any attempt to impose a monolithic system or uniform choice on the Labour movement, and this became one of his main objections both to Marxism and to social democracy. Using the existing state to achieve socialism he believed was bound to involve the imposition of an inflexible and uniform solution on society and on the working class, whereas what was needed was a framework which could encourage choice, variety and self-determination.[16]

State action and cooperation

Although personally sympathising with the anti-state tradition, Cole had come to acknowledge that the choice for socialists in his own time had come to be between different kinds of state action, and he saw little prospect of reviving the spontaneous cooperative action of the working class on which the hopes of the guild socialists had rested. He therefore presents his *History* in two halves. In the first half, which lasts up to the First World War and is covered by the first three volumes, there is still a lively tension between these two principles. In the first volume, *The Forerunners 1789–1850*, Cole distinguishes between the believers in state action like Saint-Simon and the believers in cooperation like Robert Owen. The second volume, entitled *Marxism and Anarchism 1850–1890*, is explicitly organised around this contrast, with the belief in socialism as state action being represented by Marx and his followers, as well as by insurrectionists like Auguste Blanqui and constitutionalists like Louis Blanc, while the belief in socialism as cooperation was taken up by Bakunin and the anarchists, leading to fierce battles in the First International which eventually destroyed it.

The third volume (in two parts), *The Second International 1889–1914*, is also organised around this central tension, between state action and direct action. Several of the social democratic parties, including crucially the German party, had acquired Marxist leaderships, but all of them were committed in some form to using state power to bring about socialism, whereas the advocates of direct action, which included the anarchists, the syndicalists, and the guild socialists, all wanted to build the socialist movement outside the confines of the existing state.

The guild socialists went further, in that they believed that the working class could and should organise itself so that it could dispense with the existing state and the existing capitalist organisation of society altogether and establish its own new society, based on a federation of the guilds.

The fourth and fifth volumes of the *History* take as their theme, reform and revolution. They deal mainly with the great historical schism which took place in the ranks of the socialist movement following the creation of the first workers' state in Russia, and the organisation of separate communist parties which broke away from the existing socialist and social democratic parties. Many of these remained Marxist in inspiration and leadership, but refused to accept the doctrines or the methods of the Bolsheviks. This split had huge and tragic consequences for socialism, which Cole explores in great detail; most damaging of all was the failure of the communists and the German social democrats to combine to fight Hitler's rise to power.

One of the distinguishing marks of Cole's *History* is the even-handed way in which he deals with different wings of the socialist movement whatever their differences in tactics and analysis. For him it was still the same movement, and he strove as hard as he could to promote tolerance and pluralism. He suffered repeated rebuffs and disappointments, and these are reflected in many of the pages of the final two volumes. Socialists had always been prone to squabbles and splits, but the split which took place after 1917 was of a different order of magnitude and was never healed. Many of the protagonists on both side of the argument insisted that the chasm was unbridgeable, but Cole never shared this view. He argued that the basic attitude towards capitalism and the desire to see it replaced by an alternative form of economic and social organisation was sufficiently strong to give the two sides common ground. What they shared was more important than their differences.[17] Cole ultimately sided with social democracy against communism, although he never denounced communism in the way that so many social democrats as well as former communists came to do, and he remained broadly sympathetic to Russia and was always prepared to defend it, as will be shown later. What it meant for his *History*, however, is that the last two volumes become a detailed account of the battle between reform and revolution in different countries, the course of events in the Soviet Union and the responses to the rise of fascism. Cole ruefully reflects that this titanic struggle for the soul of socialism had buried the older argument about state action and cooperation, without adding very much of substance to socialist thought.

Marxism

One of the great themes in Cole's *History* as well as in his active life as a socialist was his attitude to Marxism. He always felt deep ambivalence to Marx, to Marxism and to the Russian Revolution, yet what makes his *History* so interesting is precisely that he did not simply reject Marxism, but sought to come to terms with it and explain it. To understand fully Cole's attitude to Marxism it is necessary therefore to understand something of the context in which he formed his views on it.

For Cole's generation the Russian Revolution was the most exciting and important political event of their lives:[18]

> Whatever view one may take, either of the successive phases of the Russian Revolution itself or what came out of it in the realms of thought and action, there can be no question that it has proved itself, for good or ill, or for both, the most important world event since the French Revolution of 1789, and indeed further-reaching even than that vast upheaval because its influence has spread over the whole world and has set all mankind at sixes and sevens.

At the same time, the Russian Revolution had completely divided the socialist movement. Some socialists regarded it as 'providing the pattern for a new world order in which all the contradictions of the older forms of society are destined to be overcome', while other socialists denounced it as 'the most terrible of all tyrannies of men over men' and were prepared to ally themselves with capitalism against it, and 'to incite the peoples subject to Soviet rule to rise in the cause of liberty for its overthrow'.[19]

Cole himself was never prepared to 'ally himself with capitalism' against the Soviet Union, but it was with an increasingly heavy heart that he observed the way in which the Soviet Union had developed. He wrote the final volumes of his *History* at the end of the 1950s following the events of Hungary in 1956 and the disappointment of the hopes for an early liberalisation following Stalin's death. In 1959 the Soviet Union was still a colossus, still one of the two superpowers, with a nuclear arsenal, and a huge conventional army. Communism had spread to all parts of the world, and there were many western observers who believed that the communist centrally planned economies would outpace the capitalist market economies, because of their ability to direct a higher proportion of their resources towards investment rather than towards consumption. The launch of the Sputnik in 1957 was taken as a symbol of what centrally planned economies could achieve.

What would have been unimaginable to Cole was that thirty years after his death communism would collapse in Russia and the rest of Europe with an absolute finality, its moral authority and its economic and political capacity completely exhausted. At the time he was writing, the Soviet Union appeared a permanent fixture, and for all his acknowledgement of its shortcomings, errors and crimes, he was still willing to defend it, at times even write apologetics for it,[20] but his patience was strained by events like the Nazi-Soviet pact, one of the most cynical pieces of realpolitik ever perpetrated, and one which deeply shocked many socialists, since it seemed to be an action completely devoid of principle or morality:[21]

> I can see why the Soviet Union, under Stalin's rule, signed the Nazi-Soviet Pact, but I cannot believe him to have been justified, even in the circumstances of 1939; for I believe that Fascism and Nazism were bestial cults that had to be resisted and overthrown at all costs. Even if the Soviet Union was justified in not entering the war in 1939, it does not follow that it was justified in partitioning Poland with the Nazis or in attacking Finland, or indeed that it was justified in still keeping out of the war at the darkest hour for the West, after the fall of France.

What most distressed Cole was that the Soviet Union was prepared to force its line of neutrality on all the parties of the Comintern, refusing to recognise any common cause with other opponents of Nazism on the left. But although Cole was utterly without illusions about the Soviet Union, knowing it to be a cruel tyranny, he still acknowledged that it was difficult for socialists to condemn it. In his *History* he probes the 'deep and enduring loyalty to the Soviet Union as the centre of world Socialism – a loyalty which remained proof against every disclosure of the dictatorial ruthlessness of the Stalinist regime'.[22] For many socialists, the communists had shown themselves ready to fight against the forces that sustained both capitalism and war, while the social democrats had tamely surrendered in Germany, Italy and Austria. In the climate of world economic crisis, political upheaval and the drift to war which characterised the 1930s, many socialists, including Cole himself, clung to the Soviet Union as the one bulwark of resistance in a world descending into chaos and barbarism. Whatever the shortcomings of the Soviet Union (and much remained hidden in the 1930s) socialists remained emotionally committed to the first workers' state and were loath to condemn it:[23]

it seemed in the thirties to most Socialists – even to most who were strongly hostile to Communism – immensely important that the Russian Revolution should survive and the great adventure in Soviet planning succeed – the more so because there was so little to hearten us in events in the rest of the world, and so much to increase our fears in the almost unopposed advance of Fascism in Europe. However much Socialists were impelled to criticise both the Communist philosophy and its manifestation in the Soviet Union, most of them were not prepared to carry their criticism to the length of wishing to see the Soviet system overthrown by the forces that were actively ranged against it.

What the Soviet Union represented to socialists was a living alternative to capitalism, and in the 1930s the only one in existence. It was a guarantee that there was a stage of development beyond capitalism, and that a planned economy was superior to a market economy. The achievements of the Soviet Union in laying the foundations for an industrial economy, for creating a modern education system, for creating universal welfare programmes were greatly admired. This emotional pull of the Soviet Union and the Russian Revolution was felt strongly by Cole himself, but also as he noted even by those socialists who were most strongly opposed politically to the communists. This attachment grew much weaker after 1945, but it never entirely disappeared until communism itself disappeared. The existence of the Soviet Union legitimated other forces of resistance to capitalism despite itself, and made possible a whole series of radical experiments in the Third World, as well as the flourishing of many different varieties of socialism and Marxism. The collapse of the Soviet Union when it finally came was not simply the collapse of a regime and a state but the collapse of an idea and a symbol of resistance to capitalism. After the end of communism all forms of socialism were declared discredited and belonging to the past.[24]

Marx and Marxism

Even as he acknowledged the emotional pull of communism and the Soviet state, Cole was never close to becoming a communist, even though he often wrote very appreciatively of communism. Surveying the world scene in 1933 he declared: 'to look around the world of today with seeing eyes is to be a Marxist, for Marxism alone explains what is going on'.[25] What repelled him from Marxism is set out very clearly in the *History*. As ever with Cole, however, the judgement is a mixed one. He found much to praise as well as condemn.

On the positive side was Cole's appreciation of Marx as an economic historian. The famous chapters in *Capital* such as chapter 10 on the class struggles over the working day, and chapter 15 on the class struggles over the introduction of machinery, involved remarkable and pioneering research of a kind which had not been attempted in the same way before, and which opened the way for detailed exploration of the way capitalism actually worked and was developing, which generations of socialist historians, including Cole himself, were to pursue. The importance which Marx gave to understanding the material conditions in which people earned their livings, and the social relationships which they formed, was an inspiration to a new kind of historical understanding. The great tradition of labour studies which it helped inaugurate number Cole as one of its most distinctive practitioners.[26]

In contrast to his deep appreciation of Marx's contribution to economic and specifically to labour history, Cole had very little regard for Marx's economics. Like William Morris, who suffered agonies of the brain reading the theoretical parts of *Capital* but who greatly enjoyed the historical parts, Cole dismisses much of the famous first six chapters of *Capital* which set out Marx's theory of value and surplus value as misguided and ultimately unnecessary:[27]

> Professor Tawney ... once spoke of Marx as the last of the schoolmen ... . Was it also Professor Tawney who said that he did not need the theory of surplus value to tell him that the capitalists exploited the workers? Yet that in effect was what the theory did proclaim – that, and nothing besides.

Cole's disdain for Marx's economics stemmed from his distrust of what he saw as the metaphysical and determinist elements of Marxism. He had a rooted aversion to Hegel and to the German intellectual tradition, preferring English historical empiricism. He conceded that it was politically astute for Marx to claim that his doctrine was scientific since it lent it added authority and gave working-class leaders the impression that they had reason as well as justice on their side, a powerful combination. But for Cole this did not make it any less bogus:[28]

> To call such a theoretical structure 'scientific' is really an entire misnomer. It is in truth a gigantic metaphysical

construction, quite unrelated to any statement or hypothesis that can be tested or verified. ... Marx, in the final form of his theory of value was talking metaphysics and not science; and it is a curious paradox that this least scientific – because least verifiable – part of his social theory should have attracted, and should continue to attract, so many natural scientists who would put up with nothing at all analogous to it in the practice of their own disciplines.

Cole, however, still pays generous tribute to Marx in the *History*. He did not achieve what he imagined, namely a 'scientific' socialism, and his economics proved a dead-end. But this is insignificant beside his great achievement, the materialist conception of history. It did not explain every event, or exclude other explanations, but it did provide an 'indispensable key to an otherwise often unintelligible sequence of historical changes which were transforming the lives of men'.[29] On this score alone, declares Cole, '*Das Kapital* must rank as one of the very great books of the nineteenth century'.[30]

In terms of recent scholarship Cole's treatment of Marx is typical of his time in seeing Marx first and foremost as an economic determinist and historical materialist, founder of the doctrines which had become so important in Europe and the rest of the world in the first half of the twentieth century. His lack of German made him apparently unaware of the previously unpublished 1844 manuscripts which were published in 1932 and contained Marx's writing on alienation, or of the *Grundrisse*, the notebooks written in the 1850s from which *Capital* was drawn, but which in their scope go considerably beyond it. If Cole had lived to take account of the new Marx scholarship[31] which was to burst into life on the strength of these unpublished works in the 1960s and 1970s, he might have put more emphasis on the humanist and Romantic side of Marx. He would still have been critical of the influence of Hegel, which the *Grundrisse* display so emphatically, but he might have seen how Marx's approach was grounded in a humanism and a Romanticism not so different from his own.

Parliamentary socialism

Cole's attachment to pluralism and the liberal heritage meant that he could not in the end accept the dogmas of Marxism which made everything certain and beyond debate, still less the imposition of a single line and a single path. Above all he distrusted the emphasis upon the state, and upon imposing socialism from above. Yet as has already been stated, he was far from happy with the main alternative to Marxism in his lifetime, the various forms of democratic socialism. Partly this was because these too shared the same strategic emphasis on the achievement of socialism through the capture and utilisation of the machinery of the state.

In his *History* he gives attention to some of the forerunners of democratic socialism, including Louis Blanc and Ferdinand Lassalle. He notes how the struggle for democracy, one of the great unifying campaigns for socialists throughout the nineteenth century, already was beginning to pose dilemmas for socialists, of a kind which became much more familiar when democracy was firmly established. For a long time, however, democracy was a distant gleam in most states, and the ruling class used repression and violence to hound, persecute, and murder both socialists and democrats. Socialism and democracy were not alternatives but part of the same struggle, and many of those in the ruling class who opposed the extension of democratic rights did so because they feared that the outcome of democracy would be socialism, the expropriation of property, and the plunder of the rich by the poor.

In his richly detailed account Cole shows how differences over political tactics gradually emerged among socialists. At first this was not the familiar division between reform and revolution from a later era, because all the demands of the socialists, even the most moderate, were revolutionary – they implied the overthrow and reorganisation of the *anciens régimes* of Europe. But there were differences between those who believed in insurrection, the *coup d'état*, the seizure of power; those who wanted to create a parallel state, a community separate and independent of the existing state; those who wanted no state at all; those who wanted to create a new centralised state; and finally those who wanted to transform the existing state. In many ways it was the latter who were furthest from reality in nineteenth-century Europe, and the bloody suppressions of the 1848 uprisings and of the 1870 Paris Commune, and many similar incidents, only seemed to confirm this. It should be remembered how long it took before democracy was established in Europe, and even when it was, it often collapsed as a result of internal coups or external invasion, and authoritarianism resumed its sway. For most of the period Cole is writing about in his *History* (1789–1939) democracy did not exist and was not likely to be brought about except through a revolutionary upheaval.[32]

This was true even of Britain. Full universal suffrage was only achieved in 1918 and 1928, and only then was the Labour party able to emerge as a contender for power within a constitutional system. It is important to remember that Cole was a member of the first generation of European socialists for whom the peaceful conquest of political power through constitutional means and electoral contest were becoming possibilities. Up until that moment the socialist movement had been, not by choice but by circumstance, a movement outside the existing state. If it wanted to achieve its goals it had to do so either by overthrowing the existing state or bypassing it. Socialist hopes for a new moral world, a new kind of community and fellowship, depended either on a miraculous conversion of those holding property and political power, or on their violent dispossession, or on the creation of an alternative power, so strong that it had to be left alone.

Socialists in the nineteenth century were utopians, as Cole demonstrates, even those like Marx who abjured utopias. To believe in the possibility of socialism was a reckless leap of faith into the unknown, resting on the experience of a few experiments in cooperation, such as those of Robert Owen, and a powerful sense of the injustice and oppression of current social and political arrangements. Cole himself was proud to be a utopian, attracted by the vision of guild socialism, organising every sector of the economy into a self-governing guild which would then be joined in a federation. The centralised state would be stripped of many of its powers and functions, and reorganised as a democratic body working in partnership with the guilds. Power would be decentralised, and the people would govern themselves.[33] Marx had celebrated the Paris Commune in similar terms as providing a glimpse of a different kind of political organisation, a decentralised, egalitarian self-governing community, which had set aside hierarchy, authority and bureaucracy.

Guild socialism was strongly attacked by Sidney and Beatrice Webb as akin to syndicalism, and as incapable of providing the gradual socialisation of the economy which they favoured. They believed that this could be best achieved through the Labour movement winning an electoral majority, forming a government, and using the existing machinery of the state to implement a socialist programme. Their view prevailed in the Labour movement, the trade unions swung behind it, and the guild socialists found their support ebbing away. Cole was forced to acknowledge that, whatever his hopes for a state within a state, the only prospect for advancing socialism was through the gradualist route of parliamentary socialism.

If the Labour movement could not be won for guild socialism he now thought it might be won for parliamentary socialism, although he always had misgivings about this strategy and never lost his belief that the guild socialist route was preferable, because more likely in the end to deliver a society which was truly socialist and democratic.

But for the next thirty years he devoted himself wholeheartedly to the cause of education and persuasion within the Labour movement for parliamentary socialism. He recognised from the start, however, and this is reflected throughout volumes III, IV and V of the *History* that any electoral strategy to achieve socialism would be subject to huge pressures for compromise, as a result of the necessity to build coalitions to win power, and to dilute socialist policies. Contrary to what the right had feared, mass democracy did not favour socialism. The electorate was too diffuse, and in most countries the working class was in a minority. The difficulties of securing an electoral majority for socialism through electoral politics were immense; the pressures to preserve the status quo and to avoid dangerous experiments were always likely to prevail. The forces of property quickly learnt how to turn the new terrain of mass democracy to their advantage.

Cole had always recognised the huge obstacles in the path of socialist movements. One of the reason for his criticisms of Marxism in the *History* is because he was opposed to any determinism or fatalism; he never accepted that socialism was somehow inevitable. On the contrary he was only too aware of how fragile it was. The early socialists were visionaries, pioneers in a hostile social and political environment. Their only hope of breaking out of their isolation and realising their dreams of a better society, a new moral world, was either to establish self-governing communities in places like America which would tolerate them, or to help to organise and to educate the emerging Labour movement. Cole argued that there was no necessary relationship between socialism and the labour movement; it had to be fought for, but he did think that the labour movement offered socialists the best chance of success. The pivotal economic role which the industrial working class played in modern capitalism gave it leverage out of all proportion to its numerical size. It was this which offered the best hope of a transition to socialism.

The parliamentary road by contrast was as likely to lead away from socialism as towards it. Cole campaigned tirelessly within the Labour party and the Labour movement to firm up its socialist commitment and stiffen the party's resolve. He was horrified by the drift and irresolution of the minority Labour Government in 1929 faced by the mounting financial and industrial crisis, and by the ease with which Labour was dismissed, and a pro-capitalist coalition installed to manage the crisis, which included several of Labour's former leaders. In common with many other socialists in the party Cole in response advocated that the party must in future prepare itself to act decisively when it was next in government. He proposed that it pass an Emergency Powers Act to give the government powers to impose a socialist economic plan and override constitutional restraints like the veto of the House of Lords. Only in this way he thought would the Labour movement be able to break the political power of capital and implement the programme on which it was elected.[34]

By the end of his life, however, Cole was forced to recognise that the British Labour party was so wedded to constitutionalism that it would never challenge the power of capital in this way, and that therefore the prospect for any transition to socialism by parliamentary means was remote, and getting steadily more remote. In compensation Cole noted that at least the constitutional road of parliamentary reform was achieving in many countries the gradual extension of basic social rights to all citizens.[35] The European welfare states of the second half of the twentieth century were bringing significant and real improvements to the lives of the working class. Cole was grateful for this but he did not confuse it with socialism. His great *History* ends rather sadly. He had never had much faith in the centralised creeds of communism and social democracy to deliver his vision of socialism. But equally he could see no viable alternatives, no way back to recreating the promise and energy of the guild socialism of his youth.

The situation was not promising. A hundred years of socialism had not brought socialism much closer. Looking back to the world situation in 1939, the year in which he formally ended his *History*, he concluded that it was disappointing for socialism as a world force:[36]

> The Communist World Revolution, so confidently predicted in the early 'twenties, had not merely failed to occur, but had been put for the time being almost out of mind by its Russian protagonists, who were devoting their energies, under Stalin, to building up 'Socialism in a single country' and were throwing their influence on the side of anti-Fascist Popular Fronts designed to protect the Soviet Union against the dangers of Nazi aggression. Meanwhile Social Democracy, although in a few countries its supporters had been able to make substantial advances in the direction of the Welfare State, showed a marked tendency to settle down as a permanent large minority in most of the constitutionally governed countries of the West, and even when it held the government in its hands, showed little zeal for any rapid advance towards Socialism as an alternative basis to capitalism for the economic ordering of society.

The twenty years since 1939 up to the moment of Cole's death had not shown much improvement. Nazism had been defeated and destroyed, and social democracy and communism had increased their territorial sway and influence. But in Cole's sense socialism was still as far away as ever.

One of the difficulties in Cole's *History* is that his socialist society has no place for competition, no place for the market, and no place for private property. But as others have pointed out, this is only one way, and a very historically specific way, of expressing the egalitarian impulse which lies at the heart of socialism. Given the time in which he lived, it is hardly surprising that Cole should have given pride of place to this conception of socialism and to the class struggle as the main vehicle for achieving it. But the Labour movement is no longer the expanding force that it was at the beginning of the twentieth century, and many socialists no longer reject markets.[37] Cole's main influence on socialist thought today lies not in his recommendations for central economic planning, but in his commitment to pluralism, to self-government, to forms of association and partnership, to industrial democracy and workers' control. From our vantage point almost fifty years on from the time when the first volume of Cole's *History* appeared, the issue of transferring ownership from private to public hands as a priority for the achievement of equality is no longer the key goal of socialism that it once was. Social democratic parties have emerged as the true heirs of the European Enlightenment and of the radical tradition of Rousseau and Paine which Cole so much admired; they continue to search for the best ways to reduce inequalities and promote opportunity, to fight privilege and discrimination, and to extend democracy, but they no longer seek the abolition of markets or private property.[38]

Does Cole still have a message for modern social democracy? His fundamental beliefs in pluralism, fellowship and democracy as the heart of socialism will still resonate, long after his painstaking arguments for the merits of centralised economic planning are forgotten. For, as he himself put it at the end of his *History*:[39]

> I am neither a Communist nor a Social Democrat, because I regard both as creeds of centralisation and bureaucracy, whereas I feel sure that a Socialist society that is to be true to its equalitarian principles of human brotherhood must rest on the widest possible diffusion of power and responsibility, so as to enlist the active participation of as many as possible of its citizens in the tasks of democratic self-government.

7

Social Democracy in a Global World[1]

> The private citizen today has come to feel rather like a deaf
> spectator in the back row ... He does not know for certain
> what is going on, or who is doing it, or where he is being
> carried. No newspaper reports his environment so that he
> can grasp it, no school has taught him how to imagine it;
> his ideals often do not fit with it; listening to speeches,
> uttering opinions and voting do not, he finds, enable him
> to govern it. He lives in a world which he cannot see, does
> not understand, and is unable to direct.[2]
>
> Walter Lippman

In its original forms as it emerged in the nineteenth century social
democracy was resolutely internationalist. Existing and established
states were associated with the privileged orders of the *ancien régime*
and the embodiment of property interests. The early social democratic
movements in Europe saw themselves as operating outside existing
forms of the state, creating new forms of cooperation and community
beyond the reach of the state, and anticipating the overthrow of the
existing forms of the state in a remaking of both politics and society.
This transformation was expected to be international. A fundamental
tenet of early social democracy was that the working class had no
country.[3] The solidarity of the working class existed across all spatial
divisions, whether national or regional, and the new world order which
socialists wished to bring about would transcend national divisions.

For most of the period since the First World War, however, social
democracy has been predominantly national in character, following the
breakdown of the liberal world order in the two world wars of the first

half of the twentieth century. The hopes for building an international solidarity of labour in the nineteenth century had been based on a world in which economic integration was proceeding apace, and in which connections were being established between all regions and all peoples of the globe. The old territorial political divisions were seen as increasingly irrelevant to this new world of freedom of movement of people, goods and capital, which by the first decade of the twentieth century was in certain respects more globalised than the contemporary international order.[4]

Much of this liberal order collapsed during the carnage on the western front, and, after attempts to resuscitate it after 1918 failed, the even greater political and military struggle for territory and resources which then developed. This collapse of the liberal economic order had a profound effect upon all forms of social democracy and socialism. The Second International fell apart in 1914 when the majority of the representatives of the workers in Germany, England and France discovered that they did have a country after all and backed their national governments in voting for the war. This willingness of organised labour to subordinate class solidarity to national solidarity was a defining moment in the evolution of social democracy, stamping it with a new national character, which it has never since lost.

The fragmentation of the global order meant a new emphasis upon the national, and the nation-state, both as the source of political legitimacy and the instrument for protecting and advancing the interests of particular groups. The unity of the social democratic movement was broken beyond repair. The earlier schism between the supporters of reform and revolution was now eclipsed by the much deeper schism between two wings of social democracy – those who supported the October Revolution in Russia and the regime which it established and formed parties which affiliated to the Communist International, and those who opposed the communists because of their disregard for democracy and their willingness to implement socialism through dictatorship, and formed parliamentary social democratic parties, such as the SPD in Germany, many of them like the SPD still Marxist in orientation.[5]

The other profound split in the ranks of the socialist international was the emergence of the fascists and the National Socialists, many of them like Mussolini former socialists. They condemned cosmopolitanism, emphasising the priority of nation over class, and promulgating doctrines of racial purity, as well as advocating the need for national solutions to political problems and strong national states. The parties of the Comintern, although formally committed to internationalism, became increasingly wedded after Lenin's death to the national interest of the Soviet Union and the doctrine of socialism in one country. The most internationalist element of the old Second International remained the social democratic parties, but even here the focus shifted and national strategies became more important than protecting international solidarity.

The era of national protectionism left a profound imprint on social democracy, from which in recent decades it has struggled to emerge. The strength of this imprint derived both from the necessities created by the breakdown of the liberal world order, but also from the success of different social democratic parties in adapting to this new environment and devising strategies to build coalitions which brought them electoral success and the chance to use state power to implement their programmes. Socialism in one country became indelibly associated with Stalinism, Soviet planning and autarchy. Social democracy in one country had a longer life because, although few examples of it existed before 1939, it blossomed in the new circumstances of the post-war world, with the reconstruction of a liberal world order under the leadership of the United States. One of the main successes of this liberal world order in its struggle against communism was the emergence of successful social democratic regimes in many countries of the West, delivering high levels of welfare and social security as in the East, but combining it with economic efficiency, democracy and civil liberties. Social democratic regimes proved successful in providing new legitimacy for the established social order through their ability to reconcile organised labour to the existing state, by showing how it could operate in their interest.

Social democracy in one country reached its zenith in the three decades after 1945. Its achievements were vigorously contested by many on the left who revived the old debate about reform and revolution in the Second International, arguing that the existing state could not be used as an instrument in the creation of socialism, but only to shore up capitalism.[6] Social democrats maintained, however, that in many areas reforms could permanently improve the position of the working class and advance the cause of social justice, and that the pursuit of social justice and greater equality and fairness was the core objective of social democracy,[7] and mattered much more than the transfer of productive assets into the hands of the state. Although many social democrats continued to advocate nationalisation of key sectors as one of the instruments of a progressive programme, they came to see it as only one of a number of different instruments which were available to them, and not necessarily the most important.

This change reflected both the experience of social democratic parties in government, which many of them acquired after 1945, allied to the persuasiveness of a number of new social and economic theories which pointed to the transformation which had been wrought in capitalism by the application of Keynesian techniques of economic management, and new concepts of universal welfare provision. The powers of the modern state were highly developed and capable of being extended in numerous ways, and social democrats embraced the idea that the state machinery was a weapon which they could take hold of and employ. Many in the post-war generation of social democrats celebrated this innovative use of the state as the taming of capitalism, the use of the countervailing force of democracy to offset and reduce the pressures in a capitalist economy towards ever greater inequality.[8] Capitalism represented the unregulated market which knew no national boundaries. The task of social democracy was to reimpose social and political priorities on the way in which the market distributed resources, using the power of the state to redistribute and regulate. This was often presented as a constant struggle to keep the raw power of capitalism caged and under control, and led to a celebration of the virtues of the public sector, public service, and the public ethos, in contrast to the market.

Each social democratic regime developed in rather different ways and became associated with different models of capitalism and national formations. The global economy although reviving under the new liberal order agreed at Bretton Woods remained unmistakeably an international rather than a global economy, composed of the different national economies and their separate jurisdictions. Out of the different national paths emerged distinctive types of regime, different worlds of welfare capitalism, for example, and noted differences in institutions from corporate governance to industrial relations. What was common to all the social democratic regimes, however, were high levels of public spending and state involvement in managing their economies and societies.

Social democracy in one country

Even with the gradual restoration of a liberal economic world order after 1945, many features of national protectionism persisted. The balance between greater international economic cooperation from a secure base of national economic management worked extremely well during the years of the long post-war boom which lasted through the 1950s and 1960s, only definitively coming to an end with the collapse of the Bretton Woods system in 1971 and the first generalised recession in 1974 and 1975. The 1970s and 1980s proved to be much more difficult decades for the international economy, and saw a number of major shifts in policies, ideas and institutions, which cumulatively produced the new era of globalisation.

Many social democratic regimes struggled to adapt to the new environment. Social democracy which at its inception had been so international in its focus and so resistant to national ties now found it difficult to shed the national carapace which it had formed, and with which its achievements were associated. The rediscovery by capital of the freedom and power of operating globally beyond the constraints of territorial division was not matched by social democracy, which as a result began to see many of the safeguards and restrictions which it had established being eroded and rolled back in the new liberal era.[9]

The extent to which national economic management in general and social democracy in particular as a form of political economy and political regime have been rendered obsolete by the changes introduced by the trends associated with globalisation has been much debated, and the picture that emerges is a complex one. National governments have been forced to adapt to new demands and pressures, but at the same time have retained important capacities to choose policies and to shape their environment rather than being shaped by it. Many of the wilder fears about neo-liberalism, for example that it would cause a race to the bottom, the dismantling of universal welfare programmes, a severe contraction in public spending and social protection, the sweeping away of all employment rights, have not been borne out by events.

That is not so say that nothing has changed. The new era of floating exchange rates and the relaxation of controls on international finance has had some dramatic effects, and has altered the constraints which governments have to face, making some of the instruments which they used to employ, such as exchange rate controls, ineffective. The power of the financial markets to destabilise currencies and governments has been demonstrated several times since 1971 (Britain in 1976, France in 1982–3, Sweden in 1992). Governments have had to learn how to maintain international financial confidence in the way they conduct their affairs, or risk an exodus of capital. The price of openness, of remaining an integral part of the global economy, is an acceptance of the discipline which the financial markets impose. This has not prevented some economies borrowing very heavily to finance their domestic programmes, but they have had to find ways of doing it which do not endanger financial confidence, and they remain vulnerable to sudden changes of market sentiment.

The growth of trade from the 1950s onwards has created a high level of interdependence in the international economy which has made the cost of reducing ties increasingly prohibitive. In this sense there has been a reduction in the freedom of governments. A national protectionist strategy of severing ties with the global economy and promoting a much higher level of self-sufficiency in order to pursue policies free of concerns about international financial pressures has been recognised as no longer viable. Acceptance of the constraints of the global economy and the realities of economic interdependence is not, however, the same as being obliged to adopt particular neo-liberal prescriptions on domestic economic management. As many social democratic regimes have found, there is considerable variety in the policies that can be pursued.

The extent to which there was ever a pure form of social democracy in one country, free of any international pressures or obligations, and able to chart entirely its own course, relying on its own efforts and resources, is highly debatable, but it has remained a dream that still resonates because it suggests that no compromises are necessary and that a social democracy can be established free of all external constraints. But even while most social democrats accept that this was an illusion of the era of national protectionism, it is still emotionally and intellectually hard for many to reconnect to a new cosmopolitan vision of an international social democracy.

Two other changes have been important in the questioning of national models of social democracy. Both predate the globalisation era itself, but both are of increasing importance within it: the new international division of labour and the growth of migration. The new international division of labour reflected changing forms of comparative advantage and their exploitation by increasingly dominant transnational companies who organised the system of production transnationally, utilising the distribution of skills, resources and labour to best advantage. The policies of these firms threatened the maintenance of particular sectors and employment within many national economies, and therefore created major policy dilemmas for social democratic governments, particularly where the employment concerned was in manufacturing industry. One response was to subsidise and protect employment, sometimes through nationalisation, but the cost was often high, because of the long-term difficulty of sustaining a sector that was no longer internationally competitive.

Most social democratic governments responded to these pressures therefore by devising industrial strategies to raise the competitiveness and productivity of domestic industries, and the skills of the workforce, trying to ensure that jobs were available which could be sustained without subsidy. There were very different records of success in this. But even the most successful economies still faced difficulties in maintaining traditional manufacturing, and managing the necessary move to an economy in which services, especially internationally traded services, were increasing in importance. The communities that had grown up around traditional manufacturing were the natural electoral base of social democracy, so the decline of these industries and the trade unions associated with them presented not just an economic challenge but an electoral and ideological challenge. Social democratic parties had always had to reach out beyond the constituency of the industrial workers, to win the support of other groups, and create a progressive coalition for change, but in the wake of the restructuring of the 1970s and 1980s, this became still more pressing. The industrial workers are still a vital component of the coalition, but they also tend to be the part of the coalition with the most national protectionist instincts on jobs and industrial subsidies.

A further pressure associated with the trend to a more globalised economy has been the increase in migration. The freeing of labour markets has proceeded much more slowly than either the freeing of capital markets or the liberalisation of trade, but it has gathered pace, driven both by the need for the rich nations to increase their labour supply and by the desire of so many from poorer regions to get access to the employment opportunities and wage levels which the rich enjoy. The rich world is increasingly besieged by the hundreds of thousands who would enter if they could, but are denied the possibilities of doing so. Fears of the effect of migration on living standards, employment and housing, although often exaggerated, have become potent in domestic politics in many of the rich nations, fuelling national protectionism and leading to increasingly draconian controls. In practice controls have often been ineffective, and unknown numbers of illegal immigrants have entered the rich nations. But it is another factor that reinforces the defensive and protectionist character of social democracy, seeking to uphold the standards and citizenship benefits that have been achieved in particular national economies.

The pressures towards a more global economy in terms of finance, trade, production and labour have undercut the arguments for social democracy in one country. But they have not rendered it obsolete. That is because, as critics of globalisation have urged, many of the trends are not truly globalising trends, but regionalising trends. The regions of the world have become much more interdependent, but the growth of interdependence between regions has been much less marked. This means that the defences which national governments have erected to protect themselves from global markets have proved more resilient than first thought, and the pressure on countries to conform to a global norm, or even to a regional norm, has so far been less that some of the protagonists of globalisation expected, reinforcing a tendency for national governments to remain defensive, holding on to what has been achieved rather than thinking about ways of building an international social democracy.

The problem for social democracy is that defensive positions cannot be sustained indefinitely. Important though nation-states remain to any substantive social democratic project, and however limited some forms of economic globalisation may in fact be, there are other aspects of globalisation which do suggest the emergence of a set of problems for which social democracy in one country is quite inadequate. These problems have not suddenly arisen. They are long-standing aspects of modernity, and they continually reappear, particularly during periods of rapid economic progress. They are the unintended consequences of the processes which modernity has unleashed. Chief among them are processes of scientific discovery and technological advance which combined with the capitalist forms of production and exchange have had profound environmental and social impacts, including the huge disparities between the global rich and the global poor, and the effects on the planet biosphere, including global warming, that may prove irreversible. Amidst these great changes political authority has remained fragmented, with most political functions being exercised within quite sharply defined territorial jurisdictions. The governance of the various processes that form and sustain the modern world is notoriously uneven, and in the current era this is leading to many insoluble policy dilemmas, particularly over the distribution of resources and opportunities, the provision of security against crime, terrorism, the prevention of infectious diseases, population growth, and environmental degradation.

Contemporary dilemmas of social democratic politics

Social democracy for much of the twentieth century was national in its formation and its preoccupations, but it now faces the need to become transnational and cosmopolitan again, applying social democratic principles to the problems of making the state more effective in a more global world. Social democratic government at the national level is constitutional government,[10] because it is conducted according to rules and principles, which are binding on all political actors, and which therefore help to constrain the unfettered exercise of power by separating or dividing it. Constitutional government provides a framework in which government can be both responsible and representative – managing conflicts, protecting rights, promoting participation and maintaining the security of its citizens. There will always be dispute at any one time over the best rules and institutions for achieving this, as well as over the principles constitutional arrangements should express, and which ones should take priority over others. There will also always be debate over the extent to which constitutional government is frustrated or facilitated by the provisions of the constitution, and whether the impact of economic, social, cultural and political changes requires amendments to the constitution, or even different constitutional arrangements altogether.

A key challenge for social democrats is how to embed these principles in the global polity, creating the kind of public sphere and public space for debating policy, adjusting interests, and evaluating decisions which characterise established democracies. But this has to take place at a time when national democracies are under considerable strain, facing challenges to their capacity to be representative, responsible and participative. There is a crucial difference, however, between the national and the global level. National constitutions traditionally seek to regulate and limit political power, and constitutional government by definition is limited government. But at the transnational level the need is not so much for limiting government as creating a capacity for government, and providing regulation of those agents who are currently able to exercise power without any scrutiny or accountability. It is necessary to enquire not only whether the institutions and procedures for limiting national governments are still the right ones, and whether they can be improved, but also whether national governments have the capacities they need to meet the expectations of their citizens and deliver the services and the public goods that they want, and whether citizens have the means and opportunities to participate in determining policies and how they are being governed. The answers to the last two point towards new transnational structures of governance.

This cannot be done, however, simply by replicating the national state at the global level. Social democrats in the past have been chiefly concerned with problems arising from the division of labour, the move away from self-sufficiency, and the creation of extended and impersonal networks of interdependence, which have made possible huge increases in wealth and in population at the same time as continual changes in the structure of occupations, services, and lifestyles, and the application of modern science to create continuous technological innovation.

But social democrats also need to be concerned with the division of knowledge. As the division of labour takes hold, so knowledge and information have become progressively more fragmented, dispersed and limited. This has major implications for how contemporary societies and politics are organised and governed. Even while certain forms of knowledge, particularly modern science, have come to pervade and shape more and more areas of human life, such knowledgehas not delivered rational control either of society or of the natural world, but has instead increasingly displayed the contingency and limited character of all human knowledge.

Engagement and disengagement: where have all the citizens gone?

If social democracy is to make a contribution to the problems of contemporary politics, then it has to move beyond the nation-state, and begin to think again in transnational and cosmopolitan terms about the conditions for ensuring the global polity, and not just the national polity, is governed by social democratic values and norms. But it cannot do this successfully without at the same time engaging with the problems which threaten national social democracy. There are three particular problems – citizen disengagement, loss of accountability, and increasing complexity. There has always been a concern since the advent of mass democracy about how to engage citizens in politics. But today it has assumed a new urgency, driven by specific contemporary economic and cultural changes. The basic problem is this: do most voters still relate to politics as active citizens, concerned to share in collective decision-making as an important part of their self-identity, or have they become instead passive consumers of politics? Why should they exercise their options for voice in the political system rather than their options for exit – either by switching parties or by not bothering to vote at all? If they no longer regard themselves as citizens, then they may not feel the need to be represented by political parties, or to identify with any particular one, and will act instrumentally towards voting and participation, disengaging from it unless they have some direct interest in a particular election or decision.

The possibility that we may be witnessing a major change in the character of participation by citizens in representative democracies, as indicated by the trend towards declining participation in formal politics, has received a great deal of attention in recent years. The size of the problem is measured by falling turnout in national, local and European elections, and by the increasing unwillingness of citizens to join political parties or identify with them. The mass parties of the past have begun to wither away, and are finding it much harder to recruit members. The old idea of representative democracy was that more and more citizens would want to become involved in determining the policies of the party they identified with, and that in this way they would feel involved in shaping the policy of the government when their party was elected. The involvement that citizens have by voting for a party that presents a manifesto at the time of a general election, which very few read, is much less. The decline of the mass party and the political education it provided for a large number of citizens has been accompanied by evidence of increasing political illiteracy in the electorate and declining standards of journalism. Although there is more political information more easily available than ever before, fewer citizens appear willing to make use of it, so that opinion polls in the established democracies regularly report high levels of ignorance about how government works, the identity of leading politicians, and current political issues and events. Advocates of democracy had expected that rising levels of education would produce an electorate able and keen to make informed choices between political programmes and political leaders. But those in charge of contemporary political campaigns have found that treating voters as consumers, and campaigning as a branch of marketing, is generally more effective in winning elections than treating voters as informed citizens; this has made electoral politics increasingly a competition of brands, styles and personalities. In response the parties have begun to shed their mass character, and much of their internal democracy, so as to make themselves more effective competitors in the political marketplace. The political career has been professionalised, and an increasing emphasis has come to be placed upon the presentation rather than the substance of policy. The ideological gap between the parties has substantially narrowed, and parties become instruments of the state rather than instruments of civil society. At the extreme they become cartel parties.[11]

This process is compounded by trends in modern media, which have seen the rise of more aggressive and intrusive journalism, and at the same time a decline in the capacity of the media to scrutinise and to inform. Instead the media has assisted politicians in developing a style of politics based around celebrity and personality. Some analysts have spoken of the rise of a media democracy,[12] in which the media come to supplant the institutions of representative democracy such as political parties and parliament as the main intermediary between the voters and the government. The media have adapted to their new role by adopting for the most part a negative, cynical, sceptical stance towards government and politicians, and present politics and public policy in ways which reinforce and spread similar attitudes in their readers and viewers.[13]

The new media culture is sometimes associated with wider cultural changes, towards greater individualism and choice and away from deference and the unquestioning acceptance of authority and expertise, but it is also associated with trends towards trivialisation and entertainment which reinforce the bias against understanding and accelerate the decline of the public sphere and weaken interest in participating in the institutions such as political parties which have played such a key role in representative democracy. This creates a major challenge for building a transnational social democracy even more than national social democracy, which depends upon an educated, informed and active citizenry.

There are other more positive changes. Studies of participation have pointed out that while certain indicators of formal participation, particularly turnout, have declined, other forms of participation have increased.[14] Disengagement to the extent that it exists seems to be largely disengagement from involvement and identification with the existing parties and established forms of representation. Many citizens have increasing involvement with many organisations and campaigns outside formal politics, many of which are increasingly transnational in their organisation and concerns, and among young people research has shown that there remains lively interest in politics; it is just that politics is not defined in terms of the conventional categories of parliamentary politics. This evidence is important, although it highlights the increasing problems with representative democracy at the national level. Many voters have become disconnected from the formal political process, and national constitutional reforms, or constitutional reforms at the European level, have done little to remedy this. A well-functioning constitution requires institutions and mechanisms that make it easy for citizens to participate, and that help to sustain a vigorous civil society and the concept of a public sphere, which is separate from both the family and the market.[15]

It is important not to exaggerate the change that is occurring, or to underestimate the life there may still be in existing national constitutional forms. Much of the evidence on falling turnout supports the view that the more certain the outcome, and the less that is perceived to be at stake, the lower the turnout is likely to be. In a severe political crisis, or if the choice at a future election became very polarised, citizens might once again participate in much larger numbers in voting, as happened in the Italian election in 2006 when turnout increased to over 80 per cent. But it is clearly disturbing that the formal representative machinery is becoming a last resort rather than a first resort for so many citizens, and it does not deal with the other major problem, the disproportionately sharp fall in the proportion of young voters willing to vote.

Another feature of the problem of disengagement is that there is considerable uncertainty as to who the citizens are in contemporary democracies and what they want. There is an assumption[16] that the main problems in democracy lie with the political class and the institutions of representative democracy, frustrating the desires of the people for involvement, participation and commitment. This may be true for some groups, but there is less evidence that it is true for the majority. Rather the problem is that it is very difficult for political parties, or political campaigns and pressure groups to reach large numbers of citizens more than fleetingly, and sustain their involvement. Most voters do not want to become deeply involved in politics, preferring to give priority to other things in their lives.[17]

For much of the twentieth century mass electorates were organised around a number of basic alignments, which determined social identity and therefore voting preference and political partisanship. There were different alignments in different countries, and they were often cross-cutting, but in several countries the class alignment was particularly strong, and so was political partisanship. This gave a particular meaning to the left/right spectrum, and to the positioning of different parties along it. It also gave a particular meaning to citizenship. Citizenship could be understood as a cumulative progress from civil to political and then to social rights. There were many battles along the way, but the meaning of constitutional government in this model was the gradual inclusion of new interests within the political system, the emergence of new majority electoral coalitions, and a moving consensus around policies that promoted social justice and the welfare state, with party competition focused on the trade-offs between social equality and economic efficiency. Citizens were partisan and committed, but the outcomes of the process promoted a set of workable compromises for public policy.

The social justice agenda is still there, but the solidity of the class alignments and their organisations in civil society on which it used to depend are much weaker than before. The interpretation of social justice has also changed, with the emergence of a set of new rights and concerns, voiced by new social movements, by multiculturalism, and above all by campaigns for global justice, which have highlighted the gap between the rich North and the poor South. This is the new context which social democracy needs to address, as a priority and not as an afterthought.

Accountability and sovereignty: do governments decide anything any more?

These problems of representation within national democracies are compounded by problems of accountability. Social democratic governments have become acutely aware that they must improve the delivery of services to their citizens; at the same time their capacity to deliver is being threatened by the trends towards a more global world, and the need to provide public goods for the whole world and not just for a particular national economy. The traditional idea of responsible government in a nation-state is that the government takes responsibility for its actions and is accountable for them to its electorate. The government has the constitutional power to take initiatives and propose new measures, and it does so mindful of its overall responsibility for the public interest and public welfare. Can national governments any longer be held accountable for their actions, or to put it another way, are national governments becoming accountable for less and less?

As argued above, globalisation is not a new phenomenon but one of the principal effects of an expanding division of labour, which has existed at least since the rise of the modern industrial economy. It is also extremely uneven – between states, between regions, and between sectors – and nation-states, particularly some of the smaller ones, have not been overwhelmed by globalisation, but on the contrary have proved very resilient in adjusting to it.[18] The contemporary global economy has national and regional foundations, and cannot be properly understood without them.

What is new is that the present phase of globalisation, which first appeared in the early 1970s and became most fully established from the 1990s onwards, has been accompanied by new kinds of political fragmentation, which have made the task of national government more complicated. There has been a proliferation of new supranational bodies, and overlapping jurisdictions. Nation-states have become less self-contained, as international regimes of various kinds have been established to cope with the problems arising from the growing economic and political interdependence of the world economy. There are now many issues which are settled by negotiations in transnational and supranational bodies, and which only come to national parliaments for ratification. The European Union is one of the most prominent examples of this. Under the Single European Act and other treaties, there are now important areas of policy in which the majority of legislation originates at the EU level, and is passed down to member states for implementation.

The more that matters are transferred to subordinate or superior bodies, the less national government can claim to be responsible for what the government does. It therefore tends to undermine their legitimacy in the eyes of voters. If there is no longer any very clear centre of decision-making, and if governments no longer seem to be in charge, then the danger exists that voters will react accordingly, and lose trust in the governments they elect to promote the public interest or to protect the private interests of the citizens. At the extreme this can contribute to increasing distrust of the formal mechanisms of representative democracy.

One of the most difficult issues for social democracy is how to adapt to this rapidly evolving world of multilevel and transnational governance, where it is hard to pin down exactly where decisions are taken, and devise new ways of connecting citizens with the decisions which affect them. To some extent there has always been multilevel governance – federalist constitutions, for example, stipulate it – but in Europe, a new dimension has been added by accession to the EU and in some cases by internal devolution. There is widespread ignorance about who is responsible for which policy, and naturally numerous opportunities for ministers to absolve themselves of responsibility, by claiming that the decision which is being objected to has come from somewhere else. This ability to put the blame on some other tier of government has become endemic, and is corrosive of the authority of national government, because national governments are still symbolically looked to as the protectors of the national interest and the public interest. Huge expectations about the competence and capacity of governments to deliver outcomes which voters want still abound, and politicians themselves, particularly at elections, do little to damp down those expectations. Since they are competing with other parties for votes the temptation is always to claim much greater competence than really exists. Only in government do politicians find that the levers they need to achieve the things they have promised often do not exist.

In a system of multilateral governance, and still more of transnational governance, it can be hard for the voters to understand where a particular decision comes from, and who is imposing it. Decisions by the EU Commission, by the European Court, by the WTO, and by the numerous boards which are busy standardising such things as accounting rules and carbon emissions, often constrain what national politicians can do. Many matters are clearly no longer exclusively a matter for national decision. National politicians increasingly are forced to provide accounts that justify the arrangements of pooled sovereignty, but by definition this can make them appear weak, especially if they face any kind of populist challenge calling for the repatriation of powers and the withdrawal from international regimes. The framework of international governance which has been erected so far, and which is absolutely vital for developing coherent common responses to the problem the world faces, is quite vulnerable to these kinds of challenges, since they generally fail most tests of accountability, transparency and legitimacy. All that national politicians can do is to claim influence over decisions, but such influence often looks weak measured against full-blooded assertions of national interest.

The challenge therefore is how to bring greater transparency to the governing process. National government remains crucial to the way societies are governed, but the structures of accountability and the lines of responsibility have become blurred. A more precise definition of powers and where and how they are exercised has become necessary, with appropriate channels for scrutiny and reporting. Government has a solidity which governance lacks. There are now many forms of governance, including networks and markets, which cannot be controlled or corralled by governments. But this does not mean that government is dissolving into governance, only that to understand the new processes of governance, including globalisation, we need to see how they provide a new context for government, one which departs from the old bureaucratic, top-down, hierarchical models of government which were once so common.

Complexity and knowledge: can citizens participate in decision-making?

The disengagement of citizens has undermined representative democracy, and the shift to new patterns of governance has undermined responsible government. But an even bigger problem facing social democracy and progressive politics in the twenty-first century is the growth of complexity which threatens to undermine participative democracy, by taking many areas of policy out of politics altogether, as politicians divest themselves of the responsibility for making hard choices, encouraging the rise of a managerial and technocratic style of politics at national and at global level over which citizens can have no influence. Government in the past of course has often been secretive and opaque, and this still continues, but to a lesser extent. Modern governments are probably now more open than they have ever been, aided by freedom of information acts and a more intrusive media. The change does not arise so much from the amount of knowledge available to citizens, as from the nature of contemporary knowledge and the process by which it is produced.

As with the other trends already examined, the extent of this trend towards greater complexity is controversial, and certainly uneven, and some of the wilder claims that are made need qualifying. There are, however, some solid grounds for thinking that complexity is increasing in contemporary societies, as a result of the processes that have extended the division of labour and the division of knowledge. It is not something that has suddenly occurred, but has gradually emerged over a long period. It is associated with new kinds of risk, and with new ways of managing risk, and creates some major new dilemmas for policy.

The rise in new forms and new levels of governance is one of the sources of complexity, so too are the greater cultural diversity of modern societies, and the consequences of individualism for the way people live. But the principal source of increased complexity and the new forms of risk lies in the technologies that have become available in recent decades. Industrial societies have reached the point where economic and technological developments have become so rapid and so continuous that they are constantly revolutionising lifestyles and behaviour.[19] Established political and constitutional processes provide politicians with little control over these developments, yet they have to deal with their unintended consequences, particularly the new risks and new dangers which they produce. But because of the trends towards citizen disengagement from representative politics and declining trust in politicians and in government, as well as the shrinking capacity of the state in relation to the tasks it faces, governments appear increasingly ill-equipped to handle the problems which technological development throws up, not least because so many of these developments pose fundamental moral and political challenges to the way people live, and even to the fixity of some of the constants of human life itself (such as extending its span).

One of the obvious consequences of these developments is an increasing dependence on expertise of various kinds, since many of the issues – from climate change to nuclear energy, and from GM foods to genetic selection, and the effects of new drugs – are such that only experts could possibly offer an informed opinion. But experts' own knowledge is limited, experts often disagree and science deals in probabilities not certainties – all of which contributes to the feeling of a growing number of problems which are insoluble, and yet which everyone agrees have to be solved. Since politics is a practical activity aimed at finding practical solutions to problems, this is not good news for politicians. The problem which social democracy now has to address is therefore how to open up new spaces for politics, how to rethink how a new kind of public domain can be created which reinvigorates both representative and participative democracy, empowering citizens and enabling them to participate in policy discussion in new ways. The instinct of politicians is increasingly to 'depoliticise' decisions by setting up boards and committees of experts to take the decisions on their behalf, and remove them from any political process, whether representative or participative. But this means that increasing areas of public life are subject only to very indirect accountability to the people. Politicians retreat to dealing with those few areas where their decisions can make a difference, or where there is high symbolic value in them being involved. For the rest, they invoke terms like governance and globalisation to suggest that there are no alternatives to the courses they are pursuing, and that the constraints on policy-making are so tight that there is only one possible course of action.

As politicians are blamed more and more for what goes wrong in government, and the media portrays every branch of government as incompetent, chaotic, indecisive and corrupt, it is not surprising that politicians seek to divest themselves more and more of the necessity of actually taking decisions in difficult areas. These are devolved to the appropriate experts. But politicians still tend to get blamed for anything that goes wrong, and ignored when things go well, even though they have less and less control over what actually happens. This trend towards depoliticisation and charismatic, celebrity politics threatens to undermine attempts to create more participative forms of democracy, as well as schemes for empowering citizens, and for rebuilding trust in representative democracy. Clearly a healthy social democracy requires all three. But it needs to find ways to resist the present trends that are pushing citizens and politicians further apart, and creating policy structures that, for all the talk of consultation, often make it harder for genuine participation to take place.

Conclusion

The changes identified here are often presented in apocalyptic terms. A sense of proportion needs to be maintained. Political systems and constitutions are fairly resilient and are in any case always changing. Though some of the new developments appear to pose special problems and dangers, they also present opportunities for new forms of politics and for constitutional experiments, particularly initiatives to imagine how the global polity we have might be improved. This cannot be done by neglecting the health of national social democracy; it will be the foundation on which a cosmopolitan social democracy will be built. But it is also the case that cosmopolitan social democracy will not simply replicate national social democracy. Many institutions will need to be different.[20] It is hard to see how political parties could play the role they once did in developing national social democracy. Other ways of ensuring that different interests and groups are properly represented and other ways for individuals to participate in the political process need to be found. Every means to create new public spaces for the global polity must be tried, because only a global civil society can provide the networks, associations, campaigning organisations and public discussion that can begin to sustain the kind of politics the global polity is going to require. The crucial requirement for all forms of social democracy is that politics continues to be regarded as an open process of deliberation and choice among alternatives. Its main enemy is the belief that outcomes are fore-ordained and that the struggle to maintain healthy representative and participative institutions at all levels of the global polity is therefore futile. Forging a new transnational movement will not be easy, but it is the only way that there will be a future for social democracy.

8

The Quest for a Great
Labour Party[1]

One of the central preoccupations of David Marquand's writing has
been the Labour party, its tortured trajectory, its achievements and its
failures, its capacity to inspire and disappoint. He has written eloquently
about the progressive dilemma,[2] whether progressives in British politics
should support and work within the Labour party as the best available
vehicle for achieving political, economic and social reform. This was
and remains a dilemma because progressives, both social democrats
and socialists, have tended to be drawn from the radical intelligentsia,
enthused by ethical ideals and political theories as to how society might
be made better, and committed to a politics founded on principles and
clear ideological views of the world, whereas the Labour party was
created by the trade unions primarily to represent the labour interest
in Parliament, and appealing for support on the basis of working-class
solidarity, identity and culture. When the Labour Representation
Committee was established in 1900, its objective was to establish a
distinct Labour group in Parliament, with its own whips, able to agree
its own policy. Labourism, the ideology of the Labour movement,
was conservative, pragmatic, realist and defensive, rather than radical
and transformative. Progressive intellectuals often came into conflict
with Labourism, and many despaired of the party and left it,[3] but for
more than a hundred years the Labour party has been the main focus
for progressive politics in Britain, the indispensable party for both the
left and centre-left. The enthusiasm of different groups of progressive
intellectuals for the party has ebbed and flowed, as some leave in despair
and others join (or rejoin) in hope.

David Marquand's understanding of the progressive dilemma was
shaped both by his parliamentary experience and also crucially by

the research for his biography of Ramsay MacDonald. In this essay I review Marquand's interpretation of Ramsay MacDonald and Marquand's social democratic critique of Labourism, contrasting it with the very different interpretation by Ralph Miliband in his socialist critique of Labourism, *Parliamentary Socialism*, first published in 1961. Marquand and Miliband articulate different accounts of the progressive dilemma, but they agree about the recurring problems which have beset Labour throughout its history,[4] problems still very evident today. Miliband argued that Labour had a chronic inability to act as an effective opposition, an inherent ambiguity of purpose, and a persistent inability to adjust to new circumstances. For him Labourism was a barrier preventing the Labour party developing as a socialist party. Those progressive intellectuals who wanted a socialist transformation of Britain were repeatedly frustrated and disappointed by the timidity and conservatism of the Labour party. Those who, like David Marquand, wanted a social democratic transformation of Britain, constitutional and social reform, and a new social democratic citizenry were also often despairing of the Labour party as a vehicle for social reform. Marquand left the Labour party in 1981 and joined the Social Democratic party created by Roy Jenkins, Shirley Williams, David Owen and Bill Rodgers. This was an attempt, ultimately unsuccessful, to replace Labour as the main vehicle for progressive reform in British politics.[5]

David Marquand's most extended reflection on the progressive dilemma and the nature of the Labour party is the biography he wrote of Ramsay MacDonald, Labour's first Prime Minister. He started writing the book in the early 1960s, the 'high noon' as he puts it of the Keynesian era.[6] It was finished and published in 1977, when the dusk was falling on Keynesianism and the post-war era of 'tamed' capitalism, when the fissures in the Labour coalition had become so great that the Labour Government was 'incapable of governing effectively'.[7] This was a time of great political and economic turmoil. A Labour Government was struggling to manage the fallout from the severe stagflation which was gripping western economies, a broad left insurgency had won control of the party's national executive and of the party conference, opening a major rift between the parliamentary party and the party members.[8] Marquand resigned his safe seat in Ashfield in Nottinghamshire in 1976 to go to work for Roy Jenkins as his chief advisor at the EU Commission. The seat was lost to the Conservatives at the ensuing by-election. The Government had already lost its parliamentary majority and become reliant on the Liberals for survival. The divisions over membership of the EEC, over nationalisation, over devolution, and over foreign policy, particularly unilateral nuclear disarmament and membership of NATO, were deep and polarising. The ground was being laid for the split in the party which occurred after the election defeat in 1979.

The 1931 crisis

Ramsay MacDonald had died in 1937, yet forty years later his memory was still toxic in the Labour party. Marquand was even warned by a rising Labour politician that no one foolish enough to write a biography of Ramsay MacDonald could expect a future in Labour politics.[9] That did not deter him. MacDonald had once been such a commanding figure in the Labour party, and so important in shaping its development, its strategies and its purposes, that the party's amnesia about him seemed very odd then, and still seems odd today. Labour has always had a problem with its leaders, especially some of its most successful ones. In its earliest days the party resisted having a leader in the way that the Conservatives and Liberals did. Instead it vested power in secretaries, who were responsible to the party's committees. The post of chairman of the parliamentary Labour party was subject to annual election, and was expected to rotate. The party wanted no cult of personality, and distrusted the powers that a permanent leader might accrue.[10] It was one of MacDonald's achievements to persuade the party that it needed to give the parliamentary leader more powers and a longer tenure if the Labour party was to become an effective parliamentary force against the other parties. He served as leader between 1911–14 and 1922–31, and was twice Labour Prime Minister, in 1924, and 1929–31, although never with a parliamentary majority. He established Labour as the main rival to the Conservatives, the alternative party of government, displacing the Liberals. These were extraordinary achievements which in hindsight are treated as inevitable, because of the extension of the franchise in 1918. But as Marquand argues, in the politically fluid circumstances of the 1920s they were never guaranteed. Other outcomes, particularly a revival of the Liberal party, were also possible. The new salience of class politics and class identity after 1918, the quadrupling of the electorate, and the deep split in the Liberal party allowed Labour to break through.[11] But seizing that opportunity required the welding of Labour into a coherent electoral and parliamentary force. That owed much to MacDonald.

Yet no Labour Leader, not even Tony Blair, has been more vilified by his own party than Ramsay MacDonald. In 1929 Egon Wertheimer wrote after witnessing MacDonald's performance and reception at the Labour party conference, that MacDonald was 'the focus of the mute hopes of a whole class'.[12] But two years later he was a pariah, for choosing to stay on as Prime Minister and form a National Government with the Conservatives and the Liberals and go against majority opinion in the Labour party. His fault was compounded when he then stood against Labour in the 1931 general election and called on Labour voters to vote for National Government candidates rather than Labour ones. He and the few Ministers and MPs who had supported him were expelled from the party and formed the National Labour group. National Labour proved not to be a significant split. It soon withered and died. The Labour party regrouped; although it was reduced to fifty-two seats after the 1931 election, leaving the National Government dominated by the Conservatives with a huge majority, it still had 30.6 per cent of the vote, a higher percentage than the party achieved in 1918 or 1922, or indeed in 1983, 2010 or 2015. It steadily rebuilt during the 1930s, but although there was a radical break from MacDonald the individual, there was no radical break from MacDonald's strategy and vision for the party. That continued. It was just that its author was no longer acknowledged. He was a class traitor who had joined not a National Government but a Wall Street Government. Undone by his vanity and snobbery, he allowed himself to be seduced by the aristocracy and out of social cowardice abandoned his class and his colleagues.

Marquand has no difficulty in showing how inaccurate that popular caricature was. The reason for MacDonald's decision was much more complex and goes to the heart of the debates on the political purpose of the Labour party. The issue which brought down the Labour Government was the threatened implosion of Britain's public finances following the runs on the banks and spiralling unemployment occurring across Europe during 1931. The need for some fiscal adjustment was plain, but the Government played for time by appointing the May Commission. When the Commission finally reported, its recommendations were stark. In line with Treasury orthodoxy it recommended that the bulk of the adjustment should come from spending cuts, in particular cuts in the dole paid to the unemployed and cuts in the wages of public employees. Borrowing was ruled out because the budget must be made to balance if the confidence of the financial markets in the pound and the gold standard was to be preserved. Similarly there was general agreement, even among radical economists like Keynes, that income taxes could not be raised because that would also affect confidence and risk making the slump worse.

The Cabinet was deeply divided on the May Commission proposals. In the wider Labour movement the trade unions signalled strong opposition, but without offering any alternative policies. The Government lacked a majority in Parliament and therefore needed the support of the Opposition parties to get any package through Parliament.[13] MacDonald and Philip Snowden, the Chancellor, spent much time trying to craft such a package, but when it was clear that a significant minority of the Cabinet led by Arthur Henderson, the Foreign Secretary, were implacably opposed, the Government was forced to resign. Henderson's view was that Labour's priority should be to keep the two wings of the Labour movement, the parliamentary party and the trade unions united, and since that could not be done if the Government accepted a package to stabilise the public finances which loaded the cost disproportionately onto the unemployed and public employees, it was better for Labour to go into opposition and let the Conservatives and the Liberals take responsibility for implementing the cuts.

MacDonald saw the force of this argument, and his first inclination was to resign and go into opposition. But he also believed that would be a defeat of everything he had been trying to achieve. Only if Labour showed it could act in the national interest, if necessary overriding the sectional interests of its own supporters, could it plausibly become not just a minority but a majority party of government. If the party abdicated responsibility whenever tough decisions had to be made, it would never win the respect, trust and support of the great swathe of middle opinion in Britain which it needed to convince if it was to gain their votes and win parliamentary majorities in general elections. If the Labour party preferred the comfort of opposition to the realities of power it would never reach its full potential. The same argument has raged about every subsequent Labour government.

Marquand brings out very clearly MacDonald's own frustration with the Labour party and with his Cabinet colleagues. There were radical ideas for dealing with the unprecedented economic crisis which was engulfing the country, ideas which had been put forward both by Oswald Mosley, then a Labour Minister, in the Memorandum he circulated to his colleagues and by Lloyd George in *We Can Conquer Unemployment*. In addition Keynes was strongly advocating the imposition of a revenue tariff, which would have avoided the need to target the unemployed for cuts. Keynes argued that the British economy was locked into a collapsing world economy and had to break free by leaving the gold standard.

MacDonald dithered over the Mosley Memorandum, he saw its merits, but Snowden and the Treasury as well as the Department of Transport were implacably opposed to the proactive interventionist role it proposed for government in resolving the crisis. MacDonald lacked the political strength or conviction to overrule them. Mosley resigned from the Government and put his case to the parliamentary Labour party, but received little support. Only twenty-nine MPs supported him. Two hundred and ten were against. On the revenue tariff MacDonald became convinced that this was what had to happen, but a majority of the Labour Cabinet were opposed. Most Labour Ministers, particularly Snowden, were free traders. Free trade for them was an ethical policy, a demonstration of internationalism, rather as free movement is today. MacDonald was defeated. This meant there was no policy which could save the Government.

MacDonald could very easily have saved himself, however. He could have followed the Henderson line, and resigned rather than implement the cuts on workers which the May Commission was recommending. The later accusations about the aristocratic embrace, and his fondness for country house weekends, are unconvincing. The personal appeal from the King was more telling. MacDonald accepted that it was a betrayal of everything he had worked for if he was to refuse to act in the national interest. His critics argued that there was no national interest only class interest. He was either on the side of one class or the other. Politics was binary. But MacDonald had never accepted that. His idea of a Great Labour Party was that Labour had to show that it was genuinely a national party which could govern in the best interests of the whole community. His critics argued that was impossible and that he was governing in the best interests of the bankers.

When he decided to accept the King's call to stay as Prime Minister and head an emergency National Government he thought it would be only for a short time until the immediate financial crisis was dealt with. The Rubicon was crossed when he acceded to the demands of his new coalition partners, the Conservatives, for an early general election. His relationship with the Labour party never recovered and there was no way back. He endured fierce criticism, often from former friends and allies, and he retaliated, as Marquand shows, with his own withering assessment of what Labour had become. He complained that Labour had retreated to a Poor Law frame of mind:[14]

> The Socialist Movement in this country is going to rack and ruin, because it is being controlled by people who are nothing more than critics of the Government, inspired by

166

the idea that all you have to do is to hand out largesse to the community.

He wrote in his diary:[15] 'The Labour party will run away from two things – the orders of the TUC and an awkward crisis.' By running away, he complained, they left everything unprotected. 'If this is the best Labour can do then it is not fit to govern except in the calmest of good weather.'[16] Later he concluded despairingly: 'It looks as though all our work has gone into the creation of a petty and passionate class movement whose ideal of socialism is not much more than public subsidies.'[17] The TUC's position on the other side was equally blunt. Resigning rather than cutting employment benefit was what *Labour* Ministers should do.[18] MacDonald had surrendered to the City and defied the Labour ethic of loyalty to majority decisions. It did not help that the Conservative election battle cry in 1931 was that the National Government had saved the nation from the Labour party. MacDonald was naïve about that. He complained that 'the Tories imagine that they are the only people with national views – that the Tories are the Nation',[19] but by lending his authority and prestige to the National Government he had contributed to the sharp reduction in Labour support and to the defeat of four out of five of its MPs. Reflecting on these events later he ruefully noted: 'Anyone in my position at the time, knowing all that I did, would have acted as I acted. However I sometimes wish that someone else had been in my position at that time.'[20] This is the lonely position many Labour leaders have since found themselves in.

The project for a Great Labour Party

Marquand emphasises that MacDonald was never an exponent of Labourism, subordinating everything to the labour interest as that was expressed by the trade unions. If he had been, he would have acted as Henderson did and cheerfully accepted the view that it was better to be in opposition than in government, if being in government meant doing things that were against the labour interest. MacDonald was a progressive intellectual who had a vision for the Labour party and what it might become, a party of reform and democratic citizenship, if it could transcend the narrow politics of the labour interest. At the same time he was the politician who more than anyone else had spent his career seeking to find ways in which the trade unions and the progressive intellectuals of the socialist societies, particularly the Fabians and the Independent Labour party (ILP) could work together. As the first secretary of the Labour Representation Committee he worked extremely closely with the trade unions. He saw the labour interest as integral to the Labour party, the foundation on which everything else rested. But he believed that a politics of Labourism, which some of the unions often seemed to want, focused exclusively on defending the interests of trade unions as corporate bodies, was insufficient, and might not even achieve what its advocates hoped. Being a permanent minority in Parliament did not interest MacDonald. It meant that Labour would always be excluded from making decisions and shaping the institutional framework of society and the state. It would be a pressure group rather than an alternative government.

MacDonald's political career was devoted to showing that Labour could become an alternative government, could aspire to be not just the second party of the state but the leading party of the state. To do this he had to persuade the unions to support and fund a much broader kind of party than many of them initially wanted to do. This has remained a tension down to the present. The party even under Jeremy Corbyn often wants to do things which the unions do not support. MacDonald made a close working relationship of the leader with the trade unions a cornerstone of the Labour party, yet in the two great political crises of his career, 1914 and 1931, the relationship broke down. In 1914 it was the issue of war, which the unions supported, as did Henderson, who was elected leader in Ramsay MacDonald's place and went on to join the war Cabinet. MacDonald stayed true to the principles of the ILP and the Second International in opposing the war and calling for the international solidarity of the working class to prevent it. This stand not only cost him the leadership and isolated him from the Labour movement, but also made him a target for the right-wing nationalist press. He lost his seat in Leicester at the 1918 election as a result of being branded a pacifist and traitor. But his hounding increased his standing within the ILP, and their continuing support gave him a route back when he fought and won Aberavon in 1922. Once back in Parliament he was re-elected leader. The party was much larger now than it had been before 1918, and the weakness of the Liberals and the level of working class unrest and political upheaval gave Labour a huge opportunity. Among the Labour parliamentary leaders MacDonald was the most clear-sighted about what Labour needed to do in order to consolidate its new-found strength and develop a strategy to advance.

At the heart of MacDonald's vision for the Labour party was the example of the Liberal party. Under the old limited franchise the Liberal party had assembled a broad, cross-class coalition, which had rallied to it all the non-Conservative and anti-Conservative forces in the country. These included the nonconformist churches, Wales and Scotland, the northern industrial working class, and many industrialists. The radical wing was republican, anti-imperialist, anti-landlord, anti-the established-Anglican church and anti-aristocracy. The more mainstream wing supported the Empire and property, but all Liberals were against protection and supported free trade, as well as political devolution within the United Kingdom, the most potent symbol of which was Irish Home Rule. The strength of this Liberal party was that it did not depend on a single interest but drew a wide range of different social groups into the party and created a broad party of reform. Labour succeeded in doing this three times in the twentieth century – in 1945, in 1964 and in 1997, and won office as a result.

Many parts of the Labour movement were originally part of the Liberal coalition. The reason why socialists like Keir Hardie and Ramsay MacDonald were determined to break from it and establish separate representation of the labour interest in Parliament was because they did not think that the Liberal party was any longer capable of properly representing the labour interest. As MacDonald put it before 1914: 'In this country as on the continent the fight ... will be ... between a Great Labour party and a strong reactionary party, with a small liberal party standing between, cut off from every source of inspiration and opportunity of growth.'[21] It was a hard task to persuade many trade unionists that separate representation was indeed necessary, since few trade unionists were socialists or favoured the various kinds of social transformation advocated by the Fabians, the Independent Labour party, or the Social Democratic Federation. What created the Labour party was the Taff Vale decision in 1901, which allowed unions to be sued for damages if they launched strike action. The determination to reverse Taff Vale led directly to the formation of the Labour party and the winning of twenty-nine seats in Parliament in 1906, rising to forty seats in 1910.

The new Labour party was very small and inexperienced and not considered a big threat to the Liberals, who in 1906 won one of their most emphatic election victories. In the system of multimember constituencies which existed in many parts of the country, the Labour party was often dependent for the electoral successes it did achieve in persuading the Liberals to allow a Labour member to stand unopposed. MacDonald devoted considerable energy to cultivating good relations with the Liberal party and its chief whip, in order to maximise Labour representation. He was criticised for this strategy at the time by those who wanted the Labour party to be a clean break from Liberalism, and present itself as a socialist, working-class party. MacDonald resisted this approach, because he argued first that Labour could not make headway without the tacit support of the Liberals, and second that Labour needed to attract Liberal votes. MacDonald saw Labour from the outset as the natural successor to the Liberal party, taking over its mantle, and completing its programme, rather than marking a complete ideological and political break from it. The future of progressive politics in Britain lay in Labour taking over from the Liberal party as the party of orderly progress through the ballot box.[22]

This also influenced his view of the complex issues around class and representation. Labour was a class party in a much more obvious sense than the Liberal party had been. The Labour identity and purpose were rooted from the outset in the distinctive identity and culture of the British working class, particularly in the great industrial centres of London, the Midlands, the North, Wales and Scotland. This world of labour, which G.D.H. Cole wrote about before 1914,[23] had been created by a hundred years of British industrial and commercial supremacy. Britain was a free trade nation and an imperial nation, and by 1900 had the largest urban and industrial population anywhere in the world. Numbers working on the land had shrunk to very low levels, and this gave Britain's industrial workers a potentially decisive political strength if it could be mobilised. This strength was viewed apprehensively by many in the governing class, fearing that extending the suffrage to all citizens would mean the political supremacy of the working class in Britain, as Marx had predicted.

The first half of the twentieth century was dominated by this looming clash, and an increasing political polarisation along class lines. As Marquand notes, the Liberals hoped that the clash could be averted by persuading British workers that a party devoted to the reform of capitalism rather than its transformation into socialism would better serve their interests. There was no inevitability about the conjoining of the labour interest with socialism in capitalist industrial societies. It occurred almost universally across Europe, but notably failed to do so in the United States. Many socialists welcomed class polarisation because they saw it as building to a decisive confrontation which would lead to the displacement of the existing ruling class and its replacement by the representatives of the workers.

MacDonald and many like him thought that liberalism had done its work. They wanted an independent *Labour* party, committed to a socialist philosophy and a socialist programme, but they were also deeply opposed to class polarisation. Ralph Miliband argues that the kind of Labour party which socialists like MacDonald and the trade unions created between them made Labour 'not just opposed to revolution, violence and exacerbation of class conflict but the best bulwark against them'.[24] MacDonald always argued, however, that revolution and class war were dead ends for the Labour movement. He was critical of the Russian Revolution which transformed socialist politics and parties across Europe: '... the cruelty and fanaticism of the Bolsheviks is not accidental but the inevitable consequence of the Leninist creed.'[25] He accepted that the Conservatives were implacable class warriors and constantly fought for the interests of property. But he thought it would be folly for Labour to reciprocate. Instead it should adopt the high ground of the national interest, and appeal to the goodwill and idealism of all citizens. Socialism was about moral belief not class interest, a position shared by many later social democrats, including Hugh Gaitskell, John Smith and Tony Blair. Resorting to the same tactics against property which the Conservatives were prepared to use against Labour would result either in the defeat of the Labour movement, because its members were ultimately not prepared to support a violent overthrow of the state, or in a socialist dictatorship as in Russia. Neither outcome would bring the socialism which MacDonald believed in. His socialism involved a cultural and moral change, in which aggression and acquisitiveness would be replaced by trust and solidarity, strengthening communities, and ensuring no one was left behind. Public ownership and redistribution were means to achieve this, although the policy details were often vague. Marquand notes that while MacDonald had a clear strategy for gaining power, he never developed a clear strategy for using it.

The inevitability of gradualism

This was partly, as Marquand shows, because there was a strong strand of determinism and fatalism running through much early twentieth-century socialist thought. The belief in the inevitability of gradualism was an important part of the socialist belief. One form it took was the idea that, whatever defeats might be suffered, the progress and ultimate victory of the working class was assured. Fifty years later this belief was still strong, as Eric Hobsbawm argued in *The Forward March of Labour Halted?*[26] It was also why so many Bolsheviks thought that a proletarian seizure of power in Russia would be premature because Russia had not yet passed through all the necessary stages of economic development. While never a Marxist, MacDonald did believe that the world was moving in a socialist direction. Economies were becoming more interdependent and more socialised. The need for government intervention and regulation was increasingly recognised, and public opinion was as a result steadily moving towards socialist conclusions. Gradualists like MacDonald argued that socialists should not accelerate the process. They should steadily build up their strength and persuade more and more of their fellow citizens that a socialist organisation of society was not only right but also efficient and in tune with the way that the economy and society were evolving. *Labour and the Nation* in 1928 saw socialism as the creed of practical men and women and labour as a movement of all classes, a movement of democratic citizens, against the small minority of property owners. It argued a moral case for gradualist socialism, applying the resources of science to bring civilised and dignified existence within the reach of all. Those who advocated class war and revolution were misreading the political moment, and had to be resisted.

The platform of James Maxton, the radical Clydeside MP, and Fenner Brockway, which became increasingly the majority position in the ILP through the 1920s, called for a radical programme of public ownership to implement socialism immediately. But for MacDonald, whose original political base had been the ILP, this only made sense if Britain was ripe for revolution. The failure of the General Strike in 1926 was blamed by many socialists on the betrayal of the workers by the trade union leaders. Ralph Miliband's view was that betrayal was the inherent and inescapable consequence of the Labour leadership's whole philosophy of politics.[27] But MacDonald thought the trade union leaders, having blundered into a confrontation with the Government, were forced to blink because they recognised that the majority of their members would not support an attempt to organise the overthrow of the Government and seize power. He had always believed that if the unions tried to coerce the state, the state would win. The only alternative to parliamentary socialism was revolutionary socialism, and in a democracy revolutionary socialism was a disastrous cul-de-sac.[28] Once the Government chose to define the General Strike not as an industrial dispute over the miners' terms and conditions, but as a challenge to the constitution and the elected government, the trade unions either had to go through with that challenge or admit defeat. As Jimmy Thomas, the leader of the rail union, and one of the Ministers who joined the National Government in 1931, put it: 'I have never disguised that in a challenge to the constitution, God help us unless the Government won.'[29]

All these themes were present in the famous speech which MacDonald delivered to the Labour conference in 1930, as the slump and the financial crisis were gathering force. It was to be his last address to a Labour party conference:[30]

So, my friends, we are not on trial; it is the system under which we live. It has broken down, not only in this little island, it has broken down in Europe, in Asia, in America; it has broken down everywhere, as it was bound to break down. And the cure, the new path, the new idea is organisation – organisation which will protect life, not property ... I appeal to you, my friends, today, with all that is going on outside – I appeal to you to go back on to your Socialist faith. Do not mix that up with pettifogging patching, either of a Poor Law kind or of a Relief Work kind. Construction, ideas, architecture, building line upon line, stone upon stone, storey upon storey; it will not be your happiness, it will certainly not be mine to see that fabric finished. It will not be your happiness, and it will certainly not be mine, to see that every stone laid in sincerity has been well laid. But I think it will be your happiness, as it is mine, to go on convinced that the great foundations are being well laid ... and that by skilled craftsmen, confident in each other's good will and sincerity, the temple will rise and rise and rise until at last it is complete, and the genius of humanity will find within it an appropriate resting place.

The extraparliamentary road

The retort from the left was that a gradualist strategy was interminable, and delivered little of benefit to workers, who needed relief from their sufferings and a better society now. Right from the beginning in the Labour party there had been those who argued that the industrial power of the working class had to be mobilised to force through the implementation of a socialist programme. Since any Labour government would be subjected to huge pressures from business, finance and the media, Labour's only weapon was to deploy the power which it possessed. This critique was not only of Labour's parliamentary leaders but also of its industrial leaders. The syndicalists in particular did not just reject the parliamentary road, and the need for parliamentary representation. They also rejected the need for traditional trade unionism, with its patient incremental bargaining. Instead they favoured the general strike as a means to force the propertied class to capitulate.

Many on the Labour left did not go as far as the syndicalists. But they did have a very different view to MacDonald of the proper balance between parliamentary and extraparliamentary activity. In the 1920s the Clydesiders, the group of Scottish MPs led by James Maxton and

John Wheatley, believed that Labour MPs were elected to articulate the grievances and aspiration of the class they represented. Parliament was a soap box and debates in Parliament were skirmishes in the class war. It followed that this war had to be fought outside as well as inside Parliament[31] The purpose of engaging in Parliament was not to gain power through office, but to use it as a platform to mobilise not the uncommitted voters but the militant, class-conscious workers who were already Labour voters.[32]

This was also the view of the Communist party which emerged as a rival on the left of Labour in the 1920s. The communists rejected the 'reformist view that a Social Revolution can be achieved by the ordinary method of Parliamentary Democracy'.[33] Instead they saw parliamentary and electoral action as providing a means of propaganda and agitation towards the revolution. Communist representatives in Parliament, the party declared, held a mandate from the party not from the constituency. If they violated party decisions they would be called on to resign from Parliament. The gulf between the Labour leadership and the Communist leadership was very wide, with the Communists advocating the adoption of the Soviet system to replace parliamentary democracy. The repeated attempts made by the party to affiliate to Labour in the 1920s and 1930s were regularly rebuffed.

There have always been many in Labour's ranks, like the Clydesiders and like Jeremy Corbyn, who agree with the communists about the priority that should be given to extraparliamentary agitation and campaigns, rather than parliamentary activity to build a platform on which to win office. Many in the ILP, MacDonald's initial base and ideological home, were sceptical about Parliament and argued that the ILP should be a purely propagandist force, spreading 'sound and thorough' socialist opinion through the country.[34] Fred Jowett rejected the 'jiggery pokery of party government played like a game for ascendancy and power'.[35] Socialists should always stand on principles, and vote on the merits of the issues before them.

These divisions go deep in Labour's culture and have resurfaced in every generation. The advocates of the extraparliamentary road point to the slim achievements which the parliamentary road has delivered. Every Labour government, including the 1945 Government, was disparaged at the time for being too cautious and defensive, never enacting bold and transformative policies, and soon being overwhelmed by problems and collapsing to defeat. Even before 1914 socialists grumbled that the Labour MPs elected to Parliament were invisible, and were achieving very little. It has been a refrain heard many times since. The lifelessness of Parliament is contrasted with the energy and vitality of the movement.

MacDonald's legacy

The two conceptions of politics are far apart. Marquand's appreciation of the divide was no doubt sharpened by his experience of Labour's factional struggles in the 1970s. MacDonald grappled with it at a time when the parliamentary road was still in its infancy and had not proven itself. In MacDonald's time it never delivered a majority Labour government. His achievement nevertheless was considerable in laying the foundation of a parliamentary road which would yield majority Labour governments in 1945, 1950, 1964, 1966, 1974, 1997, 2001 and 2005, although only five of these were substantial parliamentary majorities.[36]

MacDonald's Great Labour Party did eventually come into existence, and for periods it dominated British politics, 1945–51, 1964–70, 1974–79 (much less securely) and 1997–2010, Labour's longest period of electoral success during which it won three consecutive general elections all with substantial majorities. But all these periods of government are disparaged by many in the contemporary Labour party, with the partial exception of 1945–51. The Attlee Government has been rehabilitated largely because it created the National Health Service. Unlike the Conservatives, Labour has always found it difficult to look back with pride on the achievements of its previous leaders and governments. That started with its treatment of MacDonald.

MacDonald would have been pleased that a Great Labour Party came into existence, but he would have been dismayed that, after a highwater mark in the decades after 1945, the trend turned decisively against the kind of solidaristic, non-materialist, non-acquisitive community he thought that history would deliver.[37] His basic intuition about British politics, however, was proved correct. Support for the kind of class war politics that the Communists and parts of the Labour left advocated was always limited. Even Ralph Miliband acknowledged it in a revealing passage in *Parliamentary Socialism* on the record of the Ministers in the first Labour Government in 1924. He wrote: 'There was much that could be held against them on socialist grounds. But then most Labour supporters were not socialists only anti-Conservatives.'[38] MacDonald's strategy was to rally anti-Conservatives and non-Conservatives to Labour, and convince them that Labour could stand for them and would govern for them. MacDonald's supporters in the unions argued that if workers would not vote for a Labour party pursuing constitutional methods to effect social reform, they would be unlikely to support industrial action to achieve political demands. MacDonald and the Labour leadership were always aware that a large percentage of the working class in Britain voted Conservative. Labour was far from monopolising the support of the class it claimed to represent. Philip Snowden expressed it in his usual trenchant manner on entering government in 1924: 'We should not adopt an extreme policy but should confine our legislative proposals to measures that we were likely to be able to carry ... We must show the country that we were not under the domination of the wild men.'[39] It was to be Snowden, never one for understatement, who in the 1931 general election described the manifesto of his former colleagues in the Labour party, as 'Bolshevism run mad'.

MacDonald's legacy to the Labour party was not destroyed in 1931, even though his own reputation was, and he was no longer given the credit for the party he had created. In the 1920s, as Marquand notes, Labour was still a loose federation of local bodies and special interests, rather than a cohesive unitary organisation with a single purpose. The unions provided the party with an anchor and a connection with the working class, but the unions were themselves divided, on strategies and policies. MacDonald when he returned to Parliament in 1922 quickly stated the essence of the problem: '... the failure of the party in the last Parliament was that it never was an Opposition, and was never led as an Opposition. It never impressed itself upon the country as an alternative Government with an alternative policy.'[40] MacDonald was determined to rectify that. He wanted to complete the work he had started before 1914, changing Labour from a pressure group for working-class interests into a national party capable of winning and building power. Labour's opportunity in the 1920s was not to be distracted by the calls for class war and revolution but to focus on building an alliance between the organised labour movement and the radical wing of the Liberal party.[41]

In a new introduction, written in 1997, the year of Blair and New Labour's great triumph, Marquand reflected once more on the place of Ramsay MacDonald in Labour's history and on his own assessment of Ramsay MacDonald made twenty years before. MacDonald, he wrote, like Blair, had contrived to make the Labour party appear both adventurous and safe. In the course of the 1920s under his leadership Labour had forged decisively ahead of the Liberals in not just one but several elections. The party system had been reshaped and Labour had become the main alternative to the Conservatives.

MacDonald's strategy of building Labour as a constitutional party grounded in the trade unions and the labour interest but appealing to progressive intellectuals and progressive opinion far beyond the organised labour movement, sufficient to make Labour a contender for power, had succeeded.

There still remained the issue of what that power was for. In his first edition Marquand accepted that he had interpreted MacDonald and the great crisis of 1931 through a Keynesian lens. Robert Skidelsky in *Politicians and the Slump*, published in 1967, had argued that a Keynesian solution to the slump existed, and was articulated by politicians like Oswald Mosley, before he turned to the advocacy of direct action with the establishment of the British Union of Fascists. But Labour's leadership, including MacDonald, were too cautious, and failed to grasp the opportunity, with calamitous consequences.[42] In 1977 Marquand shared much of that analysis. In 1997 he had doubts. Much of the confidence in the post-war social democratic project had dissipated. The assumption that it was possible gradually to transform capitalism, the assumption both of MacDonald and post-war social democrats, no longer seemed to hold. The harsh dilemmas facing earlier generations of social democrats had been forgotten after 1945, in trying to pursue projects of social justice in a global economy ruled once again by an unbridled, untamed capitalism. Now that great period of capitalist success and excess has ended in another crash equal in scale to the crash of 1929. Social democrats have once more had to struggle to cope with hard times, and across Europe have been on the defensive. MacDonald would not have been surprised. He always thought that socialism depended on the success of capitalism not its failure.[43] If citizens were freed from want and insecurity they might become non-materialist and non-acquisitive, and create true fraternal and solidaristic communities.[44]

Problems beset both the electoral strategy and the governing strategy of social democrats. Is the best vehicle for progressive politics still a party which is anchored in the labour interest? Many of today's social democratic parties are being hollowed out as working-class voters defect, and progressive intellectuals and professional elites increasingly dominate. Trade unions are much weaker than they were, and changes to work and households have undermined the assumptions on which the politics of labour movements were based. Right-wing populist parties across Europe have begun to invade their electoral territory. The progressive coalition which underpinned the idea of a Great Labour Party has begun to fragment. In the British Labour party the trade unions, so long the anchor which kept the party in touch with working-class opinion, no longer fulfil that role. In 2015 the party elected the veteran socialist, Jeremy Corbyn, to the leadership, the result of left insurgency, led by young urban cosmopolitans and older sympathisers of the party's broad left. Many of Labour's working-class voters voted for Brexit in the referendum in 2016, with immigration a key issue. The cultural and political gulf between the old labour working-class communities and the new cosmopolitan intellectuals (Blairites and Corbynites alike) has become stark. Although only 37 per cent of Labour voters voted for Brexit, their concentration in particular constituencies means that on some estimates over 70 per cent of Labour held constituencies voted for Leave, almost all of them in the North of England, Wales and the Midlands. Many of these constituencies elected Conservative MPs for the first time in the 2019 general election. The progressive dilemma only existed in the past because the labour interest was such a powerful electoral and industrial force, and aligned to a policy of gradual progressive political change. But the new identity politics which is dividing the centre-left makes establishing a secure connection between the different parts of the progressive coalition much harder. In that sense the Blairite and the Corbynite factions in the British Labour party, although locked in a fight to the death, also share many assumptions about politics. They represent different wings of the progressive intelligentsia which has come increasingly to dominate the party and has lost touch with the labour interest and the cultural politics it represented.

The same is true of governing strategy. Marquand in 1977 was implicitly critical of MacDonald for not realising that the future was Keynesianism and grabbing it with both hands. In 1997 he was not so sure. It was always anachronistic, he writes, to think that MacDonald could have implemented a Keynesian solution in 1931. But now he goes further. There is no reason to think, he argues, that a Keynesian solution attempted in 1931 would have worked, The external conditions were too unfavourable. The problem was that faced with a series of increasingly unpalatable options MacDonald opted in the end for the orthodox policy, because that at least might preserve Labour's reputation as a responsible, constitutional, non-revolutionary governing party, prepared to play by the rules devised by others. The governing dilemma for social democrats is that if they behave responsibly as MacDonald did in 1931 they risk losing their party. If they are perceived as acting irresponsibly they risk losing their voters. The response of many Labour party members, dismayed at the party's electoral reverses in 2010 and 2015, was to support a new version of the ILP platform from the 1920s, giving priority to the extraparliamentary struggle rather than to Parliament. The policy platform of this new insurgency called itself once again socialist, although it is a pale, if still recognisable, reflection of the socialism of the ILP in the 1920s. The 1928 ILP programme *Socialism in Our Time* proposed a national living wage, nationalisation of the banks, the railways, the mines, the land, electricity generation, and the import of food and raw materials. Taxation on the rich would be increased to pay for supplements to working-class incomes, and the unemployment allowance substantially increased. The problem with this programme as with all its successors was whether a Labour government could be elected on it, and if that hurdle was cleared, whether it could be implemented and democracy preserved, given the intense resistance which it would arouse.

These tensions and these dilemmas, around governing, around socialist purpose, around representation and electability, have recurred many times in the history of Labour, and in those of other centre-left parties and movements around the world. Sisyphus in the Greek legend was punished by being forced to roll a huge boulder up a steep hill, and then watch it roll back down again, repeating this cycle endlessly. David Marquand through his many writings, but particularly in his great biography of Ramsay MacDonald, offers many deep insights into the dilemmas of social democracy. The possibility of social democratic renewal through changes in the hearts and minds of citizens is always present because of the arrival of new generations and new circumstances. But the older generation often loses heart. In recent writings David Marquand presents an increasingly bleak and disenchanted view of Britain and British politics,[45] rather like MacDonald himself, who wrote in his diary: 'In youth one believes in democracy; later on one has to accept it ... I read for consolation Gibbon's *Decline and Fall* and the minor Prophets.'[46]

Oakeshott's Ideological Politics[1]

Michael Oakeshott has always been hard to characterise in terms of political doctrines and ideological persuasions. Everyone agrees he is a sceptic, but there is much less agreement as to what his scepticism implies for politics. Is he a sceptical liberal in the line of Tocqueville and Acton? Or a sceptical conservative in the line of Hume? Or is he sceptical of all politics? He constantly refused conventional political labels, whether left or right, liberal or conservative, regarding them as the product of that rationalism in politics he so deplored. He firmly declared that his thought had nothing to with ideology, the most common form of rationalist doctrine. Ideology was intellectually empty and had corrupted politics. Ideologies according to Oakeshott have supplanted traditions of behaviour, providing cribs for behaviour rather than an education in the activity itself. An ideology is an 'abstract principle or set of related abstract principles which has been independently premeditated'.[2]

Despite these strictures, however, Oakeshott is still regularly claimed as a conservative political philosopher, regarded by many as the most significant conservative philosopher of the twentieth century, and regularly cited by conservative politicians and commentators as an important influence. He was even offered a knighthood by the Thatcher Government in the 1980s, but declined it. In many of his reviews and articles Oakeshott appears to be sympathetic to the conservative tradition, at least in England.[3] Some of his contributions to the *Cambridge Journal* in the 1940s, and several of the essays collected in *Rationalism in Politics*, feature strong attacks on collectivism in general and the British Labour party in particular, as well as disparaging remarks about prominent standard-bearers of liberalism, including F.A. Hayek.

Yet on the other side are those who claim Oakeshott for liberalism, because of his deep attachment to the English liberal political tradition, his apparent sympathy for many of the ideas of nineteenth-century economic liberalism,[4] and his understanding of the state as a non-purposive association. Oakeshott distinguishes between two understandings of modern European states as forms of association, libertarian and collectivist, nomocratic and teleocratic, whose basis is whether the state exists to promote many purposes or a single purpose.[5] There are many books in the secondary literature on Oakeshott which place him firmly in the liberal rather than the conservative tradition, for example Paul Franco, and more recently Efraim Podoksik, who has argued that Oakeshott is best understood as a liberal writer and that the tensions found in his writings are between the Whig and the Romantic elements of the liberal tradition.[6]

These questions are connected to the broader issue of what it means to be a political writer on politics, or a political philosopher, and whether these activities are distinct from political ideology in the manner that Oakeshott supposed them to be. Is it possible to write about politics without adopting an ideological position, and if it is possible, did Oakeshott succeed in keeping the two separate? This chapter will explore these questions, mainly through an engagement with some of Oakeshott's key political essays and reviews in the 1940s and 1950s, although it will also briefly discuss *On Human Conduct*. Oakeshott published relatively little during his long life, and very seldom addressed contemporary political issues and concerns. The publication since his death of his many book reviews, as well as occasional papers and lectures, has added to the material on which an interpretation can be based, but much remains obscure, as Oakeshott no doubt intended that it should. This chapter will argue that there is a strong ideological character to some of Oakeshott's writing on politics, despite his denials, and that the ideological persuasion that is revealed is predominantly conservative, although what he understands by conservatism in the English context incorporates important elements of classical liberal thought.

Ideology

At the heart of these issues lies Oakeshott's conception of knowledge, and most specifically of ideology. Since Oakeshott's epistemology was an idealist one which places great weight on the role of ideas and thought in constructing reality, it is puzzling why he would not admit ideology in certain of its forms at least to be a legitimate and unavoidable mode of experience in modern societies. David Manning, explored this idea at some length, setting out what an ideological mode of experience in Oakeshottian terms would be like,[7] but never succeeded in persuading Oakeshott of its merits.[8] Oakeshott never abandoned his view of ideology as an expression of rationalism. Ideology was responsible for much of the political and moral confusion of the modern world, introducing a range of concepts which were not just misleading but false. Oakeshott included in the list 'proletariat', 'nation-state', 'popular sovereignty', 'social justice', indeed most of the categories in which modern political thought has been conducted. The terms 'Liberal' and 'Conservative' are acceptable as party labels, but Oakeshott does not speak of 'Conservatism' or 'Liberalism'. That would be to accept rationalist abridgements of complex traditions of behaviour. Instead he talks of the conservative *disposition*, which is similar to Irving Kristol's characterisation of neo-conservatism as a *persuasion* rather than a doctrine.[9]

Oakeshott's belief in distinct modes of experience has led some interpreters to argue that Oakeshott has nothing to say about politics conceived as a mode of practice, but only as a mode of philosophy or of history.[10] On this reading, using historical or philosophical knowledge in practical politics is illegitimate because by moving between the two modes of experience the knowledge becomes abridged and a form of rationalism. It is transformed into an ideology and as such destroys the original knowledge and understanding. From this standpoint the gulf between philosophical and historical understanding on the one side and practical understanding on the other can never be bridged, and should not be attempted. It follows that those seeking to be active in politics have nothing to learn from Oakeshott, and he has nothing to teach them He is entirely remote from their concerns. His own interest in politics is to understand it in philosophical or historical terms but those worlds although satisfying in themselves are quite disconnected from practice. To ask whether Oakeshott belongs more to Conservatism or to Liberalism is therefore a fundamental error. Oakeshott has no practical advice to give.

This interpretation is an entirely coherent and plausible understanding of Oakeshott's thought. It certainly captures something of what Oakeshott believed himself to be doing, and the defences he erected around himself. But it is not convincing as an account of Oakeshott, because Oakeshott himself does not always adhere to it. Reading Oakeshott's early essays in particular, what is striking is not his detachment but his partisanship. There are many passages in which he writes as an ideologist. He is passionately engaged in political debate, clearly preferring one pattern of society and politics over another. He often does not write as a detached historian or philosopher whose only concern is to provide the most complete account of the phenomenon under investigation. Advocacy is never far below the surface, and accounts for some of the fascination his writings have exerted. The difficulty is that it appears to contradict his epistemological stance on the radical separation of the different modes of experience. As an Oakeshottian he should not be intervening in debates in the way that he does, and making his own ideological persuasion so clear. Anti-ideology turns out on examination to be an ideological position itself, and only intelligible in an ideological framework. A comparison can be drawn with Leo Strauss.[11] He also appeared detached from the problems of contemporary politics, focusing on purely historical studies, particularly of classical political thought. But his approach inspired a Straussian School, many of whom drew lessons for the practice of contemporary politics. Oakeshott too had followers, but where Oakeshott differs from Strauss is that on occasion he draws the lessons himself.

This can be seen clearly in the essays. Oakeshott is not even-handed between political parties or political traditions. For him there is truth and error in politics, and contemporary politics is characterised by increasing amounts of error. In his essay 'Contemporary British politics' Oakeshott reviews Quintin Hogg's *The Case for Conservatism* and John Parker's *Labour Marches On*. He is disapproving of their suggestion that both these two political parties are inspired by 'a philosophy', the philosophy of the Mandate, in the case of Labour, and the philosophy of natural law for the Conservatives.[12] Oakeshott likes neither of them – both are rationalist doctrines, remote from British political experience. He particularly dislikes the doctrine of the mandate, which first raised its 'ugly head' in the seventeenth century during the civil war, and which he argues has no basis in political reality or British political tradition, because if accepted it would attribute absolute authority to the will of a temporary majority. He commends Hogg for rejecting this doctrine, but argues that the doctrine of natural law although superior suffers also from being an ideological construction rather than one based on British political experience. Natural law reproduces the separation between the individual and the state, and treats the individual as prior to the state, instead of understanding the state and the individual as a unity.[13] Hogg is also too fond of planning, making promises that the Conservatives will plan better than Labour. Oakeshott comments: 'The rationalist bug has bitten the Conservative.' To defend conservative principles what is required Oakeshott thinks is to defend the customary way of doing things. It is a mistake for Conservatives to adopt the mode of rationalist reasoning of their opponents, because if they do so they will concede crucial intellectual ground. If all institutions have to be rationally justified, if all government becomes about planning, then the distinctive British form of understanding what it is to be free will be lost:

> It is the great merit of Conservatism that it has resisted the pressure of circumstances and a misled electorate to embrace the project of a centrally planned society. Its present weakness is that it has not resisted that pressure with the absolute conviction with which it should be resisted. If there ever comes a time when two parties compete for power on the basis of rival plans, an even larger lunacy than that from which we at present suffer will have established itself.[14]

Oakeshott is mildly reproving about Quintin Hogg. If Hogg reflects more, he seems to be saying, he will see that there are stronger grounds on which to defend the things they both believe in. Towards Parker he is much more vitriolic. His review becomes an ideological polemic against collectivism and the Labour party, which is presented as a thoroughly malign and alien import into British politics. Parker advocates the refashioning of the British constitution and British government, because, he says, 'the people wanted a purpose in peace as cogent as that given them in war'.[15] This will be achieved by creating a centrally planned society, which for Oakeshott is 'the ideal of all rationalistic politics'.[16] To this end, conference decisions of the Labour party are to be made binding on the Labour government, which Oakeshott claims will mean that 'Parliament is demoted to the position of an executive body for carrying out the items of a programme determined each year by an irresponsible body'.[17] Oakeshott acknowledges that this position has not yet been reached, but 'it is the character of British Government implicit in the structure of the Labour Party'.[18] It promises a constitutional revolution besides which the introduction of central planning pales into insignificance. Nor is this the only danger. Labour also owes allegiance to the trade unions, and the Trades Union Congress (TUC) is an irresponsible body which appears to exercise a powerful influence over the decisions of a Labour administration. The repeal of the 1927 Trades Disputes Act at the behest of the TUC according to Oakeshott threatens to turn the House of Commons into a syndicalist assembly, in which a large number of MPs will owe primary loyalty not to their constituents but to the trade unions which nominated them.

Oakeshott had a low opinion of the Labour Government elected in 1945. He talks about the 'incompetence' of their administration of departments, 'the delay and folly' of their foreign policy, and the 'grand stupidity' of their finance, and chastises the Conservatives for not being a more effective opposition.[19] But he also believes that the Government is pursuing an underlying purpose, which is to concentrate much of the power that was still dispersed throughout society in the hands of the government. Nationalisation is pressed not because it is necessary or because private enterprise is inefficient or monopolistic, but because without it a planned economy cannot be created. Oakeshott asks rhetorically, 'Why is not all this recognised by its promoters as despotism, and by those who suffer under it as tyranny?'[20] The answer, Oakeshott believes, is first, because of the 'vast emotional and intellectual confusion' among British citizens about the nature and conditions of freedom, second, because the changes were not preceded by a *coup d'état*, and third, because of the 'mediocrity' of the planners: 'Suspecting a tyranny, we look for a Strafford, and find only a Cripps, we look for a Cromwell and find only Clem Attlee.'[21]

Oakeshott is not comforted by this. In this essay 'Contemporary British politics' the conclusions to be drawn, he suggests, from Parker's *Labour Marches On*, conclusions reinforced by the Government's actions, are that 'the Labour party has an *incentive* to become despotic ... that it has the *means* to become despotic ... and that it has the *intention* to become despotic.'[22] This makes a big contrast with Hogg's *The Case for Conservatism*. Here the conclusion is that: 'Conservatism has no incentive to promote despotism and the aim of conservative politics is to guard society against all those concentrations of power which are liable to result in despotism.'[23]

What is the status of these judgements? Are they empirical? Historical? Philosophical? To those not of a conservative ideological persuasion they must appear ideological, interpreting a political situation through a particular ideological discourse, a set of general beliefs invoked to justify or criticise proposals for political action.[24] They clearly do not stem from any kind of even-handed assessment of the actual intentions and policy of the 1945 Labour Government, of the kind which historians provide. They take the form of a political and ideological intervention, in which Oakeshott makes use of a number of familiar conservative ideological tropes, in particular perversity, futility and jeopardy, to attack his ideological opponents.[25] His main concern is to issue a warning about the dangers which Labour poses to British democracy. By attempting to govern in accordance with an abstract idea of central planning, Labour threatens the freedom of British citizens. For Oakeshott, 'British democracy is not an abstract idea. It is a way of living and a manner of politics which first began to emerge in the Middle Ages.'[26] He feels passionate about defending it, but in order to defend it he has to become partisan, and he makes use of historical knowledge to fashion ideological arguments about the desirability of his view of British democracy as opposed to the Labour party view. The historian as historian, according to Oakeshott, can have no opinion about the merits of one policy or development compared to another. Historians study how contingencies, events and circumstances explain why one outcome emerged rather than another. This is not Oakeshott's position here. He is fully engaged, as a partisan, on one side of the argument. The political language he uses is that of friends and enemies. The Labour party cannot be accommodated within the British political tradition because its policy threatens to destroy it. Labour is guilty of a form of treason. The doctrine of the Rights of Man, which was based on common-law practices and exported around the world has now come back to 'confound our politics and corrupt our minds'.[27]

Oakeshott's more polemical writings might be defended on the grounds that since Oakeshott never justified his views by reference to an abstract principle independently premeditated, but always to a concrete manner of living, he can be absolved from the charge of ideology. This depends on accepting an extremely narrow concept of ideology which is not shared by modern scholarship.[28] Ideologies can come in many forms, and the general beliefs they invoke can take the form of abridged historical arguments as well as abstract principles. But even if Oakeshott's narrow definition of ideology is accepted it does not dispose of the problem. In many of his essays he still appears to be making a political intervention of the kind his account of experience rules out. He is using his historical knowledge to justify attacking the plans of the Labour party as revealed in *Labour Marches On*, while giving qualified support to Hogg's conservative position.

The argument in 'Contemporary British politics' is not an aberration. The ideological assumptions and preferences on which it is based recur throughout Oakeshott's writings. While there is a philosophical Oakeshott, and a historical Oakeshott, there is also an ideological Oakeshott. It is complicated because he is never simply an ideologue, and relatively little of his work is overtly presented in that way. But his willingness on occasion to engage in ideological disputes and to furnish ideological arguments is a distinctive and revealing aspect of his thought, and helps account for its appeal and its influence. Oakeshott has a vision of politics and of modernity which is a compelling one, and which is not best served by pretending it is something else. An anti-ideology can be a potent form of ideology, and that is what Oakeshott provided. But what form does this ideology take? Is Oakeshott best placed within liberalism or conservatism? There are arguments on both sides, and it is the evidence for these that now needs to be considered.

Oakeshott and the conservative disposition

There is a strong prima facie case for seeing Oakeshott's primary ideological persuasion as conservative. In many of his reviews Oakeshott appears to identify himself as a conservative. His comments on *The Case for Conservatism* indicate that he shares many of the same political assumptions as Quintin Hogg even if they have some disagreements. He criticises Hogg and Parker for agreeing that the basic categories of British politics are 'Left' and 'Right', because this involves imposing the categories of continental politics on to Britain where they do not belong, and would deprive Britain of much of its 'individuality'. While he concedes that Labour might be thought of as part of a continental 'Left' to some extent, he disputes that the Conservatives are part of a continental 'Right': 'There is nothing whatever in common between British Conservatism and any of the categories of continental politics.'[29] Talk of this sort is dangerous. It liberates 'a fog of unreality, and lost in this, British politics may become detached from their real root in British society and its history.'[30]

This hints at the main reason why Oakeshott has most often been described as a conservative. His reverence for the British manner of doing things, the British political tradition, emphasises the individuality and particularity of this tradition. The British political tradition is liberal in many respects, particularly as regards the diffusion of power, the rule of law, and the protection of individual rights, but Oakeshott rejects the universal claims of liberalism, because he is only interested in claims that are grounded in the English political experience. He pours scorn on notions such as the Declaration of the Rights of Man, and the American Declaration of Independence. These are abridgements of other political traditions and experience, in the case of the United States they are abridgements of British political experience, solidified into an eternal document. Oakeshott always opposed the idea of the abstract individual, existing before the creation of the state, and acting as the fount of all authority. Hobbes is preferred to Locke precisely because his theory of the state does not indulge the conceit of the sovereign individual.[31] Sovereignty is established once the people agree the covenant to end the war of all against all. Oakeshott has a conception of the authority of the state which is uncompromising in its implications for the obligations of citizens. The state is the condition for civil life, for peace and for all kinds of human flourishing. It is not a negative limit on the freedom of individuals. He always rejected the 'metaphysical' conception of the individual. The 'individual' was a historical achievement in which 'government' had played a decisive part.[32]

Oakeshott is also a noted critic of liberal thinkers. While he is disapproving of lapses by English Conservatives towards rationalism[33], he is even more severe on the rationalism in much liberal thought, particularly that of F.A. Hayek. Oakeshott never joined the Mont Pelerin Society which Hayek established after 1945, as a kind of liberal international to lead the fight back against collectivism. Oakeshott approved strongly of the need to resist collectivism, but he disapproved of many of the intellectual means proposed. 'A plan to resist planning may be better than its opposite,' he wrote about Hayek's *Road to Serfdom*, 'but it belongs to the same style of politics.'[34] He always opposed the subordination of politics to a purpose external to it, and emphasised the divide between a libertarian conception of politics which was part of the conservative disposition and the rationalist conceptions of liberals and neo-liberals.

The most important source, however, for Oakeshott's conservatism is generally held to be his essays in *Rationalism in Politics*, particularly 'On being conservative', a celebration of the conservative disposition in politics. It is not a conservatism to please everyone. Oakeshott rejects not just natural law but any transcendental justification for the existing order. Conservatism arises as a disposition within a settled tradition of behaviour. It seeks to preserve that way of life from external and internal attack. Reforms should only be undertaken to help it stay resilient. Politics involves more than technical knowledge about how to do things, it involves practical knowledge about a way of life. Abstract ideas are quite inadequate to grasp the particularity of a way of life, and in mistaking its character they encourage the adoption of inappropriate and often damaging policies to reform it. Abstract ideas wherever they come from do not travel, hence Oakeshott's scorn for imported continental ideas. The British have no need for external guidance on how to run their affairs.

Oakeshott never called himself a nationalist. This is another rationalist term which has no place in English politics. He disputed that Britain or any other country in Western Europe should be described as a nation-state. But in rejecting such terms he also rejects much of the terminology of modern liberalism. Oakeshott can be seen as belonging to a conservative tradition which emphasises the gradual historical emergence of the institutions and customs which define the nation, and although he acknowledges that there are broad currents of thought at work here, and can speak quite confidently of the European mind and the European conception of the modern state, he mostly resists generalisation, and talks of different national traditions, experiences and understanding, which make every state different. He has no patience with that strand in liberalism which regards the preservation of exclusive national jurisdictions as the main cause of war and conflict. Oakeshott celebrates states and national traditions.

'On being conservative' is one of Oakeshott's most elegant essays. Some have pointed out that it speaks only of a conservative disposition, which might be attached to a variety of political projects and attachments, liberal, conservative and socialist. It is at best situational conservatism rather than any kind of doctrinal conservatism.[35] What gives it substance, however, is its linking to definite national ways of life. What is most important in the conservative disposition is the desire to enjoy the world and its inheritance as we find it, and this means cherishing the traditions received from the past. For Oakeshott the past conceived in this way is intensely liberating because it is a repository of a wealth of practical knowledge which is needed to live the good life.

This essay appears to endorse a strong version of the precautionary principle. 'Innovation,' Oakeshott writes, 'entails certain loss and possible gain, therefore the onus of proof, to show that the proposed change may be expected to be on the whole beneficial, rests with the would-be innovator.'[36] He also argues that a change is more likely to be accepted if it 'resembles growth'. The change has to be 'intimated' in the situation and not imposed on it. If the innovation is 'a response to some specific defect', then it will be more desirable than one generated by 'a vision of perfection'. A person of conservative disposition, says Oakeshott, prefers innovations which are small and limited rather than large and indefinite, which proceed at a slow rather than a rapid pace, and when 'the projected change is most likely to be limited to what is intended and least likely to be corrupted by undesired and unmanageable consequences'.[37] These are quite stringent conditions for innovations to surmount, and most would fail the test, including universal suffrage or reform of the House of Lords. It is redolent of the conservative arguments against change set out by F.M. Cornford in his satirical guide to academic conservatism in Cambridge,[38] including the principle of unripe time, and the principle of the dangerous precedent: nothing should ever be attempted for the first time.

Oakeshott examines the argument that the conservative disposition is deeply rooted in human nature. Human beings are risk averse, they prefer safety to danger, they accept change not because they like it but because as with death it is inescapable. He agrees that it is one of the strongest, perhaps the strongest of human preferences. Yet he also notes that in the last few centuries it has not been particularly strong in Europe. In a passage which echoes some of the sentiments in *The Communist Manifesto*, Oakeshott provides his own disquisition on the theme of 'all that is solid melts into air'. The conservative disposition has been eclipsed by the desire for novelty and change. 'There is a positive prejudice in favour of the yet untried.'[39] Risk-taking of an increasingly reckless kind has become rife. 'We are acquisitive to the point of greed' and everything is undergoing 'incessant improvement'. We are willing to try anything once, regardless of the consequences. One activity vies with another in being up-to-date. Religious and moral beliefs are discarded as casually as cars and televisions.

Oakeshott observes the passion of contemporary culture for the new and the untried with amused detachment. He does not think it can be arrested, and he does not recommend imposing the constraints of the conservative disposition on the restless, progressive bent of the modern individual. But he does not think this means that the conservative disposition is no longer relevant. On the contrary he thinks that there are still certain spheres where it is supremely relevant. There are those activities which can only be engaged in with a conservative disposition, activities outside the sphere of the market, activities where a conservative disposition is uniquely appropriate because what is sought is 'present enjoyment and not a profit',[40] He uses the example of friendship. It depends on the loyalties and attachments which proceed from familiarity, which would be destroyed if the economic calculus of the market were applied to them. He considers other activities like fishing and craftsmanship. But Oakeshott concedes that it would be foolish and ineffectual to attempt to use this as an argument to impose conservatism across the whole of modern social life. He would like to protect as many of these traditional spheres as possible, but accepts that they are not and cannot become dominant.

There is another sphere, however, where Oakeshott thinks the conservative disposition is not only desirable but absolutely essential if the character of the activity is to be preserved: rules of conduct and, by extension, politics. There are many activities, Oakeshott believes, in which a conservative disposition has a part to play, some in which it should be the 'senior partner' and some in which it should be master. For Oakeshott there is no inconsistency in being radical in commercial, cultural and even private life, and conservative in politics. Indeed radicalism is only tolerable in commercial and cultural life if politics is conducted according to conservative principles. Oakeshott carefully distinguishes the conservative disposition in politics from a set of conservative beliefs about organic principles such as royalism or Anglicanism on which society should be founded. To be a conservative in this sense is to seek to defend those principles as the only legitimate principles for the organisation of society. Oakeshott argues strongly against this interpretation of conservatism as implying a particular set of beliefs. For Oakeshott the conservative disposition 'is not necessarily connected with any particular beliefs about the universe, about the world in general or about human conduct in general'.[41] It only implies certain beliefs about the activity of governing and the instruments of government, not about morals, or religion or natural law.

Is this a conservatism then without content? This is not Oakeshott's intention. There is a very serious content. He celebrates the apparent disorder of modern life, the absence of a plan, the chaotic process of human beings making choices and expressing themselves in a multitude of ways: 'We know as little and as much about where is it leading us as we know about the fashion in hats of twenty years time or the design of motor cars.'[42] Oakeshott acknowledges that some observers, including many conservatives, recoil from this character of modern life, deploring its wastefulness, its dissipation of energy, its excess, its lack of any clear direction, and seek to impose an order upon it. The worst offenders are socialists and collectivists who believe in the possibility of a 'collisionless manner of living proper to all mankind'[43] and seek to remove all the causes and occasions for conflict. This is a vision of human activity coordinated and directed from the centre towards a single centrally defined end. Oakeshott agrees that this is a coherent and intelligible political vision and even that 'there is much in our circumstances to provoke it'. But he regards it as inimical to a conservative disposition in politics, whose central purpose should be to preserve the diversity of human choices and activities.

The contrast Oakeshott draws here is between purposive and non-purposive forms of association. Those of a conservative disposition in politics he thinks should favour non-purposive association because this accepts the current condition of human circumstances and does not attempt to impose a pattern upon it. On this understanding of politics, the office of government is simply to rule. It is an indispensable activity, but also one that is inherently limited and specific, and difficult to preserve as such. He uses the analogy of the ruler as the umpire, whose function is to uphold the rules of the game, or the chairman of a meeting, who governs the debate according to established rules, but does not himself participate.

The emphasis is on understanding and enforcing the rules of the association, and this implies a very conservative attitude to those rules.

They may gradually evolve and be amended but only incrementally and only after much reflection and discussion. Politics becomes an activity which is inherently conservative, maintaining intact and handing on the rules which make the chaotic, turbo-charged, expanding and constantly changing civil societies of modernity possible. If politics tries to embrace innovation and direct it, then it only succeeds by destroying the dynamism of civil society. To defend this position it is not necessary to ground it in a rationalist doctrine about free markets or private property. It is sufficient merely to understand the function which politics needs to perform in the kind of societies which are characteristic of modern times, and that function is a conservative one. Governments do not therefore do nothing. They have a great deal to do, because activities and circumstances are changing so much all around them, but the aim of all their actions is to maintain the rules which make possible 'the enjoyment of orderly and peaceable behaviour',[44] rather than to prescribe what that behaviour should be, or to adopt a managerial conception of government. He criticised Conservatives for embracing 'productivity' as the prime object of policy in the 1960s, and the Thatcher Government for seeking to 'roll back the frontiers of the state' as a near disastrous blunder. In Oakeshott's view, Conservative governments should have no place for managerial activity.[45] Oakeshott sums up his argument by noting that the disposition to be conservative in government is rooted in the belief that 'where government rests upon the acceptance of the current activities and beliefs of its subjects, the only appropriate manner of ruling is by making and enforcing rules of conduct'.[46] The state is a neutral arbiter and commands the loyalty of its citizens because it does not proclaim one version of the truth, but allows all its citizens the freedom to choose how they live their lives within the rule of law. The tools of government have to be periodically renewed to adjust to new circumstances, but only occasionally and only in response to a perceived need, and then only after careful deliberation. Politics for Oakeshott is more about conservation than innovation. There is a bias towards preserving the rules that exist rather than amending them. The onus is always on the proposers of change.

Oakeshott adds one further argument. Those who understand government in terms of rational planning typically imagine government to be a 'vast reservoir of power', which they seek to capture and use to pursue their favourite projects which they believe to be for the benefit of mankind. They use politics to inflame passions and raise expectations about what government might accomplish for a particular group or class. They make promises they cannot keep, and treat governing like any other commercial activity, such as making and selling soap. The disposition to be conservative in respect of politics goes in the other direction. It seeks not to inflame passion and give desire new objects to feed upon, but to lower expectations and inject moderation into political debate, 'to restrain, to deflate, to pacify and to reconcile'.[47] This is not, Oakeshott explains, because he is opposed to passion in ordinary life, far from it. But he, like Hobbes, is opposed to it in politics because rival passions breed civil discord, and the conflict can destroy orderly and peaceable life.

This is a very distinctive conservative attitude to governing and to politics which treats governing as a secondary activity but a necessary one, and aims all the time at preserving the established order of status and privilege by seeking to defuse sources of discontent and to reduce the intensity of politics, rather than increasing it. The task of government is to be sceptical about the passions of its citizens, and by being sceptical encourage its citizens to moderate their demands on government. Oakeshott finds therefore no paradox for a people to be conservative in politics but adventurous and enterprising in most of their other activities. Indeed he thinks that the more adventurous and enterprising a society, the more necessary it is for it to be conservative in politics. If our circumstances were different, if the people were unadventurous and slothful, then he concedes a conservative disposition in politics might not be appropriate, although he personally thinks that a conservative disposition would be important for any conceivable set of circumstances. His key conclusion is that 'it is not at all inconsistent to be conservative in respect of government and radical in respect of almost every other activity'.[48] At the heart of this attitude is the need for scepticism in politics to counterbalance passion in the rest of life, which is why he thinks there is more to be learnt about the conservative disposition in politics from Montaigne, Pascal, Hobbes and Hume than from Bentham or Burke. Burke in particular is responsible for the confusion in modern conservatism that the conservative disposition should extend to all areas of life.[49]

He also thinks politics is not an activity for the young, because the sceptical attitude it enjoins means eschewing passion, optimism and commitment, and instead understanding politics as concerned with limits and trade-offs, acknowledging realities, favouring indifference, controlling desire, 'feeling the balance of things in our hands',[50] accepting many things that are distasteful or disagreeable or morally obnoxious. Only people with a certain maturity, or those like Pitt the Younger born prematurely old, have the talent to engage in politics. Oakeshott makes clear that he himself would never consider it. To have a vocation for politics you must have both a feel for 'the commonplace world', the world of practice, and an inclination to engage with it but only if you have nothing better to think about.[51] During most of his academic career Oakeshott studied politics and wrote about politics, but he never chose to become directly engaged in politics, and retained his otherworldly stance.

Oakeshott and the liberal disposition

Oakeshott wrote eloquently about the conservative disposition in politics, but he never wrote an essay on the liberal disposition, and was often disparaging about thinkers associated with the liberal tradition, including John Stuart Mill[52] and even John Locke,[53] as well as New Liberals and neo-liberals. Yet many have argued that Oakeshott is primarily a liberal rather than a conservative thinker. The main grounds for doing so depend on a particular reading of *On Human Conduct,* and on his approval of certain liberal thinkers, such as Constant, who understand non-purposive forms of association and oppose managerial conceptions of government, and rationalism applied to politics.[54] Since Oakeshott objects to all ideologies as rationalism, and since he believes almost all contemporary politics has become rationalistic, and supports the understanding of the state as an association with a single purpose, he is equally dismissive of modern conservatism as well as modern liberalism, while socialism is beyond the pale. His revival of the distinction between *societas* and *universitas*, civil association and enterprise association, as the most fundamental distinction in modern European consciousness, much deeper than the distinction between left and right,[55] is accompanied by a clear ideological preference for *societas*. Those who characterise him as a liberal claim his arguments for *societas* reflect a liberal rather than a conservative disposition. It aligns him with the classical liberal tradition in its emphasis on the non–instrumental rule of law which, prescribing no common purpose, permits the greatest possible diversity of purposes and activities.[56]

Oakeshott's understanding of the state as a *societas* is extremely rich and seductive. The growth of individuality and personal autonomy from the late Middle Ages made this new understanding possible, allowing the state to be seen as an association which could claim to be free and sovereign in so far as it was not subject to an external authority, and possessed the authority and the procedures 'to emancipate itself continuously from its legal past'.[57] These laws are general laws, they lay down conditions of conduct rather than providing devices to satisfy substantive preferences and desires of the members of the association.

Oakeshott contrasts this sharply with the state as a *universitas*, which he defines as 'an association of intelligent agents who recognise themselves to be engaged upon the joint enterprise of seeking the satisfaction of some common substantive want'.[58]

The modern state, according to Oakeshott, is formed through a tension between these two dispositions – *societas* and *universitas*, which are irreconcilable. They are not two aspects of the modern state but deadly rivals: 'They are both characteristic of a state not because they have an inherent need for each other, indeed they deny one another, but because they have become contingently joined by the choices of human beings in the character of a modern European state.'[59] *Universitas* may be a path which is more crowded with travellers, but *societas* is morally superior, and greatly to be preferred, since it permits the free development of individuality. *Universitas* by contrast involves slavery, the exercise of 'lordly rule' over subjects too fearful to assert their own individuality.

Oakeshott on a number of occasions praises libertarianism, while linking collectivism and rationalism to despotism. He sees the great achievement of the modern world in Nietzschean terms as the liberation of individuality, the 'limitless process of self-transformation without self-destruction'.[60] Proteus rather than Prometheus is the model for the modern individual, and human life is understood as an adventure in personal self-enactment, with no guarantee of salvation or perfection. Oakeshott's enthusiasm for the kind of personality which has emerged in the modern world, and the particular understanding of politics and the state which supports and advances it, makes him an unusual conservative. He celebrates the autonomous individual, the society of enterprise and continuous change. He notes the destruction of communal ties, but is not nostalgic for them. Modernity is a set of circumstances to be enjoyed, and what is chiefly enjoyable is precisely the freedom to choose between a bewildering variety of beliefs, values and activities, to invent and reinvent oneself, to gain personal autonomy and moral responsibility.

Oakeshott's libertarianism in *On Human Conduct* is undeniable, and reflects his commitment to certain liberal values, of tolerance and choice and individualism, the endless adventure of self-creation. But at no point does it contradict the conservative view of politics outlined in 'On being conservative'. There is a profound pessimism in Oakeshott about politics, because the virus of rationalism is so vigorous and contagious. He believes in rules of conduct which promote liberal outcomes, in the sense of allowing individuals to be as radical as they choose in the way they live their lives, but that this requires a conservative rather than a liberal disposition in politics. He wants a political class that understands and respects the state as a non-purposive association and which will therefore govern cautiously and sceptically. He has a very low opinion of democracy, regarding universal suffrage as a disaster, a rationalist project which assisted the trends towards the state being understood as an 'economy' rather than as a non-purposive association, and therefore as an enterprise to be managed to provide prosperity, jobs, welfare and security for its citizens. The spread of democracy has brought into government new elites which lack the experience and knowledge of the political tradition of their state to govern wisely and prudently. 'The generation of rationalist politics is by political inexperience out of political opportunity.'[61] Oakeshott distinguishes between the state as a source of authority, the state as a source of power, and the state as a mode of association. The state must be constituted in a way that protects non-purposive association, but this does not require a representative or democratic constitution. Democracy has repeatedly failed to protect non-purposive association, by encouraging rationalistic politics that constantly threatens it. Oakeshott is against 'lordly rule', except in special circumstances such as dealing with the poor[62] and external security, but he is strongly in favour of the rule of law, and a state that has the proper authority to uphold the rule of law with whatever force is required.

Non-purposive forms of association would be much more secure if all citizens were modern individuals, prepared to take responsibility for their lives. But the modern world has created two distinct personalities, the individual and the individual manqué.[63] Oakeshott's argument here is not philosophical or historical in the way in which Oakeshott uses and applies these terms in his writing; instead it is highly schematic, the kind of ideological reasoning typically found in the rationalist ideologies he so deplores. The individual manqué is the 'mass man', the anti-individual, all those who refuse to be autonomous and who demand security from the state. Anyone who supports redistribution through the state belongs to the anti-individuals, and collectivist parties thrive by appealing to them. This simple ideological device provides Oakeshott with a key dividing line to separate those policies that pursue intimations from the inherited political tradition and those that are rationalistic and born of inexperience and intellectual error. Most of modern government comes within this second category, and constantly threatens to infantilise citizens and undermine the foundations of non-purposive association.

The conservative nature of Oakeshott's politics can be seen in another early essay 'The political economy of freedom'. Despite its title this essay is much more about politics than about economics. The task of a political economy of freedom is to define the political conditions which can make economic freedom possible. Chief among these conditions is the diffusion of power. The idea that power should be dispersed throughout the community has roots in both liberal and conservative thought. In the economic sphere it means that the state should not tolerate any monopolies, either of capital or of labour, although Oakeshott, in a characteristic ideological flourish, regards labour monopolies as more dangerous than any others.[64] This principle ensures competition, but it is diffusion of power not competition which Oakeshott emphasises. If power is diffused, then competition will naturally follow. Oakeshott regards economic freedoms – property, free trade, competition and a stable currency – as much more important than political freedoms, such as freedom of speech, since as he puts it 'the major part of mankind has nothing to say'.[65] The economy of the nineteenth century, with state spending below ten per cent of national income, no welfare state, and minimal redistribution and protections for labour, is the society which Oakeshott says we had learned to enjoy, and it is this society he seeks to defend against the encroachments of governments elected under universal suffrage, with their rationalist schemes. Oakeshott's ideological preferences set him apart from New Liberals like Hobhouse or Keynes or Beveridge, they set him apart from social democrats like Durbin or Tawney or Cole, they even set him apart from many Conservatives, such as Harold Macmillan or Quintin Hogg, but they chime with familiar, mainstream twentieth-century conservative arguments about the dangers of collectivism, the welfare state, big government and democracy.

Does he not still have resonances with the classical liberal tradition, as John Gray has argued?[66] In his essays Oakeshott's attachment to the liberal principle of the rule of law does align him with a central liberal tradition. But he rejects all forms of doctrinal liberalism, aimed at promoting either democracy and human rights, or economic laissez-faire. His conservatism resides in his endorsement of whatever has emerged from traditions of behaviour, and too much of nineteenth-century liberalism took the form of premeditated abstract ideas. Oakeshott did not share the radical political passions of John Bright or Richard Cobden. He thought the conservative thinkers of the nineteenth century had been justified in many of their fears about the prospects for western civilisation.[67] Nineteenth-century liberalism was associated with the rise of democracy, the cause of political reform, and the undermining of traditional political authority. Oakeshott was sceptical of all three.

Although Oakeshott was highly critical of the way rationalism had invaded British politics and obscured the British political tradition, he still regarded the British understanding of their state as a civil association as superior to all other nations. In *On Human Conduct* Oakeshott derided the attempts of other nations to sustain representative forms of government.[68] Britain almost alone had preserved the continuity of its institutions, and succeeded in creating for long periods of its modern history a state which understood itself as a civil association rather than an enterprise association.[69] But even in Britain, the ability to protect the traditional British understanding of the state as a civil association was gravely under threat. Oakeshott's strong sense of national identity, his disparagement of other nations,[70] his references to 'foreign claptrap', his disdain for the European Community, are all part of his political vision. It is a very distinctive vision, and a very eloquent one, and it borrows from other traditions. But it is hard to dispute either its ideological or its predominantly conservative character.

Oakeshott and Totalitarianism[1]

Michael Oakeshott might seem at first glance to have little to say about totalitarianism and therefore to be an unlikely contributor to either the theory or the practice of cold war liberalism. The word does not feature in any significant sense in his very extensive writings. If he noted the term totalitarian at all he would have mentally classed it with all those other words like nation-state and popular sovereignty which litter modern political discourse and in his view are best avoided by serious students of politics. Such ideas are derived from rationalist political doctrines and therefore belong to ideological politics. An ideology is an 'abstract principle or set of related abstract principles which has been independently premeditated'.[2] Oakeshott believed that ideologies confuse more than they elucidate because they are based on a very superficial view of what politics is about, and prevent clear thinking about its nature.

The concept of totalitarianism

The concept of totalitarianism was originally used by writers sympathetic to Italian fascism to describe their political and ideological revolution against liberalism. But its meaning changed when it began to be used by supporters of liberal democracy to denote the character of the regimes which fascism and communism had created in Europe, and to contrast them unfavourably with western liberal regimes. The term became pejorative, denoting societies in which state control had become all-pervasive, over the minds as well as the bodies of its citizens, and all the intermediate institutions and associations between the individual and the state had been destroyed. The state was all-powerful and highly centralised, while individuals had become atomised and dependent, and no longer capable of acting autonomously. The idea of totalitarianism embracing both Nazism and communism, even though the two were deadly rivals, became an important current after the war, although it was already in use in the 1930s, as the regimes of Hitler and Stalin consolidated their grip. After 1945 the Soviet Union and the satellite states under its control were seen as the main instance of totalitarianism, although the concept was extended backwards in time to include the fascist and Nazi regimes of Europe which had been destroyed in the Second World War. George Orwell's satire on communism, *Animal Farm,* as well as his later *1984* helped popularise the idea of totalitarianism, and political theorists including F.A. Hayek and Jacob Talmon also sought to drive home the distinction between a free liberal society and totalitarian society as the struggle between East and West intensified.

Oakeshott deliberately distanced himself from all this. Very little of his writing on politics relates to contemporary events. He showed no interest in contemporary political issues, and developed an account of politics which played down the importance of premeditated ideas and stressed instead the role of traditions, concrete manners of living, and habits of behaviour. In a review of Hayek's *The Road to Serfdom* he rebuked him for his rationalist understanding of politics. 'A plan to resist planning may be better than its opposite, but it belongs to the same style of politics.'[3] Oakeshott never joined the Mont Pelerin Society which Hayek established after the Second World War as a league of liberals to fight back against the advance of collectivism. Oakeshott was opposed to ideological crusades and to ideological thinking. Political philosophy had nothing to do with the practical world of politics and attempts to use it to try to influence practical politics were either harmful or ineffective. It is true that Oakeshott on a few occasions forgot his own principles and did engage in ideological debate, revealing his own ideological persuasion, but in the context of all his writings, these were small episodes, and the bulk of his writing on politics is a philosophical exploration of the nature of political experience, far removed from the concern of ideological politics with the issues of the present.

A number of Oakeshott scholars, however, among them Ephraim Podoksik and Noel O'Sullivan, have argued that notwithstanding Oakeshott's lack of interest in trying to influence or intervene in current politics, he can nevertheless be seen as one of the foremost theorists of totalitarianism, along with Hayek, Popper, Talmon and Berlin during the period of the cold war.[4] This claim is based first on the way Oakeshott's thinking, in common with that of many of his contemporaries, was profoundly shaped by living through the rise and fall of the two great totalitarian regimes of the twentieth century, Nazism and communism; and second,, on the vision of a liberal society which was contrasted sharply with the totalitarian regimes.

Oakeshott differs from many of the other writers associated with the critique of totalitarianism partly because he never addresses the topic directly, and because he rarely involved himself in any practical engagement in politics. This disengagement made many intellectuals who were actively involved in fighting against what they saw as the evil of totalitarianism mildly despairing of Oakeshott. His writings contained some of the most eloquent accounts of the nature of western liberal society, but Oakeshott held himself aloof from direct involvement in politics, and did not encourage his followers to become involved either, although some of them, such as Kenneth Minogue, did later become prominent public intellectuals espousing libertarian and conservative positions. Yet this does not detract from the point that Podoksik and O'Sullivan make. Oakeshott's writings, like those of Hayek, were profoundly shaped by the experience of twentieth-century totalitarianism, and his work does contain a powerful statement of the nature of the western liberal tradition.

Social and political doctrines of contemporary Europe

The case for Oakeshott as an anti-totalitarian thinker is, first, his attack on rationalism and ideological politics which is contained in many of the essays published in *Rationalism in Politics*, and second, his exploration of the character of the modern European state, most extensively in *On Human Conduct,* in which he develops the contrast between civil association and enterprise association. There are a number of other works which are also relevant, including the volume he edited on *The Social and Political Doctrines of Contemporary Europe* first published in 1939, and the manuscript on *The Politics of Faith and the Politics of Scepticism* which was completed in the early years after the war and finished in 1952, a period when anxiety about Soviet totalitarianism was at its height, but it was not published until after Oakeshott's death.

One of the first signs of 'anti-totalitarian' thinking in Oakeshott is to be found in *The Social and Political Doctrines of Contemporary Europe*. It is a collection of texts chosen by Oakeshott to illustrate the five doctrines with which the book is concerned – Representative Democracy, Catholicism, Communism, Fascism, and Nazism. Three of these in the cold war era came to be firmly identified with totalitarianism, but in his Introduction Oakeshott plays down the differences between the five doctrines. He is more inclined to stress what they have in common. His criterion for selecting these five doctrines is that they are all 'represented in the life and order of some national community'.[5] As philosophies they are all disappointing. They frequently make excursions into philosophy and attempt philosophical analysis or criticism, but whenever they do so, 'they are quickly out of sight of anything like dry land',[6] and this applies almost as much to the doctrines of representative government as it does to fascism and communism. The only doctrine with any philosophical depth according to Oakeshott is Catholicism.[7] But he acknowledges that what is important in these doctrines is not their philosophical profundity. Their practical importance does not depend upon their intellectual coherence, but on something else, what he would later term ideology: 'What we are presented in contemporary European thought is at least five separate and distinct ways of conceiving the fundamental character of society, ... five distinct ways of conceiving the nature and earthly destiny of man.'[8] Five, says Oakeshott, is perhaps four too many for a single civilisation if it is to be harmonious with itself. This is because each of them is 'not merely a political doctrine, a doctrine about the nature of the state and the ends of government, but also a social doctrine, a conception of society and of the place and function of the individual in society'.[9]

Although Oakeshott is remarkably even-handed between the five doctrines he still makes his own allegiance quite plain. The three 'totalitarian' doctrines are all to some degree reactions to representative democracy, and are much more recent in origin. Oakeshott admits to some difficulty in choosing texts to illustrate representative democracy. He decided not to call it liberal democracy because he wanted to avoid what he saw as the identification of liberalism with a particular kind of 'crude and negative' individualism. What is important in the doctrine of representative democracy is the spirit of the laws in countries like England rather than the programme of any particular party. He says he does not mean to suggest that the doctrine of representative democracy is 'the final deliverance of the human mind on questions of society and government' so that it is 'outside history' as Mussolini accused it of being,[10] but he does argue that it 'has the advantage of all the others in that it has shown itself capable of changing without perishing in the process' and 'of not being the hasty product of a generation but of belonging to a long and impressive tradition of thought'.[11] But Oakeshott then goes beyond this to make an important claim: 'It contains, I believe, a more comprehensive expression of our civilisation than any of the others (although it is by no means either a complete or a satisfactory expression as it stands), and its adaptability is a sign of vitality rather than mere vagueness.'[12] He then sets out what he regards as its central principles: 'that a society must not be so unified as to abolish vital and valuable differences, nor so extravagantly diversified as to make an intelligently co-ordinated and civilised social life impossible, and the imposition of a universal plan of life on a society is at once stupid and immoral.'[13]

The same point is elaborated later in a footnote: 'With regard to the moral ideals represented in these doctrines, the fundamental cleavage appears to me to lie neither between those which offer a spiritual ideal and those which offer a material ideal, nor in the actual content of the moral ideals themselves, but between those which hand over to the arbitrary will of a society's self-appointed leaders the planning of its entire life, and those which not only refuse to hand over the destiny of a society to any set of officials but also consider the whole notion of planning the destiny of a society to be both stupid and immoral.'[14] This is one of Oakeshott's first formulations of what later became the distinction between civil association and enterprise association, and it is why he can be considered a leading critic of totalitarianism, even if he never used the term. In this early work he is already drawing a clear distinction between what he calls 'the three modern authoritarian doctrines, Communism, Fascism, and National Socialism', and on the other side Catholicism and Liberalism. 'To the Liberal and Catholic mind alike the notion that men can authoritatively plan and impose a way of life upon a society appears to be a piece of pretentious ignorance; it can only be entertained by men who have no respect for human beings and are willing to make them means to the realisation of their own ambitions.'[15]

Faith and scepticism

This distaste for government planning runs through all Oakeshott's work, and it frames his approach to totalitarianism. It is the theme of the essay published posthumously as *The Politics of Faith and the Politics of Scepticism*.[16] In this essay Oakeshott distinguishes between two ways of understanding the politics of the modern world, the politics of faith and the politics of scepticism. He suggests that the reason our political language is so hopelessly confused and our politics so ambiguous is because every political term has a different meaning depending on whether the user subscribes to faith or scepticism about the purposes and limits of government. Oakeshott clearly intends his distinction between faith and scepticism to be much more fundamental than the more usual oppositions encountered in contemporary political thought between individualism and collectivism or between democracy and dictatorship or between freedom and totalitarianism. These are often presented as polar opposites, and much of the political rhetoric of the cold war invited citizens to defend liberty against despotism. Oakeshott was on the side of liberty but he did not think matters were so simple. He did not think that the doctrines and regimes associated with totalitarianism were creations of the twentieth century. For him they were merely the latest manifestation of a much older tradition, and although they had some novel features, their basic principles were inherited from the past. They were the latest example of the politics of faith which first emerged as early as the sixteenth century, and had gradually come to dominate western politics. By faith Oakeshott meant much more than religious faith, although that was one form this style of politics could take. But many of the most important advocates of a politics of faith, from Robespierre to Lenin, have been aggressively secular in their politics.

Oakeshott noted the common view that the nineteenth century had been an age of individualism, and that the twentieth century had seen the rise of collectivism to challenge it, but he did not agree with this view. The modern world does not begin for Oakeshott with the French Revolution, still less with the Bolshevik Revolution, or any of the other dates which are sometimes seen as especially significant. Instead it begins with the gradual modifications of the medieval world by the incremental centralisation of power in new state institutions, and the development of new state capacities. The modern state is significantly more powerful than the medieval state, and it is this potential which early modern theorists such as Francis Bacon begin to think about in a new way. For Oakeshott Bacon is one of the main architects of the new politics of faith, which has had so many manifestations in the centuries that have followed, including the totalitarian doctrines and regimes of the twentieth century. This does not mean that Oakeshott thought that Bacon was responsible for Hitler or Stalin in the way that Popper thought Plato, Hegel and Marx directly inspired twentieth-century totalitarianism and were therefore enemies of the open society. This was so for two reasons. First, Oakeshott did not think that abstract reflection, whether in the form of philosophy or ideology, had direct practical consequences. The ideas important for behaviour were embedded in habits and traditions and did not operate independently from them. Intellectual doctrines were interesting to explore but they did not explain how or why events took place. The second reason is that Oakeshott always recognised the complexity of political and social reality. The politics of the modern world was constituted for him by both faith and scepticism, and if either one was carried to an extreme, bad consequences would follow. Most important political figures were influenced both by faith and by scepticism. Oliver Cromwell for example from one standpoint pursued a politics of faith, but as Oakeshott notes he was also one of the leading sceptics of the English Revolution, imposing restraint upon those who wanted to turn England over to the rule of the saints.

Oakeshott's distinction between faith and scepticism arises from different attitudes to the power of government, specifically the enlarged power which the modern state has come to possess and the potential power it is able to deploy. Adherents to the politics of faith believe that this power is beneficial and unlimited, and should be used to promote the perfectibility of human beings and human society. There is one truth which government has a duty to impose on all its citizens and regulate their behaviour in minute detail to ensure that all are contributing to the achievement of the common good. Adherents to the politics of scepticism believe that the power of the modern state is only beneficial if it is strictly limited and devoted to a set of narrow purposes, in particular the maintenance of order and the avoidance of civil strife. They mistrust the uses to which power will be put if it is not tightly controlled, and fear the consequences of government being used to pursue substantive projects, because of the ignorance and folly of human beings. They therefore conceive government in primarily judicial terms. The role of government is not to prefer one purpose or one good over any other but to hold the ring, and adjudicate between the competing claims and interests of the citizens on the basis of a concern for how best to maintain order and fair dealing in the light of the traditions and habits of the community that is being governed. In the first conception, governments should not be restricted at all in their pursuit of the common good and their powers should be unlimited; in the second, governments should do as little as possible, and their powers should be tightly controlled.

Oakeshott's position has sometimes been represented as similar to those conservatives who reject the modern world, and yearn for a return to the medieval order, when the capacity and reach of government were limited, and societies were ruled by custom and precedent. The rationalist madness of modernity has promoted liberty and equality, tearing down hierarchy and rank, and destroying tradition and older understandings of political order. Totalitarianism on this view is the final triumph of atheistic rationalist materialism, and ushers in a new despotism and the destruction of western civilisation. This, however, is not Oakeshott's view. He may have some nostalgia for the medieval past, but he does not believe it can be recovered, or that it would be desirable if it could be. The great achievement of the modern world is the development of individuality, the ability of individuals to live the life they choose within the rule of law, and Oakeshott welcomes this and celebrates it. This is the inheritance which has been bequeathed to the citizens of western states and they should enjoy the exceptional degree of freedom which it gives to them.

Oakeshott believes that this inheritance can only be safeguarded if the politics of scepticism assumes a more prominent place in the way we are governed, but he acknowledges that the politics of scepticism is not enough. If all we had was scepticism, then the modern world would never have come about. It is the tension between the politics of faith and the politics of scepticism which has created the marvellously diverse and rich society in which more and more opportunities and choices for individuals have become available. There needed to be projects inspired by faith to reveal the potentialities of the modern world. The politics of scepticism is very good at moderating and restraining the overambitious and destructive tendencies of the politics of faith, and achieving a balance which creates both an ordered and an innovative society, but if there was only scepticism there would be very little movement at all. Government would not be abolished, but it would stay confined to a very few functions, and innovation would be inhibited.[17]

The modern world therefore needs the politics of faith. But Oakeshott warns that there have always been great dangers associated with it. In the end projects inspired by faith are self-defeating, because they assume a perfection which can never be achieved and in trying to achieve it they overreach themselves and that leads to tyranny or destruction. Oakeshott's difficulty is that he believes passionately in individuals pursuing projects inspired by faith. That is what leads to creativity and great human achievement. But that same passion and creativity applied to politics can lead to disaster. Yet Oakeshott can see no way of preventing it, and in *The Politics of Faith* he suggests that if it could be prevented something would be lost that has helped create the vitality of the modern world.

This line of argument has important implications for how Oakeshott thought about totalitarianism. It means that totalitarianism is not separate from modern society and modern politics. In the form of the politics of faith it is inseparable from it. Right from the beginnings of the modern state in the sixteenth century there have been totalitarian tendencies, unleashed by projects of faith – Oakeshott mentions in particular the Puritan revolution in England in the seventeenth century.[18] The attempt to impose a uniform pattern on society and to use the powers of the state to do it, claiming that the purpose is to realise the common good, and to make human beings masters of their fate, can be relatively benign if it is restrained by the politics of scepticism, but if it escapes those restraints it can lead to the kind of totalitarian regimes of which the twentieth century had much experience.

The twentieth century was not unique in its susceptibility to totalitarianism, but Oakeshott did think it was a period in which the risks associated with the politics of faith had once again increased, so that this style of politics was once again becoming too dominant and was threatening to overwhelm the ability of the politics of scepticism to prevent ever greater concentrations of power in the hands of the state. Oakeshott fulminated against the British Labour party because he believed its leaders were pursuing a politics of faith that threatened to destroy the inheritance of custom and law which had been built up in England over three centuries since the end of the Puritan revolution and absolute monarchy and to impose a new despotism. He regarded the Labour party as a political movement which was alien to English tradition because it had been captured by a politics of faith which owed more to continental models than to English experience.[19] In this he was close to Hayek, who also saw totalitarianism as a tendency at work in the moderate as well as the extreme parties of the left, and warned that even moderate socialists were advancing down a road which would end in serfdom and totalitarianism and the extinction of freedom.[20] The difference is that Oakeshott also saw Hayek, at least at the time he wrote *The Road to Serfdom,* as being committed to his own version of the politics of faith which sought to use the state to reimpose the conditions for a lost liberal order. From Oakeshott's perspective the totalitarians and the anti-totalitarians of the cold war were both pursuing different but mutually exclusive projects inspired by the politics of faith. Both wished to impose their own pattern on society and regarded all other views as error, to be rooted out. Oakeshott preferred Hayek's politics of faith to that of the socialists, but he thought that this was not the best way to defeat the totalitarian tendencies in western politics. What was needed was the antidote of scepticism, not a rival faith.

Civil association and enterprise association

Oakeshott elaborated his arguments in some of his later writings, but he did not substantially depart from the views he had first expressed in the 1930s and elaborated in *The Politics of Faith.* His distinction between civil association and enterprise association in *On Human*

Conduct is recognisably the same distinction as that between the politics of scepticism and the politics of faith. There is the same ambivalence too in that Oakeshott recognises that civil association and enterprise association are two different ways of understanding the modern state, and neither one can be excluded. The state understood as a civil association is concerned mainly with administering and when necessary adjusting the procedural rules which make possible a peaceable and secure order, allowing individuals to choose how they employ their talents and live their lives. An enterprise state by contrast has an overriding purpose and enlists all its citizens in a collective endeavour to achieve that purpose. The common purpose takes precedence over whatever purposes individuals may have or might have. A totalitarian regime may be considered an extreme example of an enterprise state, but all modern states in part resemble at times enterprise states, for example when fighting wars, or when pursuing a goal such as economic growth, to which everything else comes to be subordinated in the name of economic efficiency. So extensive have modern states become, so intrusive their regimes of taxation and spending, so wide the scope and so large the scale of their activities, that governments are constantly dreaming up new enterprises to pursue, and electorates have come to expect their politicians always to be doing things and proposing new initiatives. The older ideal of the state as a civil association preserved by a politics of scepticism towards the power of government is still there, but its advocates sometimes struggle to be heard. The more extreme forms of totalitarianism may have self-destructed, as Oakeshott predicted that they would, but the milder forms of totalitarianism which he analysed through the concepts of the politics of faith and the enterprise state do not look to be losing their grip. States never seem to shrink, and even governments committed to reduce them have little to show for their efforts.

Although he wanted no part of practical politics, Oakeshott had many profound things to say about politics, and he offered a distinct vision of what good government in the western tradition involved. One of his most striking characterisations of his view is found in the essay 'On being conservative'. The essay is remarkable for combining a strong defence of being conservative about politics but radical or libertarian about almost everything else. This is because Oakeshott valued the conservative disposition in politics because it preserved the conditions which made every other form of individual liberty possible. Preserving traditional institutions which conferred authority gave to people the anchor they needed to experiment as much or as little as they wanted in their private lives. The formal nature of the constitution under which we live, and whether it coincided with some ideal liberal constitution, was not important to Oakeshott. Indeed he thought that pursuit of an ideal constitution which represented all minorities and respected all human rights, risked becoming a new politics of faith, turning the state once more into an enterprise, rather than a civil association, created through experiment, adjustment, chance, circumstance and contingency as much as through premeditated reflection. Oakeshott was highly conservative therefore about the political institutions which had come down from the past. Much better to keep them than engage in radical reform of them.

His understanding of English liberty made him conservative towards English political institutions. He celebrated the virtues of the English character and the English way of life he had come to know. His work draws on the European tradition of political thought, and his conception of the modern state is European. But he also believed that politics was necessarily local and national. The political tradition which had emerged in England after the religious and political turmoil of the sixteenth and seventeenth centuries was in many ways an accident, but that for Oakeshott was its strength. Nobody had planned or designed it, but it worked, and delivered a high measure of order and continuity. Oakeshott regarded this tradition as the best available expression of a free society and a civil association, a government in which the politics of faith was always tempered by the politics of scepticism. This made it the best antidote to the totalitarian regimes of the twentieth century. England offered an example to the rest of the world of a state which was not pursuing a single enterprise or seeking to impose a uniform pattern on its citizens, or promoting a particular doctrine. Instead its citizens were mostly concerned with their own private affairs, and gave their allegiance to a government which had many anachronistic features but which was the guarantor of their liberties and the rule of law.

Oakeshott may have celebrated the English tradition, but he never believed that this tradition could be distilled into a doctrine and exported to the rest of the world. Its lesson was rather different. What the English experience showed was that it was possible in the modern world to combine a limited government which maintained the rule of law and traditional institutions, with a dynamic civil society based on a high degree of personal liberty. Oakeshott thought of the modern world as quintessentially liberal because it was based on the free expression of individuality. He implicitly challenged the vision of Max Weber and Joseph Schumpeter, at times shared by Hayek, who thought the modern world was moving in an increasingly illiberal, collectivist and bureaucratic direction. Oakeshott was confident that a government of the English kind would always triumph over a government of the Soviet kind because the latter denied individuality while the former celebrated it. The English way was much better adapted to the circumstances of the modern world. There were internal and external threats to it, but Oakeshott never doubted that these could be overcome.

Part of this confidence is derived from the view that a modern society which turns its citizens into anti-individuals, making them dependent on the state, will ultimately fail. The anti-individuals are consumed by resentment and achieve little. Only a society of confident independent individuals can make the state a civil association which is then incomparably more dynamic and innovative than enterprise states. Oakeshott advanced these arguments without any deep study of the economics and sociology of modern societies, and as noted above he always remained ambivalent about what role faith and enterprise had played and should continue to play in the development of the modern state. He had a deep distrust of contemporary democracy because it had encouraged a politics of faith which had infected all parties, treating the state not as a civil association without any purposes of its own, but as an 'economy', an enterprise to be managed to provide prosperity, jobs, welfare and security for its citizens. Oakeshott celebrated modern society but he hated modern politics.

Conclusion

Oakeshott offers a very different perspective on totalitarianism from many of his contemporaries. He was optimistic about the kind of political arrangements he cherished to win through. He never believed that the totalitarian regimes could avoid destroying themselves. They had suppressed too many of the qualities and the institutions which had made western modernity so successful. But Oakeshott did not provide an anti-totalitarian message or an anti-totalitarian blueprint. He would never have joined an anti-totalitarian crusade like Hayek, or cast his argument in a universal form, promising a new salvation of the world. That would have been to capitulate to the politics of faith. While Oakeshott believed in English liberty he did not think it could be exported. Countries that did not have the English experience could not adopt English institutions. If they did they were likely to fail. Similarly there was no point imposing English (or American) institutions on anyone else. Every country had to decide which parts of its political inheritance it should preserve, and most important always would be those institutions which helped maintain internal order and authority, and these varied across nations. Government needed to be strong but limited. So long as it stayed within its own boundaries and focused on maintaining order and the security of its citizens, then it was a government which deserved support. This Hobbesian view always commended itself much more to Oakeshott than what he regarded as the confused liberalism of John Locke. It meant that there was no single solution to the problem of modern government. Authoritarian regimes which suppressed democracy might also be much more in tune with the traditions of their society than their opponents, and might be much more likely to safeguard personal liberty. Oakeshott did not believe democracy was a panacea. It had come to stand for so many things that it should be approached with great caution. Too often it had become a vehicle for the politics of faith.

Oakeshott's positions on totalitarianism and many other matters have often been misunderstood. He has had less influence than some of the self-proclaimed anti-totalitarians because he does not offer a universal message, or a simple call to arms. He offers a complex understanding of the nature of our political experience, and how in his view the things he regards as most valuable in that experience can best be preserved. But the country he is addressing is England, and he has little directly to say to other countries. He thinks the world is not the same everywhere, so that one solution will not work. Many protagonists for liberty despair of Oakeshott, but he despaired of many of them. He deplored the ease with which many of those who saw themselves as friends of liberty so easily and thoughtlessly adopted the same approach to politics and the state held by its enemies.

11

The Drifter's Escape[1]

One of Dylan's albums in the 1990s was called *World Gone Wrong*. The title has a wider resonance. It expresses the particular conception of politics and the political which informs so much of his work. Many of his songs depict a world which is fundamentally disordered, and from which as a consequence people are alienated and disaffected. Alienation is one of Dylan's major themes, but his account of how human beings become alienated and his recommendations as to how we should respond to it are many-sided and complex. There is no single perspective or attitude which he consistently presents. The changes through which his work has passed, and the constant reinventions of himself have contributed to this, but the ambivalence also goes deeper, and is reflected in songs at every stage of his career.

Alienation has a long history in western thought, both in the Judeo-Christian tradition and in the secular social theories which grew out of it.[2] Its oldest meaning is estrangement, the experience of the world as alien. Individuals become divorced from their essential natures and from authentic existence, and begin to live in inauthentic ways. The source of this alienation is alienation from God, and from the ways of God, brought about by original sin and the fall of man. Disobedience to God's commands led to the expulsion of human beings from the Garden of Eden and the loss of innocence. The attempt to understand and to overcome this estrangement between God and man lies at the centre of Judeo-Christian teaching and its parables about human existence, and has always been a deep influence on Dylan's songs, not just in the Christian albums.

The Judeo-Christian tradition also shaped the secular ideologies and social theories of the modern period, including liberalism and socialism, which proclaimed the possibility of a redemption for the human race through the reordering of society. Rather than being alienated from the ways of God, human beings in the modern world were seen as alienated from nature, both from the physical world and their own human nature. They experienced feelings of estrangement, powerlessness, insecurity, and anxiety arising from political and social structures which denied equality and liberty to their citizens. The two great authors of secular theories of alienation, Rousseau and Marx, contributed hugely to the traditions of ideas and feeling on which Dylan draws in his songs.

At the heart of Rousseau's thought, for example, is a contrast between nature and civilisation. Human beings are naturally good and free, but corrupted by civilisation, which separates them from their own nature, and imprisons them and condemns them to live inauthentic lives, in thrall to useless and pointless desires (and useless and pointless knowledge, as Dylan puts it in 'Tombstone blues', 1965). Vice and evil are the product of the institutions of organised societies. 'Man is born free but is everywhere in chains', Rousseau proclaims at the beginning of *The Social Contract*. These chains are the chains of institutions, of civilisation, of cities, of industry, and of states, in short of modernity itself. What civilisation has produced is an artificial and inauthentic being in place of the natural and original human being. The revulsion against the complexity and corruption of the modern world and the beliefs and processes which underpin it, and the corresponding desire for simplicity, for a return to nature, for goodness, for truth and beauty, and for authenticity – these are themes which resonate in the American Romantic tradition of Emerson and Whitman,[3] and became an important strand in the sensibility of modern America, and in the counter-culture of the 1960s. Dylan articulated this sensibility more searchingly than any of his contemporaries, and explored the alienated world of late twentieth-century America, a civilisation recognisably descended from the civilisation condemned by Rousseau and Emerson, but on a hugely expanded scale, and vastly more complex and more corrupt than anything they could have imagined.

A second major meaning of alienation is associated with Hegel and Marx, and draws on the legal meaning of alienation as the process by which individuals divest themselves of property. They alienate their property, by transferring the ownership to another. As such, alienation is built into the structure of market economies which rely so heavily upon individual exchange, and upon buying and selling all goods and services which have a use, including the labour power of individuals. Society appears as a vast collection of commodities, the products of alienated labour. The conversion of everything into commodities, the treatment of nothing as sacred, the subordination of all values to the laws of supply and demand, were essential aspects of the secularisation of society and the creation of the great wealth-creating institutional nexus of modern capitalism. The idea of everything being for sale, and therefore everything being in principle commensurable, is fundamental to commercial society and the formation of capitalist relations of production, and as such provided the basis of Marx's critique of alienated labour and exploitation, his analysis of the relationships of power and oppression which arise from them, and his moral condemnation of capitalism as denying true emancipation, the possibility of a true human community.[4] Dylan's songs, drawing on the folk and blues traditions and on the political ferment of the 1960s, are suffused with this understanding of the modern world as one of unjust power and the denial of human potential.[5]

In the Judeo-Christian tradition there has always been much theological dispute as to whether original sin and the alienation of man from God is a sentence which defines the human condition, and from which there is no escape, or whether it is possible for individuals to achieve release from the burden of original sin and be saved, by renouncing their sinful ways to live in accordance with the ways of God, and by so doing to increase their chances of reaching paradise after death. Are redemption and the creation of a Christian society possible on earth? For the secular doctrines of progress which were deeply imbued with the same eschatological visions as Judaism and Christianity, there was no question. Paradise could be realised on earth, if human societies were reordered so that they corresponded with the true nature of human beings. True human emancipation meant that alienation could be overcome.

In Dylan's work, now spanning six decades, the theme of alienation is ever-present, but the theme is treated very differently in particular songs and particular periods. Dylan has written and performed many different kinds of songs, but there are some distinct recurring patterns, one of the most important of which is the distinction between what might be called songs of redemption and songs of survival. Songs of redemption reflect a committed gaze and their primary motif is change, the possibility of transforming the world and human beings, while songs of survival reflect a sceptical gaze, a much bleaker assessment of the world, and their primary motif is escape. But both share a common conception of the politics and the political, what Dylan calls 'the political world', which for him is an alienated world.

Alienation and the American Dream

The theme of alienation is there in Dylan's earliest songs, and finds expression in both the songs of redemption and the songs of survival. What Dylan almost never offers is a straightforward accommodation to the world as it is, certainly not the political world. Instead his starting point is always a 'world gone wrong', a world which fails to live up to or match its ideal. As many commentators on Dylan have noted this ideal is an ideal of America, and Dylan belongs in an American Romantic tradition which was inaugurated by Emerson, and includes Thoreau, Whitman and Melville,[6] but which also has deep roots in American Protestantism. The idea of the American people as God's chosen people, in the same way that the Israelites had been, became closely allied to the sense of America as a new beginning, a break with the past, particularly the old European past, and the birth of a nation which was forever young, and forever capable of renewing itself.[7]

This possibility of renewal was never a matter of cautious, incremental reform but a moral revolution, a cleansing of the nation's soul, stripping away the pretences and the corruption and the lies, casting down the false idols, and returning to a life of simple purity and goodness. This ideal is contrasted with the actual world of complexity, of 'mixed-up confusion', of corruption and greed. Entanglement with this world means that individuals themselves become corrupted, alienated from their true selves and their true potential. To escape from this entrapment individuals must either find redemption or escape. If they find neither they become victims, and Dylan's catalogue has numerous examples of victims, from Emmett Till and Davy Moore to Hattie Carroll, George Jackson and Rubin Carter.

Dylan's ideal of America has always been fairly consistent. In the early days he drew much of it from Woody Guthrie, and the folk tradition and radical politics that Guthrie represented. He constantly contrasted the purity of the country with the corruption of the city. 'I'll take all the smog in Cal-i-for-ne-ay/ 'N' every bit of dust in Oklahoma plains/ 'N' the dust in the caves of the Rocky Mountain mines/ It's all much cleaner than the New York kind.' ('Hard times in New York Town', 1962). This went along with the myth of the Wild West, the independent, rugged, self-reliant pioneers who extended the frontier and built new communities. Dylan has always been attracted by the persona of the drifter, the outlaw, the vagabond, 'hard-travellin' with no fixed commitments or fixed abode. His songs frequently celebrate such characters, some fictional like the Jack of Hearts in 'Lily, Rosemary and the Jack of Hearts' (1974) and 'The man in the long black coat'

(1989), some (often loosely) based on actual historical figures, such as John Wesley Harding and Billy the Kid.[8]

This mythical America of the frontier has such hold on the American imagination because of its moral starkness and simplicity, and because the special American virtues of liberty, equality and independence can flourish there without impediment. This is also the ideal Whitman championed of the archetypal American setting out on a voyage of self-discovery down the open road into a future where anything might happen.[9] At the same time it is understood as a fragile space which was doomed to be destroyed by the forces of modern urban civilisation, the application of its laws and its systems of economy and politics. These signal the dominance of what Dylan calls 'the political world', which destroys the true America and makes it forget its true self. The task of the singer is to keep alive this tradition, by celebrating its heroes and its outlaws, and to call for their values to be recognised once more as the values of America. Emerson himself had denounced the state of American culture and prophesied the arrival of a genius who would transform America.

This sense of an older, better America runs right through Dylan's work, and it projects an image of an America which is unalienated, in which human beings can be honest and simple and true, no longer estranged from themselves or from their society. This determination to strip away complexity and embellishment is a desire to return to an original state of simplicity and purity. In Dylan's songs this idea is often expressed through nakedness. In 'Ballad of a thin man' (1965) Mr Jones is alarmed to see someone naked, and exclaims 'Who is that man?' He cannot adjust to the unexpected situation in which he finds himself, cannot understand what is happening. Similarly, in 'Bob Dylan's 115th dream' (1965) Dylan the hobo sailor, searching desperately for help to free his friends, runs into a bank: 'They asked me for some collateral/ And I pulled down my pants/ They threw me in the alley.' As well they might. Nakedness here signifies being authentic, real values over the values of the straight world (which from the standpoint of the ideal America is really the crooked world). In 'It's alright, Ma (I'm only bleeding)' (1965) Dylan declares (to wild applause when he performed the song during Nixon's Watergate crisis): 'Sometimes even the President of the United States must have to stand naked.' Standing naked is to stand stripped of all honours, offices, titles, the attributes of wealth and power, naked before God. In the liner notes for *The Times They Are A-Changin'* (*11 Outline Epitaphs*) Dylan writes: 'I never eat/ I run naked where I can/my hobby's collectin' airplane glue ... that is the bare hungry sniffin' truth.'

During Dylan's Christian period the hobo/outlaw tradition of the authentic America appeared to be supplanted by fundamentalist Christianity, but a closer reading of his work shows that the Judeo-Christian themes had always been present in his songs.[10] His embrace of Christianity, full-hearted though it was for a time, did not fundamentally alter Dylan's vision of America, or what was valuable about it. It gave him another way of expressing his faith in a morally pure America and his disgust at how it had fallen into the abyss. His apocalyptic warnings of imminent doom for America were echoes, if rather starker this time, of warnings he delivered in his earlier songs. What unites the three Christian albums (*Slow Train Coming, Saved,* and *Shot of Love*) with the 'protest' albums (*The Freewheelin' Bob Dylan,* and *The Times They Are A-Changin'*) is that Dylan was singing songs of redemption, proclaiming that America could be saved if it realised its errors and repented.

Apocalypse now

One striking characteristic of Dylan's view of alienation has been his constant warnings in his songs and public utterances of a coming apocalypse.[11] This is present very early in *The Times They Are A-Changin'* (1964) with his call to his fellow Americans to 'admit that the waters around you have grown' and that they had 'better start swimmin'' or you'll sink like a stone'. These are predictions of a sudden cataclysmic event, like Noah's flood, which will also be a day of reckoning, and which those who are not prepared will not survive. Dylan returns to it again and again, even entitling one of his live albums *Before the Flood.* His songs are scattered with dark hints at apocalyptic events, travelling the 'crooked highways', 'sad forests' and 'dead oceans' of 'A hard rain's a-gonna fall' (1963). Newborn babies surrounded by wolves, black branches with blood that kept dripping, guns and sharp swords in the hands of young children, a young woman whose body was burning, people starving. He hears 'the roar of a wave which could drown the whole world'.

This sense of impending doom is nowhere better expressed than in 'All along the watchtower' (1968), one of Dylan's most complete songs. He adapts lines from the Book of Isaiah which prophesied that the appearance of two horsemen signalled the destruction of Babylon: 'Prepare the table, watch in the watchtower, eat, drink: arise ye princes and anoint the shield ... And behold here cometh a chariot of men, with a couple of horsemen. And he answered and said, Babylon is fallen, is fallen and all the graven images of her gods he hath broken into the ground' (Isaiah 21: 5–9). The first two verses of Dylan's songs have the two riders, two archetypal drifters, the Joker and the Thief, conversing with one another gravely, aware that 'the hour is getting late'. The third verse then identifies them (although not directly) as the riders of Isaiah, and therefore as the harbingers of catastrophe, expressed in the song by the growl of the wild cat (a lion in Isaiah) and by the wind beginning to howl.

This theme is picked up again in much later songs, such as 'Things have changed' (1999). Not much has changed for Dylan it seems. He sings: 'Standing on the gallows with my head in a noose/ Any minute now I'm expecting all hell to break loose'; and later. 'I've been walking forty miles of bad road/If the bible is right the world will explode'. There is a similar theme in 'Shelter from the storm' (1975). The storm is both the pressures of celebrity from which Dylan (briefly) escaped in the 1960s, but also the biblical flood once again. For a moment Dylan, 'burned out with exhaustion' and escaping from a world of 'steel-eyed death and men who are fighting to be warm', imagines he has found sanctuary: 'Try imagining a place where it's always safe and warm.' But before long he was on the road again, and confronting once more another major change in his life, the acceptance of God. In 'Senor' (1978) which appeared on *Street Legal*, the last album before the Christian albums, the sense of an apocalyptic moment both in Dylan's life and the approach of the Last Judgement is palpable: 'Senor, Senor, do you know where we're headin'?/Lincoln County Road or Armageddon?/Seems like I been down this way before.' He had been down this way before, and would be again: 'This place don't make sense to me no more. / Can you tell me what you're waiting for, senor?'

What was waiting for him was what he had already predicted in 'Shelter from the storm' (1975): 'In a little hilltop village, they gambled for my clothes/ I bargained for salvation an' they gave me a lethal dose'. These lines are reminiscent of the ones in 'Stuck inside of Mobile with the Memphis blues again' (1966) when the rainman gave him two cures and said. '... "jump right in"/ The one was Texas medicine,/ The other was just railroad gin/ An' like a fool I mixed them/ An' it strangled up my mind/ An' now people just get uglier/ An' I have no sense of time.' The dose of salvation Dylan got also strangled up his mind, and led to his decision for a while to stop performing any of the songs written before his conversion at his concerts, and also produced the long rambling monologues in which he warned his audiences to prepare to face their Maker:[12]

How many people are aware that we're living in the end times right now? How many people are aware of that? Anybody wanna know? Anybody interested to know that we're living in the end times? How many people *do* know that? Well we are. We're living in the end times. That's right. I told you that the times they are a-changing 20 years ago and I don't believe I ever lied to you. I don't think I ever told you to vote for nobody; never told you to follow nobody ... Well let me tell you now, the devil owns this world – he's called the god of this world. Now we're living in America. I like America, just as everybody else does. I love America, I gotta say that. But America will be judged. ...

You just watch your newspapers, you're going to see – maybe two years, maybe three years, five years from now, you just wait and see. Russia will come down and attack in the Middle East. China's got an army of two million people – they're gonna come down in the Middle East. There's gonna be a war called the Battle of Armageddon which is like something you never even dreamed about. And Christ will set up His Kingdom, and He'll rule it from Jerusalem. I know, far out as that might seem this is what the bible says.

But Dylan, as so often before, did not stay convinced by fundamentalist Christianity for very long. He was soon distancing himself from it and recovering his more usual sceptical, detached pose. In 'Sweetheart like you' (1983) he sings rather poignantly: 'There's only one step down from here, baby,/ It's called the land of permanent bliss.' Dylan had been there and it had failed to satisfy.

But although his religious ardour notably cooled in the 1980s it did not disappear, because at root the religious vision is only a more extreme version of the American vision to which Dylan has always subscribed. Religious imagery of doom and destruction continues to form an essential backdrop to his songs and to his understanding of the American predicament. Two recent examples will suffice. In 'Shooting star' (1989) Dylan sings: 'Listen to the engine, listen to the bell/ As the last fire truck from hell/ Goes rolling by, all good people are praying./ It's the last temptation/ The last account/ The last time you might hear the sermon on the mount/ The last radio is playing.' Dylan has always believed that we are living in the last days, though not always in the very literal sense which the Bible foretold. It is what has given many of his songs their edge. The same sense of apocalypse is there in 'Caribbean wind' (1985): 'Every new messenger brings evil report/ 'Bout armies on the march and time that is short/ And famines and earthquakes and train wrecks and the tearin' down of the walls. ... And them distant ships of liberty on them iron waves so bold and free,/ Bringing everything that's near to me nearer to the fire.'

The political world

With his apocalyptic vision that we are living in the last days and are soon to be judged, and with his ideal of a lost America, it is hardly surprising that Dylan should have a jaundiced view of the role of politics. Indeed he regards the political world as the antithesis of the world of love, community and authenticity. The political world is the alienated world which individuals must decide whether to seek to overthrow, to survive within or to escape from. There is not much room in Dylan's vision of politics for cautious piecemeal reform of institutions and policies. Things are too far gone for that.

He displays this anti-politics in many ways. Almost every reference to politics and politicians in his songs is derogatory, from the 'drunken politician leaps' in 'I want you' (1966) to the reference in 'Summer days' (2001): 'Politician got on his jogging shoes/ He must be running for office, got no time to lose/He been suckin' the blood out of the genius of generosity.' In 'Stuck inside of Mobile with the Memphis blues again' (1966) the Senator is wandering about showing off his gun. Politicians are treated marginally better than judges, but are generally seen as part of the same axis of evil and corruption. In 'Union sundown' (1983) Dylan states: 'Capitalism is above the law/It say "It don't count 'less it sells" ... Democracy don't rule the world ... This world is ruled by violence.'

The reason, for Dylan, has always been plain. 'We live in a political world,' he sings, where 'Love don't have any place/ We're living in times where men commit crimes/ And crime don't have a face' ('Political world' 1989). Wisdom is thrown into jail, mercy walks the plank, courage is a thing of the past, it's all a stacked deck, in the cities of lonesome fear, where suicide is one of the kinder options. Unrelieved bleakness is often characteristic of Dylan's view of modern America. It is there in the 'Song to Woody' (1962) where he sings about the world being sick, hungry, tired and torn. In another very early song 'Train a-travellin' (first published 1968) he sings 'There's an iron train a-travellin' that's been a-rollin' through the years/ With a firebox of hatred and a furnace full of fears/ ... Did you ever stop to wonder 'bout the hatred that it holds?/ Did you ever see its passengers, its crazy mixed-up souls? … Does the raving of the maniacs make your insides go insane?/ … Do the kill crazy bandits and the haters get you down?/ Does the preachin' and the politics spin your head around?' And he asks rather plaintively at one point: 'Did you ever start a-thinkin'that you gotta stop that train?' The train is the train of Southern White supremacy, but it stands as a metaphor for the whole political world as Dylan came to see it.

In some moods Dylan is fiercely condemnatory of the political world; in others he is more reflective. In 'Slow train' (1979), for example, he says, 'Sometimes, I feel so low-down and disgusted', and goes on to rail against man's inflated ego, his outdated laws which no longer apply. He depicts modern America as a land where people starve when grain elevators are bursting: 'You know it costs more to store the food than it do to give it … They talk about a life of brotherly love, show me someone who knows how to live it.' This style can be contrasted with one of Dylan's greatest songs, 'Blind Willy McTell' (1983), where the history of slavery in America is evoked with masterful economy and haunting images. From the very first line 'the arrow on the doorpost' signals that 'this land is condemned' and the theme is continued through the images of burning plantations, the cracking of the whips, the sweet magnolia blooming, the ghosts of slavery's ships, the tribes a-moaning, the undertaker's bell, and the chain gang on the highway.

At the end of 'Blind Willy McTell' Dylan chooses to make a more general statement from his vantage point in the St James Hotel: 'God is in his heaven/ And we all want what's his/ But power and greed and corruptible seed/ Seem to be all that there is.' That sums up Dylan's view of the political world – it is a bleak Augustinian vision of sin, only power and greed and vulnerable sinful human beings ('corruptible seed') exist within it. But although, as in this song, Dylan is often to be found gazing out of the window, reflecting on the infirmities and perversities of the political world, he is also fascinated by this world, and in his extraordinary output of songs he has explored it vigorously. Among the many metaphors he uses to describe it three will be drawn on here: the political world as a prison; the political world as a graveyard; and the political world as the Insanity Factory.

The prison

Dylan's songs contain many references to the world as a prison. It is there in 'George Jackson' (1971): 'Sometimes I think this whole world/ Is one big prison yard/ Some of us are prisoners/ The rest of us are guards.' This idea that all of us are part of the prison system is echoed elsewhere in his belief that it is impossible to tell the sane from the insane. He has often written about prisoners, and the effects of prison, for example in songs like 'Walls of Red Wing' (1963) and 'I shall be released' (1967). Dylan tends to see the inmates of prisons as victims, as in 'The ballad of Donald White' (1962), many of whom like Rubin Carter have been falsely imprisoned on trumped-up charges. Many of Dylan's more committed songs treat the political world as sanctioning oppression. Special opprobrium is reserved for judges, who are seen as bending the rules to favour vested interests, and protect the wealthy and privileged, as most famously in 'The lonesome death of Hattie Carroll' (1964). Dylan here satirises the gap between the ideology of the courts and their actual practice. Judges proclaim that all are equal before the law and that even 'the nobles get properly handled.' But when William Zanzinger, a rich, white Baltimore socialite, was found guilty for the unprovoked and senseless death of Hattie Carroll, a black kitchen worker, he was given only a six-month sentence. Now is the time for your tears, Dylan tells his audience. He sees a similar pattern of miscarriages of justice in the imprisonment of the innocent like Rubin Carter in 'Hurricane' (1975) 'For somethin' that he never done', and in the excessive punishment of a defendant as in 'Percy's song' (1964).

Dylan sees law for the most part as coercive, part of a structure of power which disadvantages the poor and the weak, and is used systematically against them. Much of this stemmed from the experience of the civil rights movement, as Mike Marqusee has shown in his major study, *Chimes of Freedom*, which explores the political background to Dylan's songs in the 1960s, the systematic denial of black rights, and the frequent murder of black activists.[13] Dylan wrote many songs about the civil rights struggle, including 'Oxford Town' (1963), and 'Only a pawn in their game' (1963). Dylan may have told Joan Baez that he only wrote his protest songs for the money, but as Marqusee points out, this does not ring true either with the songs themselves, or with the fact that he was to return on several occasions to these themes in his later career, most notably in 'Blind Willy McTell'.

The graveyard

A second metaphor for the political world and one quite strongly related to the first is that of the graveyard. This informs above all the many anti-war songs, which include 'John Brown' (1963), 'Masters of war' (1963), and 'With God on our side' (1963). These are songs about the consequences of war, and the evil motivations of those who prosecute and profit from war, and the hypocrisy of the ways in which war is justified. War is regarded in these songs as an ultimate evil, which destroys lives, and with them communities, and the ideal of an America at peace, and a model of peace, harmony and community to the rest of the world. War is the means by which all the worst elements of American society come out on top, and transform the United States from a loose confederation of isolationist, pacific and independent states into a centralised, federal state, and by degrees a world power and an interventionist power.

Mike Marqusee notes that Dylan hardly ever mentions Vietnam directly in his songs. There is one brief reference in the liner notes to *Bringing it All Back Home*. In the 1990s he added a verse to 'With God on our side' to include Vietnam, but he studiously refused to be drawn on the issue in the 1960s, even though it was convulsing America and in particular Dylan's fans, and Dylan's songs were widely regarded as articulating the sensibility and political awareness of a large part of his generation. Yet despite Dylan's increasing unwillingness to be cast in the role of a leader and 'sound a battle charge', his '60s songs do refer obliquely to Vietnam and to the desperate morass into which America was sinking. 'Highway 61 revisited' (1965) and 'Tombstone blues' (1965) are dark satires on the mentality promoting the war in Vietnam. The first begins with the willingness of fathers to sacrifice their sons, and ends with the 'rovin' gambler' trying to create the next world war: 'He found a promoter who nearly fell off the floor/ Saying I never engaged in this kind of thing before/ But yes I think it can be very easily done.' 'Tombstone blues' has the memorable image of 'John the Baptist after torturing a thief/ Looks up at his hero the Commander-in-Chief/ Saying "Tell me great hero, but please make it brief/ Is there a hole for me to get sick in?"/ The Commander-in-Chief answers him while chasing a fly/ Saying "Death to all those who would whimper and cry"/ And dropping a bar bell he points to the sky/ Saying, "The sun's not yellow it's chicken".'

'Tombstone blues' also contains the lines which have often been taken to be a direct reference to the escalating war in Vietnam: 'The King of the Philistines his soldiers to save/ Puts jawbones on their tombstones and flatters their graves/ Puts the pied pipers in prison and fattens the slaves/ Then sends them out to the jungle.' From where many did not return. The sequence is continued in 'From a Buick 6' (1965) which concerns 'this graveyard woman' who 'if I go down dyin', you know she bound to put a blanket on my bed'. It ends with the plea for 'a steam shovel mama to keep away the dead', 'a dump truck mama to unload my head'. Images of death, destruction, desperation abound in the song, reflecting the experience of so many young conscripts, disproportionately poor and black, thrust into the inferno of Vietnam.

These satires mark a bridge between the more conventional anti-war songs which Dylan wrote at the beginning of his career and his new sense of the absurdity, disorientation and perversity of modern America, which he expressed in *Bringing It All Back Home, Highway 61 Revisited,* and *Blonde on Blonde.* As with the prison metaphor, the graveyard metaphor for the political world has continued to be employed by Dylan and to shape his understanding of the nature of politics.

The Insanity Factory

One way in which it particularly did so was in influencing his conception of the political world as an 'Insanity Factory', a place of death and inauthenticity. Lifelessness was one of its abiding characteristics, and it was the spreading of lifelessness which Dylan regarded as the great scourge of modern America, the attitude which more than anything undermined independence, self-reliance, creativity and vitality. What it left was a profound sense of emptiness, a feeling Dylan has often written about in his love songs, for example, 'Felt an emptiness inside to which he could just not relate' in 'Simple twist of fate' (1974), but which he also treats as a major symptom of political and social alienation.

The Insanity Factory is a phrase used by Dylan in the liner notes to *Highway 61 Revisited*. He proclaims there that 'Lifelessness is the Great Enemy' and associates it with calls to "go save the world" and declares 'Involvement! That's the issue'. Liberal activism is no longer enough; for Dylan it has become part of the problem. It cannot understand the seriousness of the situation. He states: 'We are singing today of the WIPE-OUT GANG – the WIPE-OUT GANG buys, owns and operates the Insanity Factory – if you do not know where the Insanity Factory is located, you should hereby take two steps to the right, paint your teeth & go to sleep.'

What Dylan means by the Insanity Factory is the peculiar institutional character which American capitalism had come to assume in the second half of the twentieth century, with its aggressive consumerism and market imperialism, its militarism and nationalism, and its deep racial and social conflicts. Dylan's instinctive anti-authoritarian streak and his roots in the Emersonian tradition made him a strong critic of developments in modern America, but the growing dislocation occasioned by the assassination of President Kennedy, the race riots, and above all the Vietnam War, transformed his attitude from one of wanting a moral reform and the cleansing of his society to one of despairing that this society was reformable at all.

In his exploration of modern America Dylan uses satire, anecdote, allegory, free association, and deliberate obscurity to try to capture aspects of this weird and complex culture. The starting point is that the lunatics have taken over the asylum, and that sane people, or those that want to remain sane, had better watch out. In this way Dylan provides a series of commentaries and notes on how to survive in modern America. In some of his earlier songs, such as 'Bob Dylan's 115th Dream', the satire is quite good-humoured, although with a sharp edge. America is a weird place, in which hypocrisy and self-serving behaviour abound. The building with a sign advertising brotherhood turns out to be a funeral parlour and the undertaker is only interested in Dylan's imprisoned friends if they die. He knocks on a house displaying the US flag and asks for help, only to be told: 'Get out of here/ I'll tear you limb from limb/ I said "You know they refused Jesus too"/ He said "You're not him".'

The general picture repeated in many other songs is of a society driven at best by selfishness, at worst by crazed prejudice. At first Dylan seems to have thought that the crazies were confined to particular groups of racists and bigots, such as the John Birch Society, with their obsessions with communism, black people and Jews, which he memorably satirised in 'Talkin' John Birch Society blues'. But subsequently his mood becomes darker, and he appears to believe that insanity has spread to all those in charge of the society. In songs such as 'It's alright, Ma (I'm Only Bleeding)' (1965) and above all 'Desolation Row' (1965) Dylan probes deeply into the perversities of America.

A constant theme is the corrupting power of markets which seek to turn every human attribute into a commodity in order to reap a profit. In this way traditional values are subverted: 'Made everything from toy guns that spark/ To flesh coloured Christs that glow in the dark/ It's easy to see without looking too far/ That not much/ Is really sacred' ('It's alright, Ma'). Dylan here draws on one of the classic themes of alienation – everything has become for sale. Balzac satirised the France of his day in which 'even the Holy Spirit has its quotation on the stock exchange'.[14] Dylan does the same for America. The loss of the sacred means also that individuals are defenceless against the tide of consumerism: 'Advertising signs that con/ You into thinking you're the one/ That can do what's never been done/ That can win what's never been won/ Meantime life outside goes on/ All around you.' ('It's alright, Ma'). The members of this society are trapped, 'For them that must obey authority/ That they do not respect in any degree/ Who despise their jobs/ Their destinies' are forced to 'gargle in the rat race choir, bent out of shape from society's pliers'.

Dylan's classic song about the Insanity Factory and about modern America is 'Desolation Row' (1965). It combines the apocalyptic 'They're selling postcards of the hanging/ They're painting the passports brown' and 'the Titanic sails at dawn' with a succession of images of the threatening, the absurd and the freaky, from the restless riot squad and the superhuman crew rounding up 'everyone that knows more than they do' to Dr Filth and his sexless patients, Einstein the former electric violin player bumming cigarettes, and Ophelia whose sin is her lifelessness. This is a society portrayed as on the edge of the abyss, where everybody's shouting "Which side are you on", an old socialist anthem, as if political action of any kind could redeem and save this world. Dylan's response is to state that the only refuge from this madness is no refuge. It is Desolation Row, but it is the only place to be.[15]

The outlaw

Dylan's achievement in his extraordinary run of albums in the 1960s from *The Freewheelin' Bob Dylan* (1963) up to and including *John Wesley Harding* (1968) was to take the persona of the drifter and the outlaw from the folk and radical tradition personified by Woody Guthrie and translate them into the very different world and experience of 1960s urban America. What Dylan takes in particular from the Guthrie tradition is the idea of the outsider, the drifter who is always travelling, travellin' hard, always on the move, driven by that 'restless hungry feeling' ('One too many mornings', 1964), never content to be tied down. These drifters, the vagabonds, the hobos, the jugglers, the clowns, the gamblers, the hustlers, the jokers and the thieves are the true Americans, or at least the ones that are keeping alive the true American spirit and the possibility of a different America. Dylan plays endlessly throughout his career with the myths of this other America, and its favourite images, such as the railroad. The obsession with the railroad in all its forms is ultimately nostalgic and locates this America firmly in the past.[16] There are hardly any references in Dylan to aeroplanes, (apart from bombs), except for the rather plaintive 'Time is a jet plane, it moves too fast' in 'You're a big girl now'.

The American ideal of a life of self-creation and self-discovery is a central motif in Dylan and draws on a particular ideal of American masculinity, typified by such figures as James Dean, Jack Kerouac, Jim Morrison and Marlon Brando. Along with these, Dylan is said to be part of a 'masculine iconography of white, rebellious America'.[17] Dylan's songs and parables are said to be primarily about men, and to exclude women, by treating women in fairly standard ways, as 'bookends' to the innovative, creative, life-enhancing, challenging male experience. Dylan, it is argued, has contested many aspects of the dominant culture, but not its preferred styles of masculinity.[18] That a particular narrative of male experience is one of the sources of Dylan's songs is undeniable, but just as Dylan drew hugely on the folk tradition, he was not confined by it, and he succeeds in providing much more than just a male view of the world.[19] Many of his later songs, including 'License to kill', 'Floater' and 'Highlands', demonstrate greater self-knowledge and a more complex view of male/female relationships, and of female experience. Dylan is too complex and ambivalent an artist ever to be satisfied with one way of looking at the world.

What Dylan began to do during that extraordinary surge of creative energy which possessed him in the 1960s was to explore an alternative sensibility and an alternative model from that of the folk tradition – the moralist with one foot in the American past, confronting contemporary America with its fall from grace. Although Dylan proved exceptional in that role, it failed to satisfy him, and instead he began to explore what it meant to experience contemporary America as a drifter. As he puts it much later in one of the greatest of his later songs, 'Highlands' (1999): 'Feel like I'm drifting/ Drifting from scene to scene/ I'm wondering what the devil could it all possibly mean'. These lines capture the sense of the drifter constantly moving on, never satisfied, never fixed, but also permanently confused about the meaning of existence. As he put it in 'Visions of Johanna' (1966): 'We sit here stranded though we're all doin' our best to deny it.'

Dylan has always denied that he is a leader or that he wants people to follow him, or that he has any useful advice to give them. That has certainly become true. But it was different in the 1960s, and in part because even when he had consciously abandoned the role of the spokesman for his generation, setting out the moral challenges facing it, he was still seen as providing 'road maps for the soul'. His songs no longer preached, but they did show others how to live and how to survive in modern America. How to dodge authority, how to watch out for the traps laid by conventional society, how to keep running, and keep independent and true to oneself. The song where all this came together was 'Subterranean homesick blues' (1965).

From its very first lines, 'Johnny's in the basement/ Mixing up the medicine/ I'm on the pavement/ Thinkin' about the government', this song conveys a mood of urgency and menace: 'Look out kid/

It's somethin' you did/ God knows when/ But you're doin' it again.' This is a world as nightmarish and threatening as Desolation Row; the phones are tapped, busts by the authorities are imminent, the repeated advice is to watch out, otherwise you will be hit, 'users, cheaters, six-time losers' are looking for a new fool – you could be it. No one can be trusted, you are on your own. Dylan insists 'Don't follow leaders', they will always let you down, or lead you astray. Instead trust your own instincts, just look around you and you will see what is going on: 'You don't need a weatherman to know which way the wind blows.' This eerie echo of 'Blowin' in the wind' (1962) shows how far Dylan had moved in two short years. The wind was blowing, but no longer promising progress and hope for a better world. In saying these things, however, and in so concentrated and powerful a way, Dylan was providing his own lead to many in his generation. He was saying, this is how it is, this is our experience, and you have to draw the right conclusions if you want to stay out of trouble. In his satire on the American Dream in the final verse, Dylan lists the things that are expected of everybody as they grow up, but look out kid, they keep it all hid: 'Twenty years of schoolin'/ And they put you on the day shift.' The realities of the production line in modern America snuff out opportunity and individuality. The only way out is to escape, 'better jump down a manhole'. Don't draw attention to yourself, keep on the move. In a last enigmatic line, with its hint of resistance to authority and the crushing conformity of modern American life, Dylan wrote: 'The pump don't work/ 'Cause the vandals took the handles.'

Dylan is renowned for his strong opposition to established authority of any kind, and his refusal to fit in with people's preconceptions. Along with the often surreal press conferences, a mine of disinformation, one of the most notorious incidents came when, in accepting the Tom Paine Award from the liberal establishment just after Kennedy's assassination, he stated that he saw something of Lee Harvey Oswald in himself.[20] The audience booed. Another instance was at the climax of the Live Aid Concert in 1985 when he asked for some of the money being raised for famine relief in Africa to be given to help the farms crisis in America.[21] In both cases it was not what he was supposed to have said – he punctured expectations, and disappointed his friends. But then Dylan has always been puncturing expectations and disappointing his friends, always restless, never content to be categorised and taken for granted. Even when he has accepted the embrace of the establishment, as when he received an honorary doctorate of music from Princeton, he sent up the ceremony afterwards in 'Day of the locusts' (1970).

In his early career he did deliberately cultivate the image of the hobo, with his tales of running away from home, hitchhiking, and living rough, in songs like 'Long time gone' (1963) and also in interviews and liner notes ('My life in a stolen moment'). Joan Baez, in her song 'Diamonds and rust' (1975), later depicted the young Dylan as bursting on the scene, 'Already a legend/ The unwashed phenomenon/ The original vagabond'. As many at the time and since have pointed out, Dylan was not actually the vagabond he pretended to be. In songs like 'Guess I'm doin' fine' (1964) Dylan sings 'I been kicked and whipped and trampled on/ I been shot at just like you', which could be doubted. But in the same song he also shows awareness both of the pose he is adopting to make his way as a singer, and the grimmer reality beyond: 'My road might be rocky/ But some folk ain't got no road at all.'

In many of his early songs Dylan slips easily into the persona of the hobo which was such a standard identity of the folk tradition. But he soon turned it into something quite different, especially in those songs in which he uses it to explore not the America of the past but the America of the present. These songs, which include 'Bob Dylan's 115th dream' (1965) and 'Motorpsycho nightmare' (1964), depict Dylan encountering the absurdities, the cruelties, and the prejudices of modern America. The gun-toting farmer of 'Motorpsycho nightmare' is reassured when Dylan tells him he's a doctor, 'A clean cut kid/ And I've been to college too'. In order to escape from the house Dylan's ruse is to shout out, 'I like Fidel Castro and his beard'. It has the desired effect and Dylan is chased out, with a *Reader's Digest*, bible of middle America, flung after him and the farmer's curse, 'You unpatriotic/ Rotten doctor Commie rat'. As the last line of the song observes, 'Without freedom of speech we might be in the swamp'. The same persona is developed further in Dylan's Candide-like odyssey through America in 'Bob Dylan's 115th dream'. The contrast is between America as it pretends to be and America as it really is. The hobo sailor fails to find anyone to help him, and finds himself adrift in a corrupt and self-interested society.

What the outlaw has to do is survive. To do that she has to have higher standards than the society around her. 'To live outside the law you must be honest' ('Absolutely Sweet Marie', 1966). She has to learn 'how to live out on the street', a rolling stone. Dylan's famous chorus 'How does it feel/ To be all alone/ With no direction home/ A complete unknown' is both taunt and injunction. Being like a rolling stone is the only way to be. 'When asked to give your real name never give it' was Dylan's advice for Geraldine,[22] advice he faithfully followed.

He told one audience in 1964, 'I have my Bob Dylan mask on'.[23] Throughout his career he has had his Bob Dylan mask on, or rather one of his many Dylan masks. Many of his characters are enigmatic and mysterious, like the 'Man in the long black coat' (1989): 'He had a face like a mask.' Occasionally this has approached caricature, as when Dylan was cast as Alias in Peckinpah's film *Pat Garrett and Billy the Kid* and had to reply 'That's a good question' when asked 'Who are you?'.

Dylan's long catalogue of outlaw songs contains many western heroes, but also some modern ones, such as Lenny Bruce. Not only did Dylan write a song to Lenny Bruce, there are also several references to Lenny Bruce in his liner notes and other writings (for example *Some Other Kind of Songs* on *Another Side* and *11 Outlined Epitaphs* on *Times they are A-Changin'*). In the song 'Lenny Bruce' (1981) Dylan quite possibly is addressing himself when he sings: 'He was an outlaw that's for sure/ More of an outlaw than you ever were.' What he admired about Bruce was his uncompromising opposition to established authority. He lived outside the law and was honest, 'Never robbed any churches/ Nor cut off any babies' heads'.

One of Dylan's strongest allegiances is to what the Japanese call the floating world, the world which is outside straight society, and peopled by jugglers, clowns, vagabonds, criminals, misfits of all kinds, beats, bohemians, hippies, the world of Desolation Row and the St James Hotel, where people apply different standards and higher levels of honesty. One of his late songs is even called 'Floater' (2001), its lyrics influenced by a Japanese novel, *Confessions of a Yakuza* by Junichi Saga. Yet while no one has explored the floating world of modern America more searchingly than Dylan, he is also ambivalent about it. In 'Man in the long black coat' (1989) Dylan criticises the notion of just floating and drifting, treating life as a joke, and never taking life and death decisions: 'There are no mistakes in life some people say/ And its true, sometimes, you can see it that way/ But people don't live or die/ People just float.' The implication is that those who do live their lives on the edge are not like the majority of people who never consider doing anything that would risk them making a mistake. Most people accept the dull conformism of an alienated life, and never glimpse the possibilities of anything different.

A final prevalent image in Dylan's self-creation as outlaw is his persona as the Thief. This operates on several levels. Dylan is the thief of other people's music and other people's words as he transforms them into his own highly personal narratives. The title of his 2001 album *Love and Theft* is taken from Eric Lott's book on American blackface minstrelsy during the Civil War.[24] Dylan has always seen himself as working within the broad tradition of American song, drawing at will from its many strands, and refusing to be categorised as belonging to a single branch. To be a thief in this sense is necessary in order to interpret a tradition and to develop it. But Dylan is also not just a thief but the Thief, a mask he assumes to signify that in a corrupt world the honest man must live outside the law. When Allen Ginsberg asked him at a news conference in 1965 'Would there ever be a time when you'll be hung as a thief?' Dylan replied 'You weren't supposed to say that'.[25] There are numerous references to himself as a thief, for example, in 'Sad eyed lady of the lowlands' (1966) ('Now you stand with your thief'), and many references to thieves in his songs, above all, the archetypal figures of the Joker and the Thief in 'All along the watchtower'.[26]

The opening lines, 'There must be some way out of here/ Said the Joker to the Thief/ There's too much confusion/ I can't get no relief', crystallise the sense of being trapped and the yearning to escape which are such powerful themes throughout Dylan's work. The representatives of the alienated world from which the Joker and Thief seek to escape are the oppressive figures of the ploughman and the businessman (also present as it happens in 'Sad eyed lady of the lowlands' – 'the farmers and the businessmen'). None of them know 'what any of it is worth'. It is the Thief who then tries to calm the Joker – 'No reason to get excited' – and who suggests that treating life as a joke is no solution either. Things are too serious for that: 'Let us not talk falsely now.'

Yet as always with Dylan there is ambivalence. Desolation Row is the place to be and the place not to be. 'She knows there's no success like failure, and that failure's no success at all' ('Love minus zero/no limit', 1965). Stealing and thieves are often condemned in Dylan's songs as expressions of corruption and power. In 'Changing of the guards' (1978) on *Street Legal* he talks of 'merchants and thieves, hungry for power'. Elsewhere he sings: 'You're on your own, you always were/ In a land of wolves and thieves.' In 'Sweetheart like you' (1983) he observes: 'Steal a little and they throw you in jail/ Steal a lot and they make you king.' Dylan is aware that taking the persona of thief as a badge of honour has its own difficulties.

He continues to have a deep regard for those striving to live outside the law according to their own codes, although at times as in 'Joey', one of his least successful songs, he ends up romanticising a brutal gangster.[27] But he is more sure-footed in dealing with the numberless anonymous victims of arbitrary systems of justice. 'Drifter's escape' (1968) portrays an archetypal Dylan figure, the drifter himself, about to be sentenced by the judge but still unaware of what he has done wrong, in a manner reminiscent of 'Subterranean homesick blues': 'It's somethin' you did/ God knows when/ But you're doin' it again'. The judge sorrowfully advises the drifter not to even try to understand what is happening to him. There is the atmosphere of a lynching with the crowd stirring and the jury crying for more. But just at that moment, lightning strikes, and in the confusion, the drifter escapes. It is a parable for modern America and for Dylan's own life.

Ultimately despite bursts of indignation and injunctions to action, Dylan's political message is one of resignation but not conservatism. The world cannot be fundamentally changed, but individuals can still survive if they are bold and independent enough to go against the 'idiot wind' and to 'live outside the law'. The world is meaningless – 'I think also/ That there is not/ One thing any place/ Anywhere that makes any/sense' he wrote in his liner notes to *Another Side of Bob Dylan*. The world is also endlessly confusing: 'There's too many people/ And they're all too hard to please/ ... I'm looking for some answers/ But I don't know who to ask' ('Mixed up confusion', 1962). At the same time, it exerts stifling pressure for conformity: 'Well, I try my best/ To be just like I am/ But everyone wants you/ To be just like them' ('Maggie's farm', 1965). In his later albums Dylan's mood of resignation has deepened as he confronts ageing and disillusion, and his sense of a lifeless, alienated world has increased: 'I'm walking through streets that are dead' ('Love sick', 1997). In 'Trying to get to heaven' he wonders 'If everything is as hollow as it seems'. He has been walking forty miles of bad road, he tells us in 'Things have changed' (1999), forty years of songwriting, and at times he feels there is nothing left: 'The party's over, and there's less and less to say' ('Highlands', 1997). Yet at the same time he is still yearning for escape: 'Well, my heart's in the Highlands at the break of day/ Over the hills and far away/ There's a way to get there, and I'll figure it out somehow/ But I'm already there in my mind/ And that's good enough for now.'

Epilogue: The Western Ideology Revisited

An important aspect of politics and of the study of politics is how agendas are set and issues framed. What seems vitally important at one particular time can be of no interest at another. Politics and the study of politics are both subject to fashion, both in the issues that seem important and in the languages and conceptual frameworks we use to discuss them. We spend most of our lives immersed in our own times and it is very hard to stand outside them and look at them objectively, very hard to understand which of all the trends are likely to be the decisive ones, which of the many forks in the road will be the one taken. One of the features of the human condition which Hayek described so well is the limited knowledge we possess.

As students of politics we need a little humility to acknowledge our own blind spots, and the necessary incompleteness of our understanding. A good dose of scepticism is also necessary in studying politics and in engaging in politics, but as Oakeshott reminds us scepticism itself is not enough. Without faith, without the passion for certainty, there would be few human achievements. But the pursuit of projects of faith carries great dangers. The modern world is littered with their debris. The pluralism and diversity which have made possible the richest human experiences have arisen whether by luck or design in societies able to create institutions which restrain the constant drive to uniformity and ideological certainty. When those checks fail or are never put in place the consequences can be dire.

The debate on neo-liberalism is a central theme of this book and one I have been engaged with since the 1970s. Although I accept the term neo-liberalism is here to stay I have never liked using it for a number of reasons, first because it is mostly used by those who are not neo-liberals themselves but critics of neo-liberalism. Neo-liberals generally prefer other terms to identify themselves – economic libertarians, economic liberals, classical liberals, or free market liberals are just some of them. A second reason is that the original use of the term by Alexander Rüstow was very precise and referred to a new emerging strand of German liberalism which later became known as Ordo-liberalism. But today neo-liberal is applied indiscriminately to monetarists, public choice theorists, rational expectations theorists as well as to Hayekians and Friedmanites. A third reason is that neo-liberal became a term whose reach has been endlessly extended until every regime in the world is defined as neo-liberal, from the United States under Reagan, Britain under Thatcher, and Chile under Pinochet to Russia under Putin, and Turkey under Erdogan to Third Way social democratic governments in Europe. Every regime in the world, except for a handful like Cuba, North Korea and Iran, has been labelled as neo-liberal. That does become slightly absurd. Rather than assuming there is a single monolithic doctrine called 'neo-liberalism' a better strategy is to identify the many different forms of liberal political economy and the tensions between them. Some of these only became apparent over time. In the 1970s I still mistakenly put Hayek and Friedman together, but their theoretical and political differences were pronounced and became quite clear during the 1980s when they differed on a number of key questions such as whether monetarism offered the best way to tackle inflation.

My general position has not changed. I still think that the new liberal political economy was an extremely important development in political ideology in the 1970s, that it had deep intellectual roots which were important to explore in their own right, and that it is still shaping our world through the numerous political and administrative strategies it spawned to achieve its objectives. But the more I have studied these doctrines, the more aware I have become of their internal contradictions, particularly in relation to their theories of the state and their attitude to democracy. Only the state can guarantee the conditions for a spontaneous market order to prosper and thrive, but nobody can be trusted to run the state, because power will corrupt them. Hayek ended up defending the idea of emergency dictatorships because he said a liberal dictator was better than an illiberal democracy. An illiberal democracy was one which threatened property rights. Hayek was uneasy at this conclusion and in *Law, Legislation and Liberty* he indulged in some utopian thinking about how to construct an ideal state which would prevent democracy being a threat to liberty. This involved making the key principles of economic liberalism (such as property rights) foundational principles, enshrined in a constitution of liberty which could not be changed except with the consent of an upper house whose members were to be elected at age forty to serve for fifteen years. Each age cohort on turning forty would elect some of its number to serve in the upper house. The lower house would be elected by universal suffrage but its powers would be tightly constrained by this upper house of unaccountable philosopher kings who alone had the power to interpret the constitution. In the meantime, while waiting for these new arrangements to spontaneously emerge, Hayek, and Friedman too, supported authoritarian rulers like Pinochet in Chile to keep democracy under control. Their blindness to the nature of the regimes they favoured equalled the blindness of many intellectuals on the left to the nature of the Soviet Union in the 1930s. Supporting dictatorships never ends well.

Economic liberalism, like socialism, is deeply imbued with central tenets of the western ideology. It has bought into the promise of modernity, that progress in human affairs is possible and that the future will be different from the past, and that inequalities and suffering can be reduced. It pioneered the understanding of politics through political economy and is responsible for many of the categories, such as the distinction between public and private through which we experience and think about the modern world. What was striking about neo-liberalism in all its forms in the 1980s was the Enlightenment certainty with which it repeated its dogmas at a time when much of intellectual culture was dominated by scepticism, relativism and postmodernism.

Since the 2008 financial crash neo-liberalism has been tested. It has proved highly resilient but at the cost of its credibility, and its doctrines are no longer very effective at defending the rules-based international order against the rise of populist nationalism in so many of the advanced democracies and the spread of authoritarianism elsewhere. This is hardly surprising. The rules-based international order has not done well at protecting the interests of the poorest and most vulnerable. Its governance structures are regarded by those outside as a club for the rich. The idea that there is just one modernity, a liberal modernity, appears Eurocentric and western centric to many of its critics. Modernity is understood in very different ways in India, in China, in Africa. The cultural power of the West and its attractiveness to the rest of the world remains high, but it is waning. Other models of development are coming to the fore. Negotiating a world of multiple modernities which is also multipolar will be complex. The economic liberalism of the last few decades is a thin gruel which does not match the need. If the western ideology is to survive it needs to shed its western-centric character and enter into a dialogue with other traditions and other modernities. Western power is in decline.

Last words

In 2120, assuming there is still some intelligent life left on earth apart from robots, if anyone should come across these essays what might they make of them? They will certainly seem of their time. The issues that animate and preoccupy one generation are rarely those of the next. Thatcherism, neo-liberalism, capitalist crises, Brexit, devolution, European integration, and early twenty-first century culture wars will probably by then be only of interest to historians. Other things will have arisen to take their place. Some of those it is impossible to guess at, but two at least we know from our own experience – the existential dangers of nuclear weapons and climate change. Any human society in 2120 is likely to look back in amazement at the behaviour of earlier generations. We did know about the dangers of climate change and nuclear weapons yet we did very little. And very little space is devoted to either issue in these essays. To our 2120 observer that may seem extraordinary. From their vantage point these may seem the only issues worth discussing.

The politics of these two issues has been rather different. For decades the issue of nuclear weapons and the possibility of a catastrophic nuclear exchange and human extinction was present in everyone's mind. It inspired mass movements of protest and global concern. The doctrine of mutually assured destruction (MAD) highlighted the absurdity and fragility of human life and led to famous satires like the Kubrick film *Dr Strangelove*. The Cuban missile crisis in 1962, the closest the world ever came during the cold war to a nuclear exchange between the superpowers, made everyone aware of what the stakes were. It was followed by an easing of tensions, the signing of a limited test ban treaty, and efforts to make resort to nuclear weapons a very last resort. Wars like Vietnam were fought without the use of nuclear weapons. But heightened tension returned during the second cold war in the 1980s with the deployment of Cruise and Pershing missiles in Europe to deter a possible Soviet invasion of Western Europe. Mass protests erupted again. The danger was defused, and Reagan and Gorbachev signed significant nuclear reduction treaties which were continued into the post Soviet era, when the West paid for the decommissioning of a significant part of the Soviet arsenal. For a time the world forgot about nuclear weapons. But they were still there, and more countries were acquiring them. Nuclear proliferation remains a huge problem. The only country ever to unilaterally get rid of its nuclear stockpile has been South Africa in 1994. In the 2010s the growing rivalry between great powers started undermining the nuclear reduction treaties and threatened a new nuclear arms race. The risk has not gone away.

The environmental crisis is even graver than the nuclear crisis, because much harder to resolve. It cannot be said that we have only just become aware of the risks we are running. The Club of Rome's report *Limits to Growth* was published in 1972. Although much criticised at the time its basic message has been proved correct. It warned that if we continued on the path of business as usual the planet's ecosystem would collapse. Since then numerous reports have confirmed and refined that message, with the emphasis switching to the effects of rising temperatures on sea-level rise and on the spread of deserts, alongside the effects of pollution, species loss and an increased likelihood of pandemics. The Brundtland report *Our Common Future* in 1987 and the Earth summit at Rio in 1992 kickstarted a concerted effort to get global collaboration to address the dangers. The Kyoto protocols, signed in 1997, committed all the signatories to a substantial reduction in carbon emissions. The Paris Agreement signed in 2016 reinforced and extended those commitments. But action remains uneven and nowhere matches the scale of the challenge. Carbon emissions continue to grow and the heating of the planet continues. With the evidence now of the melting of the polar ice caps and the Siberian permafrost, and the increasing violence of forest fires and hurricanes, we appear to be approaching the tipping point which scientists have long warned about. The chances of keeping temperature increase below 2 degrees are receding. The mounting evidence that we are living through a major extinction of species caused by human activity and the pollution of the natural environment has also become compelling. Yet the political will to act decisively to avert the catastrophe remains weak, particularly in an era of populist nationalism with leaders like Donald Trump and Jair Bolsonaro in open denial of the evidence. Those leaders who do not deny the evidence fail to take urgent action because other issues always seem more pressing.

A nuclear exchange could destroy the human species by making the planet uninhabitable for humans. The multiple threats to the biosphere caused by human activities are unlikely to make the human species extinct but will destroy most other species and will fundamentally change the world we inhabit. I wrote on these issues first of all in the 1970s with an essay 'Towards a sustainable state economy in the UK' co-authored with my brother, David Gamble, which was presented at the World Alternatives to Growth conference in Houston in 1977, and was awarded a Mitchell Prize. I wrote about these issues again in *Politics and Fate* (2000), in my critique of Hayek in the essay in this volume, and most recently in *Politics: Why it matters* (2019). But I accept that I did not make them the central focus of my writing. There were other things I wanted to write about more.

Francis Fukuyama was not wrong when he spoke of the end of history in 1989. An era had ended, a major historical alternative to capitalism had finally disappeared, and a new and very different era opened. But there had been ends of history and ends of ideology before, promoted by thinkers as different at Herbert Marcuse and Daniel Bell. Where Marcuse, Bell and Fukuyama were wrong was to suppose that the new eras they described would have no history of their own, no further deep and irreconcilable conflicts. The triumph of the western ideology after 1991 was short-lived. Within twenty years capitalism and democracy were in crisis again, challenged by forces from within as well as without.

The environmental crisis sheds a new light on capitalism and on the western ideology. In the last two hundred and fifty years we have created this huge engine of wealth accumulation and environmental destruction. They are two sides of the same process. There is little secret to the formula at the heart of free market capitalism. From the very beginning it has been a system which privatised gains and socialised costs. But we are risking a future in which the gains shrivel and the costs mount exorbitantly. Neo-liberal fixes such as cutting taxes and constantly paring back state spending on public services have reached their limits. Markets cannot solve the environmental crisis. They are making it worse. Technological fixes are urgently needed, but by themselves they will not be enough. Only new ways of living and new ways of cooperation within borders and across borders will offer hope. But these are the hardest things to achieve on the scale that is needed.

I have always been optimistic about the future although I concede it is increasingly hard to be. Some like Dylan contemplate a world filled only with power and greed and corruptible seed, and it is true sometimes you can see it like that. Others, like Christopher Lasch in his last writings, lapse into deep pessimism and despair. He wrote that it was difficult to understand why serious people still believed in the future. Neo-liberalism and social democracy in all their many variants are optimistic doctrines. They believe in the possibility of progress, against all the evidence. There is certainly no consistently upward progress in human affairs. Radical hopes are dashed, new dawns fade. Sometimes there are advances, at other times we start slipping back. The last decade has seen a lot of slipping back, just at the moment when the need for international cooperation to meet the challenges we face is more urgent than ever before. The situation we face is a bit like Pascal's wager on the existence of God. We can either resign ourselves to scepticism, disillusion and despair, cultivating our garden as best we can, or we can wager that a better world is possible and that our individual efforts may still count in trying to bring it about.

Notes

Introduction

1 Andrew Gamble, *After Brexit and Other Essays*, Bristol: Bristol University Press, 2021.
2 John Parkinson, Gavin Kelly and Andrew Gamble (eds), *The Political Economy of the Company*, London: Hart, 2000.
3 https://www.theguardian.com/news/2004/apr/09/guardianobituaries
4 Stefan Collini, 'Disciplines, Canons and Publics', in D. Castiglione and I. Hamphser-Monk (eds) *The History of Political Thought in National Context*, Cambridge: Cambridge University Press, 2001.
5 Andrew Gamble, *The Limits of Politics*, Cambridge: CUP, 2008.

Chapter 1

1 This is the edited text of the Leonard Schapiro Lecture delivered on 1 April 2008 at the PSA Conference, University of Swansea.
2 Reddaway, 'Leonard Bertram Schapiro', p. 524.
3 Francis Fukuyama, *The End of History and the Last Man* London: Hamish Hamilton, 1992.
4 W.C. Sellar and R.J. Yeatman, *1066 and All That*, London: Methuen, 1930.
5 F.A. Hayek, *New Studies in Philosophy, Politics, Economics and the History of Ideas*, London: Routledge, 1978, p. 305.
6 Seymour Martin Lipset, *Political Man*, London: Heinemann, 1960.
7 Perry Anderson, 'The ends of history', in *A Zone of Engagement*, London: Verso, 1992.
8 Francis Fukuyama, 'The end of history', *The National Interest*, 16, Summer 1989, 3–18.
9 Rachel Turner, *Neo-liberal Ideology: History, Concepts and Policies*, Edinburgh: Edinburgh University Press, 2008.
10 James Bennett, *The Anglosphere Challenge: Why the English-speaking nations will lead the way in the twenty-first century*, Lanham, MD: Rowman & Littlefield, 2004; Kees van der Pijl, *Global Rivalries From the Cold War to Iraq*, London: Pluto, 2006.
11 John Gray, *False Dawn: The delusions of global capitalism*, London: Granta, 1988; David Harvey, *A Brief History of Neo-liberalism*, Oxford: Oxford University Press, 2005.
12 Vivien Schmidt, *The Futures of European Capitalism*, Oxford: Oxford University Press, 2002; Peter Hall and David Soskice, *Varieties of Capitalism: The institutional foundations of comparative advantage*, Oxford: Oxford University Press, 2001.
13 John Hobson, *The Eastern Origins of Western Civilisation*, Cambridge: CUP, 2004.

14   Alan Macfarlane, *The Riddle of the Modern World*, London: Macmillan, 2000.

15   Ernest Gellner, *Plough, Sword, and Book: The structure of human history*, London: Collins Harvill, 1988.

16   United Nations; World Urbanization Prospects: The 2007 revision Population Database, www.esa.un.org

17   Anatol Lieven *America Right or Wrong: An anatomy of American nationalism*, London: Harper Collins, 2004. The term was first used by Gunnar Myrdal, *An American Dilemma: The negro problem and modern democracy*, New York: Harper, 1962.

18   Lloyd Gardner, *A Covenant with Power: America and world order from Wilson to Reagan*, New York: Oxford University Press, 1984.

19   Patrick O'Brien, 'The myth of Anglophone succession', *New Left Review*, 24 (2003), 113–134.

20   Donald Cameron Watt, *Succeeding John Bull: America in Britain's place*, Cambridge: Cambridge University Press, 1984.

21   Robert Kagan, *Paradise and Power: America and Europe in the New World Order*, New York: Atlantic Books, 2003.

22   David Held and Anthony McGrew, *Globalisation/AntiGlobalisation: Beyond the great divide*, Cambridge: Polity, 2007.

23   John Gray, *Al Qaeda and What It Means to be Modern*, London: Faber, 2003, p. 104.

24   Norman Geras and Robert Wokler (eds) *The Enlightenment and Modernity*, London: Macmillan, 2000.

25   John Stuart Mill, *Autobiography*, Oxford: Oxford University Press, 1971; Raymond Williams, *Culture and Society, 1780–1950*, London: Chatto & Windus, 1958.

26   Quentin Skinner, *Liberty before Liberalism*, Cambridge: Cambridge University Press, 1998.

27   Michael Pinto-Duschinsky, *The Political Thought of Lord Salisbury, 1854–1868*, London: Constable, 1967.

28   Anderson, 'The ends of history'.

29   Daniel Conway, *Nietzsche and the Political*, London: Routledge, 1996.

30   Alan Finlayson and Jeremy Valentine, *Politics and Post-Structuralism*, Edinburgh: Edinburgh University Press, 2002.

31   Anthony Giddens, *The Consequences of Modernity*, Cambridge: Polity, 1990.

32   John Ikenberry, 'Liberalism and empire: logics of order in the American unipolar age', *Review of International Studies*, 30 (2004), 609–630.

33   John Gray, *Heresies: Against progress and other illusions*, London: Granta, 2004.

34   Jürgen Habermas, *Time of Transitions*, Cambridge: Polity, 2006.

35   Mario Telo, *A Civilian Power? European Union, global governance, and world order*, London: Palgrave-Macmillan, 2006.

36   Furio Cerutti, *Global Challenges for Leviathan: A political philosophy of nuclear weapons and global warming*, Lanham, MD: Rowman & Littlefield, 2007.

37   Martin Rees, *Our Final Century: Will the human race survive the twenty-first century?*, London: Arrow, 2004.

38   Gareth Stedman Jones, 'The end of history?', *Marxism Today*, November 1989, p. 33.

39   Peter Reddaway, 'Leonard Bertram Schapiro', *Proceedings of the British Academy* London, 1985, p. 515.

Chapter 2

1   This essay was originally published in 2013, in Mark Thatcher and Vivien Schmidt (eds) *Resilient Liberalism in Europe's Political Economy*, Cambridge: CUP, 2013, pp. 53–76, under the title 'Neo-liberalism and fiscal conservatism'.

2   Karl Polanyi, *Origins of our Time: The great transformation*, London: Gollancz, 1945.

3   Robert Cox, *Approaches to World Order*, Cambridge: CUP, 1996.

4   Peter Hall, 'Policy paradigms, social learning, and the state: the case of policy-learning in Britain', *Comparative Politics*, 25:3, (1993), pp. 275–96.

5   David Harvey, *A Brief History of Neoliberalism*, Oxford: OUP, 2005.

6   Robert Skidelsky, *Keynes: The return of the master*, London: Allen Lane, 2009.

7   Colin Crouch, *The Strange Non-Death of Neo-Liberalism*, Cambridge: Polity, 2011.

8   Francis Fukuyama, 'The end of history', *The National Interest*, 16 (Summer), 1989, pp. 3–18.

9   Andrew Gamble, 'Two faces of neo-liberalism', in R. Robison (ed), *The Neo-Liberal Revolution: Forging the market state*, London: Palgrave-Macmillan, 2006, pp. 20–35.

10 Rachel Turner, *Neo-Liberal Ideology: History, concepts and policies*, Edinburgh: Edinburgh University Press, 2008. See also Andrew Gamble 'The free economy and the strong state', *Socialist Register*, 1979, pp. 1–25, reprinted in Volume 2 of this collection.

11 Anthony Nicholls, *Freedom with Responsibility: The social market economy in Germany, 1918–1963*, Oxford: Clarendon Press, 1994.

12 Ludwig von Mises, *Omnipotent Government: The rise of the total state and total war*, New Haven: Yale University Press, 1944; F.A. Hayek, *The Road to Serfdom*, Chicago: Chicago University Press, 1944.

13 F.A. Hayek, *Law, Legislation and Liberty*, London: Routledge, 1982.

14 Robert Nozick, *Anarchy, State and Utopia*, Oxford: Blackwell, 1974.

15 Murray Rothbard, *For a New Liberty*, New York: Macmillan, 1973.

16 James Buchanan and Richard Wagner, *Democracy in Deficit*, New York: Academic Press, 1977.

17 Milton Friedman, *Inflation and Unemployment: The new dimension of politics*, London: IEA, 1977.

18 Richard Cockett, *Thinking the Unthinkable: Think-tanks and the economic counter-revolution, 1931–1983*, London: Harper Collins, 1994.

19 Michel Foucault, *The Birth of Biopolitics Lectures at the Collège de France 1978–79*, London: Palgrave-Macmillan, 2008.

20 Istvan Hont, *Jealousy of Trade: International Competition and the Nation-State in Historical Perspective*, Cambridge, Mass.: Harvard University Press, 2005.

21 Helen Thompson, *Might, Right, Prosperity and Consent: Representative democracy and the international economy*, Manchester: Manchester University Press, 2008.

22 Ha-Joon Chang, *Kicking Away the Ladder: Economic development in historical perspective*, London: Anthem, 2002.

23 F.A. Hayek, *Law, Legislation and Liberty*, Vol. 2, *The Mirage of Social Justice* London: Routledge, 1982, p. 108.

24 Leslie Hannah, *The Rise of the Corporate Economy*, London: Methuen, 1976.

25 Colin Crouch, *The Strange Non-Death of Neo-Liberalism*, Cambridge: Polity, 2011.

26 John Parkinson, Andrew Gamble and Gavin Kelly (eds) *The Political Economy of the Company*, London: Hart, 2000.

27 Daniel Bell, 'The public household', in *The Cultural Contradictions of Capitalism*, London: Heinemann, 1976.

28 Joseph Schumpeter, 'The crisis of the tax state', in R. Swedberg (ed), *The Economics and Sociology of Capitalism*, Princeton: Princeton University Press, 1990.

29 Joseph Schumpeter, 'The crisis of the tax state', p. 100.

30 Joseph Schumpeter, 'The crisis of the tax state', p. 125.

31 Joseph Schumpeter, 'The crisis of the tax state', p. 126.

32 F.A. Hayek, *Law, Legislation and Liberty*, London: Routledge, 1982.

33 Andrew Shonfield, *Modern Capitalism: The changing balance of public and private power*, Oxford: Oxford University Press, 1965.

34 Paul Krugman, *End This Depression Now*, New York: Norton, 2012.

35 Andrew Gamble, 'The UK: The triumph of fiscal realism?', in Wyn Grant and Graham Wilson (eds), *The Consequences of the Global Financial Crisis: The rhetoric of reform and regulation*, Oxford: Oxford University Press, 2012, pp. 34–50.

36 Paul Pierson, *Dismantling the State? Reagan, Thatcher and the politics of retrenchment*, Cambridge: CUP, 1994.

Chapter 3

1 This essay first appeared in *Ideas, Interests and Consequences*, IEA Readings 30, London: IEA, 1989, pp. 1–21.

2 For a brief but enlightening discussion of the concept of interest, Roger Scruton, *Dictionary of Political Thought*, London: Macmillan, 1982.

3 Lionel Robbins, *Political Economy Past and Present*, London: Macmillan, 1976; Joseph Schumpeter, *History of Economic Analysis*, London: Allen & Unwin, 1954.

4 Milton Friedman, *Newsweek*, 14 July 1976.

5 Schumpeter, *History of Economic Analysis*, p. 38.

6 J.R. McCulloch and N. Senior, quoted in Lionel Robbins, *The Theory of Economic Policy*, London: Macmillan, 1952, p. 174.

7 A.V. Dicey, *Lectures on the Relation Between Law and Public Opinion in England*, 2nd ed, London: Macmillan, 1926, p. 1.

8 Dicey, *Lectures on the Relation Between Law and Public Opinion in England*, p. 2.

9 Joseph Schumpeter, *Capitalism, Socialism and Democracy*, London: Allen & Unwin, 1950; Samuel Beer, *Modern British Politics*, London: Faber, 1965.

10 Susan Howson and Donald Winch, *The Economic Advisory Council 1930–1939*, Cambridge: Cambridge University Press, 1977, p. 158.

11 Howson and Winch argue this point forcefully.

12 Mancur Olson, *The Rise and Decline of Nations*, New Haven, Conn.: Yale University Press, 1982.

13 British institutions received particular praise from political scientists from other countries, for example, Giovanni Sartori and Samuel Beer.

14 Ralph Miliband, *The State in Capitalist Society*, London: Weidenfeld & Nicolson, 1969.

15 See, for example, the analysis by Simon Clarke in his *Keynesianism, Monetarism, and the Crisis of the State*, Brighton: Wheatsheaf, 1988.

16 In particular, Evgeny Pashukanis, *Law and Marxism*, London: Ink Links, 1978, and for the state derivation school, John Holloway and Sol Picciotto (eds), *State and Capital*, London: Arnold, 1978.

17 See, for example, the discussion of the political theories of Nicos Poulantzas in Bob Jessop, *Nicos Poulantzas*, London: Macmillan, 1985.

18 Jose Harris, *Unemployment and Politics, 1886–1914*, Oxford: Oxford University Press, 1972, p. 362.

19 Harris, *Unemployment and Politics*, p. 365.

20 See, for example, the work of Jim Tomlinson: *Problems of British Economic Policy 1870–1945*, London, Methuen, 1981; *British Macroeconomic Policy Since 1940*, Beckenham: Croom Helm, 1985; and 'Why was there never a Keynesian Revolution in Economic Policy?', *Economy and Society*, 10 (1), (1981), pp. 72–87.

21 White Paper on *Employment Policy*, Cmd. 6527, London: HMSO, 1944. See Alan Booth, 'The "Keynesian Revolution" in economic policy-making', *Economic History Review*, 36 (1), (1983), pp. 103–23.

22 R.C.O. Matthews was one of the first sceptics – see his 'Why has Britain had full employment since the War?', *Economic Journal*, 78 (3), (1968), pp. 555–69.

23 W.H. Greenleaf, *The British Political Tradition*, Vol. 1, *The Rise of Collectivism*; Vol. 2. *The Ideological Heritage*, London: Methuen, 1983.

24 Albert Hirschman, *Shifting Involvements*, Oxford: Blackwell 1983.

25 Noel O'Sullivan, 'The New Right and the quest for a civil philosophy', paper presented to the 1989 Political Studies Association Conference, University of Warwick.

26 For example, John Keane (ed), *Civil Society and the State*, London: Verso, 1988, and Richard Holme and Michael Elliott (eds), *1688–1988: Time for a New Constitution*, London: Macmillan, 1988.

27 See Elizabeth Durbin, *New Jerusalems*, London: Routledge & Kegan Paul, 1986.

28 John Gray is particularly noteworthy in this respect. See, for example, *The Undoing of Conservatism*, London: Social Market Foundation, 1994.

29 See, for example, Alan Duncan and Dominic Hobson, *Saturn's Children*, London: Sinclair Stevenson, 1995.

30 Maurice Mullard, *The Politics of Public Expenditure*, London: Routledge, 1993, pp. 22–3.

31 Nigel Ashford, 'The Ideas of the New Right', in G. Jordan and N. Ashford (eds), *Public Policy and the Impact of the New Right*, London: Pinter, 1993, p. 41.

32 I explore these questions further in *Hayek: The Iron Cage of Liberty*, Cambridge: Polity, 1996.

Chapter 4

1 This essay first appeared in Edward Feser (ed), *The Cambridge Companion to Hayek*, Cambridge: CUP, 2006, pp. 111–131.

2 F.A. Hayek, *Law, Legislation and Liberty*, London: Routledge & Kegan Paul, 1982, p. 13.

3 F.A. Hayek, *The Counter-Revolution of Science*, Glencoe, Illinois: Free Press, 1952, p. 50.

4 F.A. Hayek, *New Studies in Philosophy, Politics, Economics and the History of Ideas*, London: Routledge & Kegan Paul, 1978, p. 33.

5 Bruce Caldwell, *Hayek's Challenge: An intellectual biography*, Chicago: University of Chicago Press, 2004; Meghnad Desai, 'Equilibrium, expectations and knowledge', in Jack Birner and Rudy van Zijp (eds), *Hayek, Co-ordination and Evolution*, London: Routledge, 1994, pp. 25–50.

6 Alan Ebenstein, *Friedrich Hayek: A Biography*, New York: Palgrave, 2001, p. 273.

7 Alan Ebenstein, *Friedrich Hayek: A Biography*.

8 Terence Hutchison, *The Politics and Philosophy of Economics: Marxians, Keynesians, and Austrians*, Oxford: Blackwell, 1981.

9   F.A. Hayek, *Individualism and Economic Order*, Chicago: University of Chicago Press, 1948.
10   F.A. Hayek (ed), *Collectivist Economic Planning: Critical studies on the possibility of socialism*, London: Routledge & Kegan Paul, 1935.
11   Frank H. Knight, *Risk, Uncertainty and Profit*, Boston: Houghton Mifflin, 1921.
12   Hayek, *Individualism and Economic Order*, p. 33.
13   Hayek, *Individualism and Economic Order*, p. 35.
14   Hayek, *Individualism and Economic Order*, p. 54.
15   Hayek, *Individualism and Economic Order*, p. 54.
16   Hayek, *Individualism and Economic Order*, p. 35.
17   F.A. Hayek, *Studies in Philosophy, Politics and Economics*, London: Routledge & Kegan Paul, 1967, p. 35; Meghnad Desai, 'Equilibrium, expectations and knowledge'.
18   Hayek, *Law, Legislation and Liberty*, p. 12.
19   F.A. Hayek, *The Constitution of Liberty*, London: Routledge & Kegan Paul, 1960, p. 64.
20   F.A. Hayek, *The Road to Serfdom*, London: Routledge & Kegan Paul, 1944.
21   Hayek, *The Counter-Revolution of Science*, p. 64.
22   Hayek, *The Counter-Revolution of Science*, p. 59.
23   John Watkins, 'Parsons on two theses of Hayek', in Stephen F. Frowen (ed), *Hayek: Economist and Social Philosopher*, London: Macmillan, 1997, pp. 87–94.
24   Ludwig von Mises, 'Economic calculation in the socialist commonwealth', in Hayek (ed), *Collectivist Economic Planning*, pp. 87–130.
25   Hayek, *Law, Legislation and Liberty*, p. 15.
26   Hayek, *The Counter-Revolution of Science*.
27   Hayek, *Law, Legislation and Liberty*, p. 21.
28   Hayek, *New Studies in Philosophy, Politics, Economics and the History of Ideas*, p. 13.
29   Hayek, *Law, Legislation and Liberty*, p. 16.
30   Watkins, 'Parsons on two theses of Hayek'.
31   Hayek, *Studies in Philosophy, Politics and Economics*, p. 59.
32   Hayek, *Studies in Philosophy, Politics and Economics*, p. 19.
33   Geoffrey Hodgson, *Economics and Institutions*, Cambridge: Polity, 1988.
34   Hayek, *The Counter-Revolution of Science*, p. 43.
35   Hayek, *Individualism and Economic Order*, p. 68.
36   Hayek, *Individualism and Economic Order*, p. 64.
37   Hayek, *Individualism and Economic Order*, p. 73.
38   Hayek, *Studies in Philosophy, Politics and Economics*, p. 29.
39   Ray Richardson, 'Hayek on Trade Unions: Social philosopher or propagandist?', in Frowen (ed), *Hayek: Economist and social philosopher*, pp. 259–274.
40   Desai, 'Equilibrium, expectations and knowledge'.
41   Caldwell, *Hayek's Challenge: An Intellectual Biography*.
42   Hayek, *Studies in Philosophy, Politics and Economics*, p. 260.
43   Hayek, *Studies in Philosophy, Politics and Economics*, p. 29.
44   Hayek, *Studies in Philosophy, Politics and Economics*, p. 25
45   Hayek, *Studies in Philosophy, Politics and Economics*, p. 33.
46   Hayek, *Studies in Philosophy, Politics and Economics*, p. 76.
47   Hayek, *Law, Legislation and Liberty*, p. 16.
48   F.A. Hayek, *The Fatal Conceit: The errors of socialism* London: Routledge, 1988.
49   Hayek, *Studies in Philosophy, Politics and Economics*, p. 32.
50   Hayek, *Individualism and Economic Order*.
51   Hayek, *New Studies in Philosophy, Politics, Economics and the History of Ideas*, p. 5.

52 Hayek, *Individualism and Economic Order*, p. 7.

53 Hayek, *The Fatal Conceit*, p. 14.

54 Hayek, *Individualism and Economic Order*, p. 44.

55 Marina Bianchi, 'Hayek's spontaneous order: the "correct" versus the "corrigible" society', in Birner and van Zijp (eds), *Hayek, Co-ordination and Evolution*, 1994, pp. 232–51.

56 Hayek, *The Constitution of Liberty*, p. 22.

57 Hayek, *Law, Legislation and Liberty*, p. 42.

58 Hayek, *Law, Legislation and Liberty*, p. 13.

59 Hayek, *The Fatal Conceit*, p. 14.

60 Hayek, *New Studies in Philosophy, Politics, Economics and the History of Ideas*, p. 23.

61 Hayek, *Studies in Philosophy, Politics and Economics*, p. 265.

62 Hayek, *Individualism and Economic Order*, p. 17.

63 Hayek, *Studies in Philosophy, Politics and Economics*, p. 264.

64 Hayek, *Studies in Philosophy, Politics and Economics*, p. 130.

65 F.A. Hayek, *Choice in Currency: A way to stop inflation*, London: Institute of Economic Affairs, 1976.

66 Hayek, *New Studies in Philosophy, Politics, Economics and the History of Ideas*, p. 19.

67 Hayek, *Individualism and Economic Order*, p. 79.

68 Hayek, *The Road to Serfdom*, p. 12.

69 Hayek, *The Road to Serfdom*, p. 27; Hayek, *The Constitution of Liberty*, p. 60.

70 Hayek, *The Constitution of Liberty*, p. 60.

71 Roland Kley, *Hayek's Social and Political Thought*, Oxford: OUP, 1994.

72 Hayek, *Studies in Philosophy, Politics and Economics*, p. 92.

73 Hayek, *Studies in Philosophy, Politics and Economics*, p. 252.

74 Manfred E. Streit, 'Constitutional ignorance, spontaneous order and rule-orientation: Hayekian paradigms from a policy perspective', in Frowen (ed), *Hayek: Economist and social philosopher*, 1997, pp. 37–58.

75 Hayek, *Studies in Philosophy, Politics and Economics*, p. 120.

76 Hayek, *Studies in Philosophy, Politics and Economics*, p. 95.

77 Hayek, *Individualism and Economic Order*, p. 22.

78 Hayek, *The Fatal Conceit*, pp. 125–6.

79 Hayek, *The Constitution of Liberty*, pp. 369–70.

Chapter 5

1 This essay was first published as a journal article in *Review of International Studies* 10:2 (1999), pp. 127–144. I would like to thank Michael Cox, Michael Kenny, and Tony Payne for their comments on the first draft.

2 See for example Robin Blackburn, 'Fin-de-siècle socialism: socialism after the crash', *New Left Review*, 185 (1991), pp. 5–67; Robin Blackburn (ed), *After the Fall*, London: Verso, 1991; G.A. Cohen, 'The Future of a Disillusion', *New Left Review*, 190 (1991), pp. 5–20; Alex Callinicos, *The Revenge of History*, Cambridge: Polity, 1991; Gareth Stedman-Jones, 'Marx after Marxism', *Marxism Today* (February 1990).

3 One of the most influential characterisations of Western Marxism as a distinctive strand of Marxism is Perry Anderson, *Considerations on Western Marxism*, London: Verso, 1976. For a critical assessment of Anderson's account see Gregory Elliott, *Perry Anderson: The remorseless laboratory of history*, Minneapolis: University of Minnesota Press, 1998.

4 A classic example is F.A. Hayek, *The Road to Serfdom*, London: Routledge, 1944.

5 Michael Cox, 'Rebels without a cause', *New Political Economy*, 3:3, (November 1988), pp. 445–460.

6 The international state system which emerged after 1917 invited the development of realist interpretations. E.H. Carr's attack upon idealism in *The Twenty Years Crisis: An introduction to the study of international relations*, London: Macmillan, 1939, made the case for a realist analysis of international relations and sparked a wide-ranging and still continuing debate. See 'The eighty years crisis 1919–1999', *Review of International Studies*, 24 (1998). In his later history of the Soviet Union, Carr went on to provide a systematic defence of the Soviet Union and its policies from a realist perspective.

7 Fred Halliday, 'The end of the Cold War and international relations: Some analytic and theoretical conclusions', in Ken Booth and Steve Smith (eds), *International Relations Theory Today*, Pennsylvania State University Press, 1995, pp. 38–61.

8 Manuel Castells, *End of Millennium*, Oxford: Blackwell, 1998, pp. 287–307.

9 This view is very popular among Weberian historical sociologists. See for example John Hobson, *The Wealth of States*, Cambridge: Cambridge University Press, 1997; and 'The historical sociology of the state and the state of historical sociology in international relations', *Review of International Political Economy*, 5:2 (1998), pp. 284–320.

10 Peter Burnham, 'Open Marxism and vulgar international political economy', *Review of International Political Economy*, 1:2 (1994), p. 229.

11 Hillel Ticktin, 'Where are we going today? The nature of contemporary crisis', *Critique*, 30–31 (1998), pp. 21–48.

12 See Michael Cox, 'Rebels without a cause'.

13 Perry Anderson, 'The ends of history', in *A Zone of Engagement*, London: Verso, 1992, pp. 279–376.

14 Francis Fukuyama, *The End of History and the Last Man*, London: Hamish Hamilton, 1992. The original article was 'The end of history', *The National Interest*, 16 (1989), pp. 3–18.

15 Manuel Castells uses the term 'statist' to refer to the Soviet type of economy to distinguish it from capitalist; *End of Millennium*, Oxford: Blackwell, 1998.

16 John Roemer, *A Future for Socialism*, London: Verso, 1994. See also Anderson, 'The ends of history'; Jon Elster and Karl Ove Moene (eds), *Alternatives to Capitalism*, Cambridge: Cambridge University Press, 1989; see also Christopher Pierson, *Socialism after Communism: The new market socialism*, Cambridge: Polity, 1995.

17 Andrew Linklater, *The Transformation of the Political Community: Ethical foundations of the post-Westphalian era*, Cambridge: Polity, 1998.

18 Adam Przeworski, *Capitalism and Social Democracy*, Cambridge: Cambridge University Press, 1985.

19 Robin Blackburn, 'The new collectivism: pension reform, grey capitalism and complex socialism', *New Left Review*, 233 (1999), pp. 3–65.

20 Andrew Linklater, *The Transformation of the Political Community*; and *Beyond Realism and Marxism: Critical theory and international relations*, London: Macmillan, 1990.

21 A forum which critically discusses Linklater's most recent book can be found in *Review of International Studies*, 25:1 (1999).

22 David Harvey, *The Limits to Capital*, Oxford: Blackwell, 1982.

23 Robert Brenner, 'The economics of global turbulence', *New Left Review*, 229 (1998), pp. 1–264.

24 Bob Jessop, 'Regulation theory in retrospect and prospect', *Economy and Society*, 19:2 (1990), pp. 153–216; Robert Pollin, 'Financial structures and egalitarian economic policy', *New Left Review*, 214 (1995), pp. 26–61.

25 Immanuel Wallerstein, *The Modern World System*, New York: Academic Press, 1974.

26 Robert Cox, *Production, Power and World Order*, New York: Columbia University Press, 1987.

27 David Harvey, *The Limits to Capital*, Oxford: Blackwell, 1982 and *The Condition of Postmodernity*, Oxford: Blackwell, 1989.

28 Karl Marx and Friedrich Engels, *The Communist Manifesto*, Harmondsworth: Penguin, 1973, p. 71.

29 Simon Bromley 'Marxism and Globalization', in Andrew Gamble, David Marsh and Tony Tant (eds), *Marxism and Social Science*, London: Macmillan, 1999, pp. 280–301.

30 Tom Kemp, *Theories of Imperialism*, London: Dobson, 1967; Anthony Brewer, *Marxist Theories of Imperialism*, London: Routledge, 1980; Roger Owen and Bob Sutcliffe (eds), *Studies in the Theory of Imperialism*, London: Longman, 1972.

31 Manuel Castells, *The Rise of the Network Society*, Oxford: Blackwell, 1998, p. 93.

32 Bob Jessop, *The Capitalist State*, Oxford: Martin Robertson, 1982; *State Theory: Putting capitalist states in their place*, Cambridge: Polity, 1990; Colin Hay, 'Marxism and the state', in Gamble, Marsh and Tant (eds), *Marxism and Social Science,* pp. 152–74.

33 Peter Burnham, 'Open Marxism and vulgar international political economy'.

34 V.I. Lenin, *Imperialism: The highest stage of capitalism*, Moscow, 1917.

35 Andrew Gamble and Anthony Payne (eds), *Regionalism and World Order*, London: Macmillan, 1996.

36 Michael Cox, *US Foreign Policy After the Cold War: Superpower without a mission?*, London: RIIA, 1995.

37 Ernest Mandel, *Europe versus America*, London: Verso, 1968.

38 Ankie Hoogvelt, *Globalisation and the Post-Colonial World: The new political economy of development*, London: Macmillan, 1997.

39 Immanuel Wallerstein, *The Modern World System*, New York: Academic Press, 1974; C. Chase-Dunn, (ed), *Global Formation, Structures of the World Economy*, Oxford: Blackwell, 1989; Immanuel Wallerstein, *The Capitalist World Economy*, Cambridge: Cambridge University Press, 1979.

40 Andre Drainville, 'International political economy in the age of open Marxism', *Review of International Political Economy*, 1:1 (1994), pp. 105–132.

41 Robert Cox, *Production, Power, and World Order*, New York: Columbia University Press, 1987; Stephen Gill, *American Hegemony and the Trilateral Commission*, Cambridge: Cambridge University Press, 1990; 'European Governance and new constitutionalism: economic and monetary union and alternatives of disciplinary neoliberalism in Europe', *New Political Economy*, 3:1 (1988), pp. 5–26.

42 Henk Overbeek, *Global Capitalism and National Decline*, London: Unwin Hyman, 1990; Kees van der Pijl, *The Making of an Atlantic Ruling Class*, London: Verso, 1984; Kees van der Pijl, 'Ruling classes, hegemony, and the state system: theoretical and historical considerations', *International Journal of Political Economy*, 19:3 (1989), pp. 7–35.

43 Bob Jessop, 'Twenty years of the (Parisian) regulation approach: the paradox of success and failure at home and abroad', *New Political Economy*, 2:3 (1997), pp. 503–26; Bob Jessop, 'Regulation theory in retrospect and prospect'; Robert Boyer, *The Regulation School*, New York: Columbia University Press, 1990; Michel Aglietta,

A Theory of Capitalist Regulation: The US experience, London: Verso, 1979; Alain Lipietz, *Mirages and Miracles*, London: Verso, 1987.

44 Michael Kenny, 'Marxism and regulation theory', in Gamble, Marsh and Tant (eds), *Marxism and Social Science*, pp. 35–60.

45 Peter Burnham, 'Neo-Gramscian hegemony and the international order', *Capital and Class*, 45:1 (1991), pp. 73–93; Robert Brenner and Mark Glick, 'The regulation approach: theory and history', *New Left Review*, 188 (1991), pp. 45–99; Robert Brenner, 'The origins of capitalist development: a critique of neo-Smithian Marxism', *New Left Review*, 104 (1977), pp. 25–93.

46 Ernest Mandel, *Late Capitalism*, London: New Left Books, 1976; *The Second Slump*, London: New Left Books, 1978.

47 Robert Brenner, 'The economics of global turbulence'.

48 Diane Elson, 'The economic, the political, and the domestic: Businesses, states, and households in the organization of production', *New Political Economy*, 3:2 (1988), pp. 189–208; Jean Gardiner, *Gender, Care, and Economics* London: Macmillan, 1997.

49 Gøsta Esping-Anderson, *The Three Worlds of Welfare Capitalism*, Cambridge: Polity, 1990.

50 Manuel Castells, *The Information Age: Economy, Society and Culture: vol. I, The Rise of the Network Society; vol. II, The Power of Identity; vol. III, End of Millennium*, Oxford: Blackwell, 1996, 1997, 1998.

51 Giovanni Arrighi, *The Long Twentieth Century: Money, power, and the origins of our time* London: Verso, 1994; 'World income inequalities and the future of socialism', *New Left Review*, 189 (1991), pp. 39–66.

52 Andrew Linklater, *The Transformation of the Political Community*.

53 Perry Anderson, *Considerations on Western Marxism*, London: Verso, 1972: Afterword; Ian Steedman, *Marx after Sraffa*, London: NLB, 1977; Ian Steedman et al (eds), *The Value Controversy*, London: Verso, 1981.

54 Ankie Hoogvelt, *Globalization and the Post-Colonial World*.

55 Martin Nicolaus, 'The unknown Marx', *New Left Review*, 48 (1968), pp. 41–61.

56 J. A. Schumpeter, *Capitalism, Socialism and Democracy* London: Allen & Unwin, 1950.

57 Karl Marx, *Capital*, Penguin: Harmondsworth, 1976, ch. 10.

58 Perry Anderson, 'The ends of history'; Eric Hobsbawm, *Age of Extremes: The short twentieth century*, London: Michael Joseph, 1994.

59 Pierre Bourdieu, *Acts of Resistance*, London: Verso, 1999; Manuel Castells, *End of Millennium*.

Chapter 6

1 This essay first appeared as the Introduction to a new edition of G.D.H. Cole, *A History of Socialist Thought*, published by Palgrave-Macmillan in 2002, pp. v–xxvi.

2 G.D.H. Cole, *A History of Socialist Thought III*, p. xvii

3 'Future historians will probably regard the period from the revolution of 1848 to about 1948 as the century of European Socialism', F.A. Hayek, *The Constitution of Liberty*, London: Routledge, 1960, p. 253.

4 For accounts of his life see Margaret Cole, *The Life of G.D.H. Cole*, London: Macmillan, 1971; L.P. Carpenter, *G.D.H. Cole: An intellectual biography*, Cambridge: CUP, 1973.

5 A.W. Wright, *G.D.H. Cole and Socialist Democracy*, Oxford: Oxford University Press, 1979, p. 268. See also Margaret Cole, *The Life of G.D.H. Cole*, p. 34.

6 See Wright, *G.D.H. Cole and Socialist Democracy*; Paul Hirst (ed), *The Pluralist Theory of the State*, London: Routledge, 1989; L.C. Carpenter, *G.D.H. Cole: An intellectual biography*; Geoffrey Foote, *The Labour Party's Political Thought: A history*, London: Croom Helm, 1985, ch. 6

7 Margaret Cole, *The Story of Fabian Socialism*, London: Heinemann, 1961.

8 Hugh Gaitskell, 'At Oxford in the twenties', in Asa Briggs and John Saville (eds), *Essays in Labour History*, London: Macmillan, 1960, p. 12.

9 G.D.H. Cole (ed), *J.J. Rousseau: The Social Contract and Discourses*, London: Everyman, 1913.

10 Margaret Cole, *The Life of G.D.H. Cole*, p. 34.

11 *A History of Socialist Thought I*, p. 131.

12 Ibid, p. 131.

13 Ibid, p. 117.

14 See Paul Hirst (ed), *The Pluralist Theory of the State*.

15 *A History of Socialist Thought V*, p. 296.

16 *A History of Socialist Thought V*, p. 328.

17 In this if in little else Cole would have agreed with Hayek, who argued that the differences between authoritarian and democratic Socialists were much less important than what united them. F.A. Hayek, *The Road to Serfdom*, London: Routledge, 1944.

18 *A History of Socialist Thought IV*, p. 2

19 Ibid, p. 2

20 See Wright, *G.D.H. Cole and Socialist Democracy*, p. 265.

21 *A History of Socialist Thought V*, p. 316.

22 Ibid, p. 316.

23 Ibid, p. 27.

24 Andrew Gamble, 'Marxism after communism', *Review of International Studies*, 25, (1999) pp. 127–144.

25 Quoted in Anthony Wright, *British Socialism: Socialist thought from the 1880s to 1960s*, London: Longman, 1983, p. 17.

26 Cole not only wrote himself a great deal of labour history, but he inspired others, and it was fitting that the book of essays which was to have been presented to him on his seventieth birthday and became instead his memorial volume should have been entitled *Essays in Labour History* (edited by Asa Briggs and John Saville, London: Macmillan, 1960). One of the editors of that volume, John Saville, went on to fulfil another plan of Cole's, the publication in many volumes of a *Dictionary of Labour Biography*, which utilising notes Cole left behind includes not only entries for the national personalities of the British labour movement, but also the rank and file activists at regional and local level. See Joyce Bellamy and John Saville (eds), *Dictionary of Labour Biography*, Vol. I, London: Macmillan, 1972, p. ix. Ten volumes have so far appeared.

27 *A History of Socialist Thought II*, p. 289.

28 Ibid, p. 289.

29 Ibid, p. 297.

30 Ibid, p. 297.

31 Representatives of this new scholarship include Shlomo Avineri, *The Social and Political Thought of Karl Marx*, Cambridge: CUP, 1968; and David McClellan, *Marx Before Marxism*, London: Macmillan, 1971.

[32] Hugh Gaitskell, the future leader of the British Labour party and a pupil of Cole's was shocked when Cole declared to him on one occasion that 'there ought to be a revolution of some kind every few years, whatever it's about'. Gaitskell 'At Oxford in the twenties', p. 13.

[33] Wright, *G.D.H. Cole and Socialist Democracy*.

[34] Ibid, p. 170.

[35] *A History of Socialist Thought V*, p. 321.

[36] Ibid, pp. 293–4.

[37] Saul Estrin & Julian Le Grand (eds), *Market Socialism*, Oxford: OUP, 1989; David Miller, *Market, State and Community*, Oxford: OUP, 1989; Chris Pierson, *Socialism after Communism: The new market socialism*, Cambridge: Polity, 1995.

[38] Donald Sassoon, *One Hundred Years of Socialism: The West European left in the twentieth century*, London: I.B. Tauris, 1996.

[39] Ibid, p. 337.

Chapter 7

[1] This essay was first published in Olaf Cramme and Patrick Diamond (eds), *Social Justice in the Global Age*, Cambridge: Polity, 2009, pp. 117–135, under the title 'Moving beyond the national: the challenges for social democracy in the global age'.

[2] Walter Lippmann, *The Phantom Public* (1925), cited in Bruce Ackerman and James Fishkin, *Deliberation Day*, New Haven: Yale University Press, 2004, p. 10.

[3] Karl Marx and Friedrich Engels, *The Communist Manifesto*, London: Penguin Books, 1967: 'The workers have no country. We cannot take from them what they have not got.'

[4] Paul Hirst and Grahame Thompson, *Globalisation in Question*, Cambridge, Polity, 1996.

[5] Donald Sassoon, *One Hundred Years of Socialism: The West European left in the twentieth century*, London: Tauris, 1996.

[6] Perry Anderson, *Arguments within English Marxism*, London: NLB, 1980.

[7] Tony Crosland, *The Future of Socialism*, London: Cape, 1956.

[8] John Strachey, *Contemporary Capitalism*, London: Gollancz, 1956.

[9] David Harvey, *A Brief History of Neo-Liberalism*, Oxford: Oxford University Press 2005.

[10] Richard Bellamy and Dario Castiglione, 'Constitutions and politics', *Political Studies*, 44:3 (1966), 413–7.

[11] Peter Mair and Richard Katz, 'Changing models of party organisation and party democracy: the emergence of the cartel party', 1:1 (1995), 5–28.

[12] Thomas Meyer, *Media Democracy: How the media colonise politics*, Cambridge: Polity, 2002.

[13] John Lloyd, *What the Media Are Doing to Our Politics*, London: Robinson, 2004.

[14] Charles Pattie, Patrick Seyd and Paul Whiteley, *Citizenship in Britain: Values, participation and democracy*, Cambridge: Cambridge University Press, 2004.

[15] David Marquand, *Decline of the Public*, Cambridge: Polity, 2004; Paul Ginsborg, *The Politics of Everyday Life*, New Haven: Yale University Press, 2005.

[16] www.powerinquiry.org/report/index.php

[17] Gerry Stoker, *Why Politics Matters*, London: Palgrave-Macmillan, 2006.

[18] Peter Katzenstein, *Small States in World Markets*, Ithaca: Cornell UP, 1985.

[19] Ulrich Beck, *Risk Society: Towards a new modernity*, London: Sage, 1992.

[20] David Held, *Global Covenant: The social democratic alternative to the Washington consensus*, Cambridge: Polity, 2004.

Chapter 8

[1] This essay was first published in Hans Schattle and Jeremy Nuttall (eds), *Making Social Democrats* (Festschrift for David Marquand), Manchester: Manchester University Press, 2018, pp. 89–110.

[2] David Marquand, *The Progressive Dilemma*, London: Heinemann, 1991.

[3] Robert Dowse, *Left in the Centre: The Independent Labour Party 1893–1940*, London: Longmans, 1966; Patrick Seyd, *The Rise and Fall of the Labour Left* London: Palgrave, 1987.

[4] Ralph Miliband, *Parliamentary Socialism*, London: Merlin, 1964, p. 16.

[5] Ivor Crewe and Anthony King, *The SDP: The birth, life and death of the Social Democratic Party*, Oxford: OUP, 1995.

[6] David Marquand, *Ramsay MacDonald*, London: Richard Cohen Books, 1997, p. xvi.

[7] Marquand, *Ramsay MacDonald*, p. xvi.

[8] David Kogan and Maurice Kogan, *The Battle for the Labour Party*, London: Fontana, 1982.

[9] Marquand, *Ramsay MacDonald*, p. xv.

[10] Henry Pelling, *A Short History of the Labour Party*, London: Macmillan, 1961; Robert McKenzie, *British Political Parties: The distribution of power within the Conservative and Labour parties*, London: Heinemann, 1955.

[11] Marquand, *Ramsay MacDonald*, p. 488.

[12] Marquand, *Ramsay MacDonald*, p. 488.

[13] Robert Skidelsky, *Politicians and the Slump: The Labour Government of 1929–31*, London: Macmillan, 1967.

[14] Marquand, *Ramsay MacDonald*, p. 609.

[15] Marquand, *Ramsay MacDonald*, p. 645.

[16] Marquand, *Ramsay MacDonald*, p. 653.

[17] Marquand, *Ramsay MacDonald*, p. 674.

[18] Marquand, *Ramsay MacDonald*, p. 646.

[19] Marquand, *Ramsay MacDonald*, p. 746.

[20] Marquand, *Ramsay MacDonald*, p. 685.

[21] Marquand, *Ramsay MacDonald*, p. 162.

[22] Marquand, *Ramsay MacDonald*, p. 329.

[23] G.D.H.Cole, *The World of Labour: A discussion of the present and future of trade unionism*, London: G. Bell & Sons, 1913.

[24] Miliband, *Parliamentary Socialism*, p. 119.

[25] Marquand, *Ramsay MacDonald*, p. 256.

[26] Eric Hobsbawm, *The Forward March of Labour Halted?*, London: NLB, 1981.

[27] Miliband, *Parliamentary Socialism*, p. 144.

[28] Marquand, *Ramsay MacDonald*, p. 423.

[29] Miliband, *Parliamentary Socialism*, p. 134.

[30] Marquand, *Ramsay MacDonald*, p. 569.

[31] Dowse, *Left in the Centre*; Keith Middlemas, *The Clydesiders: A left wing struggle for parliamentary power*, London: Hutchinson, 1965.

[32] Marquand, *Ramsay MacDonald*, p. 288.

33 Miliband, *Parliamentary Socialism*, p. 86.
34 Miliband, *Parliamentary Socialism*, p. 30.
35 Miliband, *Parliamentary Socialism*, p. 29.
36 Andrew Gamble, 'The progressive dilemma revisited', *Political Quarterly*, 88:1 (2017), pp. 136–43.
37 Mark Abrams and Richard Rose, *Must Labour Lose?*, London: Penguin Books, 1959; Hobsbawm, *The Forward March of Labour Halted?*
38 Miliband, *Parliamentary Socialism*, p. 119.
39 Miliband, *Parliamentary Socialism*, p. 101.
40 Marquand, *Ramsay MacDonald*, p. 287.
41 Marquand, *Ramsay MacDonald*, p. 247.
42 Skidelsky, *Politicians and the Slump*.
43 Marquand, *Ramsay MacDonald*, p. 454.
44 J. Ramsay MacDonald, *Socialism and Society*, London: ILP, 1908; J.Ramsay MacDonald, *Political Writings*, London: Allen Lane, 1972.
45 David Marquand, *Mammon's Kingdom*, London: Allen Lane, 2014.
46 Marquand, *Ramsay MacDonald*, p. 246.

Chapter 9

1   This essay first appeared in Ephraim Podoksik (ed), *The Cambridge Companion to Oakeshott*, Cambridge: CUP, 2012, pp. 153–176.
2   'Political education', in *Rationalism in Politics*, London: Methuen, 1962, p. 116.
3   See for example his reviews of *The Conservative Opprtunity* (1965), *Conservative Essays* (1978), *and Conservative Thoughts* (1988), in Luke O'Sullivan (ed), *The Vocabulary of a Modern European State*, London: Imprint Academic, 2008, pp. 187–9, 280–2, 295–7.
4   John Gray, 'Oakeshott as a liberal', in *Post-liberalism: Studies in political thought*, London: Routledge, 1983.
5   .W.H. Greenleaf uses this same distinction in his reconstruction of the British political tradition. W.H. Greenleaf, *The British Political Tradition: Vol 1 The Rise of Collectivism, Vol 2 The Ideological Heritage*, London: Methuen, 1983.
6   Efraim Podoksik, *In Defence of Modernity*, London: Imprint Academic, 2003; Paul Franco, *The Political Philosophy of Michael Oakeshott*, New Haven: Yale University Press, 1990.
7   D.J. Manning and T.J. Robinson, *The Place of Ideology in Political Life*, London: Croom Helm, 1985.
8   Personal information.
9   Irving Kristol, *The NeoConservative Persuasion: Selected essays 1942–2009*, New York: Basic Books, 2011.
10 'The study of politics in a university', in *Rationalism in Politics*, London: Methuen, 1962.
11 R. Devigne, *Recasting Conservatism: Michael Oakeshott, Leo Strauss, & conservative political thought's response to postmodernism*, New Haven: Yale University Press, 1994.
12 'Contemporary British Politics', in Luke Sullivan (ed), *The Concept of a Philosophical Jurisprudence: Essays and reviews 1926–51*, London: Imprint Academic, 2007, p. 203.
13 Oakeshott moves away from this Hegelian understanding in his later writings.
14 'Contemporary British politics', p. 208.
15 'Contemporary British politics', p. 206.
16 'Contemporary British politics', p. 207.
17 'Contemporary British politics', p. 209.

18 'Contemporary British politics', p. 209.

19 'Contemporary British politics', p. 211.

20 'Contemporary British politics', p. 213.

21 'Contemporary British politics', p. 214.

22 'Contemporary British politics', p. 214.

23 'Contemporary British politics', p. 214.

24 Michael Oakeshott, 'Preface to the form of ideology', in *The Vocabulary of the Modern European State*, p. 294.

25 Albert Hirschman, *The Rhetoric of Reaction: Perversity, futility, jeopardy*, Cambridge, Mass: Harvard University Press, 1991.

26 'Contemporary British politics', p. 218.

27 'Contemporary British politics', p. 219.

28 Michael Freeden, *Ideologies and Political Theory: A conceptual approach*, Oxford: Clarendon, 1996. Freeden writes of Oakeshott: 'It is only through denying that conservatism is an ideology, bearing a systematic morphology and armed with a novel conceptual map of its own, that Oakeshott evaded realizing that he himself was a conservative ideologist who had justifiably become an object of inquiry on the part of analysts of conservative ideology' p. 328.

29 'Contemporary British politics', p. 208.

30 'Contemporary British politics', p. 208–9.

31 'Introduction to Leviathan', reprinted in *Rationalism in Politics and Other Essays* Indianapolis: Liberty Fund, 1991.

32 'Anarchy and Order', in *The Vocabulary of a Modern European State*, p. 73.

33 See his reviews of *The Conservative Opportunity* and *Conservative Essays*, in Luke O'Sullivan (ed), *The Vocabulary of a Modern European State*, London: Imprint Academic, 2008, pp. 187–9, 280–2.

34 Michael Oakeshott, *Rationalism in Politics,* London: Methuen, 1962, p. 21; see also Andrew Gamble, *Hayek: The Iron Cage of Liberty,* Cambridge: Polity, 1996, pp. 188–9.

35 Samuel Huntington, 'Conservatism as an ideology', *The American Political Science Review*, 51:2 (June, 1957), pp. 454–473. Oakeshott noted in one of his last reviews that such is the corruption and ambiguity which has overtaken our political vocabulary that the name conservative has lost its meaning since even Stalinists are called conservatives. *The Vocabulary of a Modern European State*, p. 295.

36 'On being conservative', in *Rationalism in Politics,* p. 172.

37 'On being conservative', p. 172.

38 F.M. Cornford, *Micro-cosmographia Academica*, Cambridge: Bowes and Bowes, 1908, pp. 15,16.

39 'On being conservative', p. 174.

40 'On being conservative', p. 175.

41 'On being conservative', p. 183.

42 'On being conservative', p. 185.

43 'On being conservative', p. 186.

44 'On being conservative', p. 188.

45 *The Vocabulary of a Modern European State*, pp. 188, 282,

46 'On being conservative', p. 189.

47 'On being conservative', p. 192.

48 'On being conservative', p. 195.

49 See Oakeshott's review of Russell Kirk, *The Conservative Mind*, reprinted in *The Vocabulary of a Modern European State,* p. 83.

[50] 'On being conservative' p. 195.

[51] 'On being conservative', p. 196.

[52] 'Political Education', in *Rationalism in Politics,* p. 130–1.

[53] 'Political Education', pp. 120–1.

[54] Michael Oakeshott, 'Conservative thoughts and conservative thinkers', in Luke O'Sullivan (ed), *The Vocabulary of a Modern European State*, London: Imprint Academic, 2008, pp. 295–7.

[55] Michael Oakeshott, *On Human Conduct*, Oxford: Clarendon, 1975, p. 320.

[56] John Gray, 'Oakeshott as a liberal', in *Post-liberalism: Studies in political thought*, London: Routledge, 1993, pp. 40–6.

[57] *On Human Conduct*, p. 229.

[58] *On Human Conduct*, p. 205.

[59] *On Human Conduct*, p. 323.

[60] *On Human Conduct*, p. 241.

[61] *Rationalism in Politics*, p. 30.

[62] *On Human Conduct*, p. 305.

[63] *On Human Conduct*, pp. 276–8.

[64] 'The political economy of freedom', in *Rationalism in Politics,* p. 53.

[65] 'The political economy of freedom', p. 43.

[66] Gray, 'Oakeshott as a liberal'.

[67] *The Vocabulary of a Modern European State*, p. 82.

[68] *On Human Conduct,* p. 191.

[69] Oakeshott acknowledges the importance of war and foreign policy in making all modern states, including Britain, enterprise states. But generally he has little to say about international relations, or the argument that it was British imperial expansion and 'lordly rule' abroad which made possible the cultivation of the rule of law and civil association at home. On this see Perry Anderson, 'The intransigent right', in *Spectrum*, London: Verso, 2005, pp. 3–28.

[70] See for example his remark that 'Russians and Turks have never enjoyed the experience of freedom, and therefore can only think in abstractions', 'The political economy of freedom', p. 40.

Chapter 10

[1] This essay first appeared in Terry Nardin (ed), *Michael Oakeshott's Cold War Liberalism*, London: Palgrave-Macmillan, 2016, pp. 63–78.

[2] Michael Oakeshott, 'Political education', in *Rationalism in Politics*, London: Methuen, 1962, p. 116.

[3] Michael Oakeshott, *Rationalism in Politics*, p. 21.

[4] Efraim Podoksik, 'Anti-totalitarian ambiguities: Jacob Talmon and Michael Oakeshott', *History of European Ideas*, 34 (2008), 206–219; Noel O'Sullivan, 'Visions of freedom: the response to totalitarianism', in *The British Study of Politics in the Twentieth Century*, J. Haward, B. Barry and A. Brown (eds), Oxford: Oxford University Press, 1999.

[5] Michael Oakeshott, *The Social and Political Doctrines of Contemporary Europe*, New York: CUP, 1950, p. xii.

[6] *The Social and Political Doctrines of Contemporary Europe*, p. xv.

[7] *The Social and Political Doctrines of Contemporary Europe*, p. xv.

[8] *The Social and Political Doctrines of Contemporary Europe*, p. xiv.

[9] *The Social and Political Doctrines of Contemporary Europe*, p. xiv.

[10] *The Social and Political Doctrines of Contemporary Europe*, p. xviii.

[11] *The Social and Political Doctrines of Contemporary Europe*, p. xviii.

[12] *The Social and Political Doctrines of Contemporary Europe*, p. xviii.

[13] *The Social and Political Doctrines of Contemporary Europe*, p. xix.

[14] *The Social and Political Doctrines of Contemporary Europe*, p. xxii.

[15] *The Social and Political Doctrines of Contemporary Europe*, p. xxiii.

[16] Michael Oakeshott, *The Politics of Faith and the Politics of Scepticism,* T. Fuller (ed), New Haven: Yale University Press, 1996.

[17] *The Politics of Faith and the Politics of Scepticism*, ch. 5.

[18] *The Politics of Faith and the Politics of Scepticism*, pp. 59–61.

[19] Michael Oakeshott, 'Contemporary British politics', in Luke Sullivan (ed), *The Concept of a Philosophical Jurisprudence: Essays and reviews 1926–51*, London: Imprint Academic, 2007.

[20] F.A. Hayek, *The Road to Serfdom*, London: Routledge & Kegan Paul, 1944.

Chapter 11

[1] This essay first appeared in David Boucher and Gary Browning (eds), *The Political Art of Bob Dylan*, London: Imprint Academic, 2009, pp. 22–49. Quotations from Dylan's songs are taken from Bob Dylan, *Lyrics: 1962–1985*, London: Cape, 1987, and from http://www.bobdylan.com/songs/

[2] Herbert Marcuse, *Reason and Revolution: Hegel and the rise of social theory*, London: Routledge & Kegan Paul, 1955; Istvan Meszaros, *Marx's Theory of Alienation*, London: Merlin, 1970.

[3] Imre Salusinzky, 'Chimes of freedom flashing' *The Telegraph*, 49, (1994,) pp. 23–37.

[4] Bertell Ollman, *Alienation: Marx's conception of man in capitalist society*, Cambridge: CUP, 1971.

[5] Mike Marqusee, *Chimes of Freedom: The politics of Bob Dylan's art*, New York: The New Press, 2003.

[6] David Pichaske, 'Bob Dylan and the search for the past', in John Gray and John Bauldie (eds), *All Across the Telegraph: A Bob Dylan handbook*, London: Sidgwick & Jackson, 1987, pp. 98–106.

[7] Clifford Longley, *Chosen People: The big idea that shaped England and America*, London: Hodder & Stoughton, 2002.

[8] Chris Whithouse, 'Alias, Pat Garrett, and Billy the Kid', in Gray and Bauldie (eds), *All Across the Telegraph*, pp. 107–26

[9] Mark Ford, 'Trust yourself: Emerson and Dylan', in Neil Corcoran (ed), *'Do You, Mr Jones? Bob Dylan with the poets and the professors*, London: Pimlico 2003, p. 129.

[10] Michael Gray, *Song and Dance Man III: The art of Bob Dylan*, London: Continuum 2000, ch. 7; Bert Cartwright, 'The Bible in the lyrics of Bob Dylan, 1985–1990', *The Telegraph*, 38, (1991), pp. 53–90.

[11] John Herdman, *Voice Without Restraint: Bob Dylan's lyrics and their background*, Edinburgh: Paul Harris, 1981.

[12] Clinton Heylin, 'Saved! Bob Dylan's conversion to Christianity', in John Bauldie (ed), *Wanted Man: In search of Bob Dylan*, London: Penguin, 1992, pp. 141–7.

[13] Mike Marqusee, *Chimes of Freedom: The politics of Bob Dylan's art*, New York: The New Press, 2003.

[14] Meszaros, *Marx's Theory of Alienation*, p. 33.

[15] Patrick Crotty, 'Bob Dylan's last words', in Corcoran (ed), *Do You, Mr Jones?*, pp. 307–333.

[16] David Pichaske, 'Bob Dylan and the search for the past', in Gray and Bauldie (eds), *All Across the Telegraph,* p. 103.

[17] Paul Hodson, 'Bob Dylan's stories about men', in Elizabeth Thomson and David Gutman (eds), *The Dylan Companion*, London: Macmillan, 1990, p.187.

[18] Hodson, 'Bob Dylan's stories about men', p. 187.

[19] Pamela Thurschwell, 'A different Baby Blue', in Corcoran (ed), *Do You, Mr Jones?* pp. 253–74.

[20] Marqusee, *Chimes of Freedom: The politics of Bob Dylan's art*, pp. 88–9.

[21] Marqusee, *Chimes of Freedom: The politics of Bob Dylan's art*, pp. 281–2.

[22] Dylan 1987, 124/5.

[23] Sean Wilentz, 'American Recordings: On "Love and Theft" and the Minstrel Boy', in Corcoran (ed), *Do You, Mr Jones?,* p. 290.

[24] Sean Wilentz, 'American Recordings: On "Love and Theft" and the Minstrel Boy'.

[25] Sean Wilentz, 'American Recordings: On "Love and Theft" and the Minstrel Boy', p. 298.

[26] David Pichaske, *The Poetry of Rock: The Golden Years*, Peoria, Illinois: The Ellis Press, 1981.

[27] Lester Bangs, 'Bob Dylan's dalliance with mafia chic', in Thomson and Gutman (eds), *The Dylan Companion*, pp. 210–221.

Acknowledgements

The author and publisher wish to thank the publishers of the following essays for permission to reproduce them, with minor changes, in this volume:

'The western ideology' from *Government and Opposition*, 44:1 (2009), pp. 1–19, reproduced with permission of Cambridge University Press.

'Neo-liberalism and the tax state' originally published as 'Neo-liberalism and fiscal conservatism', in Mark Thatcher and Vivien Schmidt (eds) *Resilient Liberalism in Europe's Political Economy* (2013), pp. 53–76, reproduced with permission of Cambridge University Press.

'Ideas and interests in British economic policy' first published by the Institute of Economic Affairs, London, in 1989 and reproduced with their permission.

'Hayek on economics, knowledge and society' in Edward Feser (ed) *The Cambridge Companion to Hayek* (2006), pp. 111–131, reproduced with permission of Cambridge University Press through PLSclear.

'Marxism after communism' from the *Review of International Studies* (1999), pp. 127–144, reproduced with permission of Cambridge University Press.

'G.D.H. Cole and the history of socialist thought' originally published as 'Introduction to G.D.H. Cole's *A History of Socialist Thought*' in *G.D.H. Cole: A History of Socialist Thought* (2002), pp. v–xxvi, reproduced with permission of Palgrave Macmillan.

'Social democracy in a global world' originally published as 'Moving beyond the national: the challenges for social democracy in the global age' in Olaf Cramme and Patrick Diamond (eds), *Social Justice in the Global Age* (2009), pp. 117–135, reproduced with permission of Polity.

'The quest for a Great Labour Party' originally published as 'A Labour of Sisyphus: the quest for a Great Labour party', in Hans Schattle and Jeremy Nuttall (eds), *Making Social Democrats* (2018), pp. 89–110, reproduced with permission of Manchester University Press.

'Oakeshott's ideological politics', in Efraim Podoksik (ed), *The Cambridge Companion to Oakeshott* (2012), pp. 153–176, reproduced with permission of Cambridge University Press through PLSclear.

'Oakeshott and totalitarianism', in Terry Nardin (ed), *Michael Oakeshott's Cold War Liberalism* (2016), pp. 63–78, reproduced with permission of Palgrave Macmillan.

'The drifter's escape', in David Boucher and Gary Browning (eds), *The Political Art of Bob Dylan* (2009), pp. 22–49, reproduced with permission of Imprint Academic.

Index

A

Abrams, Philip 7
accountability 150, 154–156
accumulation of capital 115, 116, 120
alienation 215–220, 223, 227, 228
Althusser, L. 115
altruism 44, 49
Amsterdam School 114
anarchism 43, 53, 126, 128
anciens régimes 2, 28, 32, 93, 124, 135, 141
Anderson, Perry 251n3, 260n69
Anglo-American worldview 25, 29
Anglobalisation 25
Anglo-Saxon economic model 25
Anglosphere 45
anti-western ideology 28
apocalypse 220–223
Aristotle 48, 50
Arrighi, Giovanni 117
association 67, 76–77, 139, 182, 192, 195–199, 203, 209–212
Attlee Government 175
austerity 12–13, 55, 56, 57–58
Australia 42, 83
Austrian School 42, 43, 52, 88, 89
authoritarianism 26, 135, 205, 213, 239
automation 118 *see also* technology

B

Bacon, Francis 206
Baez, Joan 225, 232
balanced budgets 44, 45, 49, 53, 55–56, 77, 164
banking 44, 50, 55, 164, 166
Beer, Samuel 63, 66
behavioural approaches 90, 181
Bell, Daniel 50, 51, 242
Berlin, Isaiah 5, 31, 202
Berlin Wall 23, 122, 202
Bernanke, Ben 58
Blair, Tony 11, 163, 171, 176, 178
Blanc, Louis 128, 135

Bolsheviks 124, 129, 171, 206
Bray, John Francis 127
Brenner, Robert 116
Bretton Woods 144
Brexit 178
Bright, John 198
Brockway, Fenner 172
Bruce, Lenny 233
Brundtland report 241
Burke, Edmund 194
Bush, George H. 10
Bush, George W. 35, 45, 55

C

Cambridge, University of 6–7, 13, 15
Cambridge Centre for Political Thought 13
Campbell, Bea 10
capitalism
    accumulation of capital 115, 116, 120
    and alienation 217
    capital as a social relation 115–117, 118, 119
    and the environment 242
    global economy/global markets 98, 110–112, 118–119, 120, 177
    as a global system 110–112, 118–119, 120
    hegemony 113–114
    inequality 117, 120, 148
    lack of rivals to 23
    and Marxism 101, 105, 106, 108, 109–110, 115–117
    and modernity 106
    public interest 69, 71
    reproduction of capital 115–117
    resistance to 120, 132
    tax states 52
    and technology 117
    uniformity of 34–35
    see also neo-liberalism
Carr, E.H. 252n6
Carroll, Hattie 218, 225

Castells, Manuel 110, 117
catallaxy 48, 49, 50, 53, 55
Catholicism 203–204, 205
centrally-planned economies 83, 86, 130, 185
centre-left politics 12, 161, 179
Chicago School 42, 44
Chile 42, 61
China 28, 35, 37, 104, 110, 122, 239
chrematistics 50
Christianity 26, 27, 28, 215, 218, 220, 221–222
Church 169
Churchill, Winston 73
citizen disengagement 150–154, 156–158
citizenship 153
City of London 167
civil association 76–77, 203, 205, 209–212
civil society 77, 151, 193, 211
civilisation, as corrupting influence 216
class conflict
    Cole and the history of socialist thought 133, 139
    and Labour 166, 170, 171, 172, 175
    Marxism 106, 111, 118–119
    social democracy in a global world 142
    special interests 68–69
climate change 36, 98, 148, 240, 241
Clinton, Bill 10
Club of Rome 241
coalition governments 56, 166, 169
Cobden, Richard 111, 198
coercion 43, 172, 225
cold war 3, 25, 102, 113, 202, 203, 206, 209, 240
Cole, G.D.H. 121–139, 170, 198
Cole, Margaret 121, 125
collectivism
    British economic policy 59, 62–64, 66, 75–76
    democracy 64
    economic liberalism 85
    and free markets 39
    Oakeshott on 181, 185, 189, 196, 202, 210
    public goods 70–71
    public policy 72
Collini, Stefan 15
colonialism 29
commercial society 46, 52, 58, 170, 217
commodity exchange 217
communism
    Cole and the history of socialist thought 122, 124–125, 129, 130–132, 138, 139
    collapse of 23–24

and Labour 174
and Marxism 101
Oakeshott on 203–204
social democracy in a global world 142, 143
and totalitarianism 201–202
United States 28
Communist International 142
complexity 14, 18, 59, 63, 73, 81, 86–88, 91, 97, 150
Conservatives
    1931 election 164
    and class 171
    coalition governments 164, 166
    and modernity 32–33
    Oakeshott on 186
    Oakeshott's conservative disposition 188–195
    rejection of modernity 2
constitutional politics 138, 148–149, 177
constructivism 87, 93, 98, 99
    see also positivism
consumerist societies 151, 228–229
cooperation 126, 127, 128–129, 242
Corbyn, Jeremy 168, 174, 178
Cornford, F.M. 190
corporate households 49–50, 57
cosmopolitanism 32, 35, 36–37, 111, 142, 146, 148, 150, 178
Counter-Enlightenment 32
coups d'état 135, 186
Cox, Robert 113–114
Crick, Bernard 8, 12
critical rationalism 92–93
Crouch, Colin 41
Cuban missile crisis 5, 240
currency stabilisation 145

D

debt financing 53
decentralisation 86, 107, 136
decline 3, 8–9, 68, 151, 239
deflation 54, 57, 77
democracy
    accountability and sovereignty 154–156
    citizen participation 150–154, 156–158
    collectivism 64
    and dictatorship 238–239
    doctrines 63
    Hayek on 43, 96
    and liberalism 93, 238
    mass democracy 64–66, 124, 135–136, 137, 150–151
    and modernity 106
    Oakeshott on 186–187, 203–204, 212, 213
    and revolution 135

and socialism 124, 135, 137, 139
special interests 69
Department of Politics and International
Studies (POLIS) 13
determinism 34, 116, 126, 134, 137, 171
Developments in British Politics 10–11
devolution 155
Dicey, A.V. 59, 62–63, 66, 72, 75, 78
dictatorships 238
diffusion of power 139, 188, 198
direct action 123–124
discrimination 29
division of knowledge 82–86, 150, 157
division of labour 26, 31, 46, 84, 146,
149, 150, 154, 157
doctrines 59–79, 85, 104, 183, 203–
204, 217
Drucker, Henry 10
Durham University 7
Dylan, Bob 215–235, 242

E

East, as the opposite to the West 27
economic growth 54, 58
economic liberalism 3–4, 8, 85, 182, 239
economic libertarianism 42, 43–44, 56
economic policy 59–79
economics
'data' of 83
and Hayek 82–83
and knowledge 81–99
and liberalism 31
as science 60–61, 65, 83, 91–92
separation from politics 47
economism 118–119
electoral systems 152–153
Emerson, Ralph Waldo 216, 218, 219
Empire 29 *see also* imperialism
employment 72, 74, 146
end of history 24, 31, 37, 105–106, 242
Engels, Friedrich 109–110, 116
Enlightenment 2, 29, 31, 35, 92,
139, 239
enterprise association 195, 199, 203,
209–212
enterprise economy 194, 205
enterprise politics 76
environment 36, 78, 97–98, 148, 241
equilibrium analysis 84
establishment politics 5
Eucken, Walter 97
European integration 57
European Union (EU)
and the eurozone 57–58
fiscal conservatism 57
hegemony 113
neo-liberalism 55

as polity 57
supranational conceptions 154–155
eurozone 57–58
exchange controls 145
experts 157
extraparliamentary agitation 173–175,
178–179

F

Fabians 5, 64, 76, 77, 123, 125, 167
Factory Acts 120
faith, politics of 205–209, 211, 213
fall of Rome 26, 27
families 49
fascism 129, 131, 132, 142–143, 177,
201, 203–204
fatalism 76, 96, 120, 126, 137, 171
feminist analysis 10
financial crash 2008 12–13, 39, 40, 41,
55, 239
financial sector 145
see also banking
First International 121, 128
First World War 32, 38, 51–52, 53,
112, 124
fiscal conservatism 39, 45, 53–58
fiscal stimulus packages 55, 56
Fordism 115, 116
Foucault, Michel 45
Fourier, Charles 126, 127
France 29, 122, 125
Franco, Paul 182
Frankfurt School 108
free market economies 39, 40, 42, 84–86
free trade 40, 47, 74, 77, 166, 170
Freeden, Michael 259n28
freedom 30, 31–32, 93, 186, 197
see also liberty
freedom of information 157
freedom of movement 142
Friedman, Milton 44, 54, 60, 78, 82,
238, 239
Fukuyama, Francis 24, 41, 105, 242
full employment 74

G

Gaitskell, Hugh 125, 171, 256n32
Galbraith, J.K. 11
Gamble, David 241
Geddes axe 53
Geithner, Tim 58
gender 36, 230
General Strike (1926) 53, 172
geopolitics 10
Germany 32, 43, 45, 57, 122, 125,
129, 142
Gibbins, John 7

global economy/global markets
  and capitalism 98, 110–112, 118–119,
    120, 177
  Cole and the history of socialist
    thought 154
  Hayekian principles 98
  hegemony 113
  international economy 40, 43, 47, 49,
    55, 103, 144–145, 146
  Marxism 103, 104–105, 109,
    110–112, 118
  social democracy 141–159
global justice 35–36, 153
globalisation 30, 46, 109–110, 119,
  146–148, 154
gold standard 53–54, 74, 77, 165
Goldscheid, Rudolph 52
Gorbachev, Mikhail 240
government, paradox of 62–63
government, role of 154–156, 193
  see also state role
governmentality 45
gradualism 171–173
Gramsci, A. 114, 115, 116
Gray, John 31, 198
Great Depression 40, 41, 54, 177
Greenleaf, W.H. 75
guild socialism 124, 127, 129, 136, 138
Guthrie, Woody 218, 229

H

Hall, Peter 40
Hall, Stuart 9, 10
Hardie, Keir 169
Harris, Jose 72–73
Hayek, F.A. 3–4, 6, 24, 42, 43, 44, 48,
  49, 52, 54, 55, 58, 78, 81–99, 181,
  189, 202, 209, 211, 238, 239, 241
Heath, Edward/Heath Government 8
hedge funds 41
Hegel, G.W.F. 2, 24, 106, 133, 134, 206,
  216–217
hegemony 29, 35, 113–114
Henderson, Arthur 165, 166, 167, 168
higher education sector 14–15
Hirschman, Albert 75–76, 79
historicism 105–108, 117–118
history 24, 29, 34, 91, 183, 187
history, end of 24, 31, 37, 105–106, 242
Hitler, Adolf 129
Hobbes, Thomas 37, 104, 119, 188,
  194, 213
Hobsbawm, Eric 10, 171
Hogg, Quintin 184, 185, 187, 188, 198
Hont, Istvan 13, 46
House of Commons 185
households 48–53, 56–57, 116

Howson, Susan 65
human rights 29, 51
Hume, David 62–63, 83, 87, 88, 93, 95,
  97, 181, 194
Hutchison, Terence 82

I

identity politics 178
ideology
  British economic policy 59–79
  Marxism 104, 106, 118–119
  Oakeshott 181, 182–188, 201, 202,
    215–216
  totalitarianism 201, 202, 215–216
IMF (International Monetary
  Fund) 35, 55
immigration 147, 178
imperfect information/markets 43, 81,
  88, 94, 98
imperialism 102–103, 105, 109, 110,
  111–112, 117–118, 260n69
income tax 164
Independent Labour party (ILP) 167,
  168, 178
India 35, 37, 239
individualism
  British economic policy 59, 62–63, 66,
    75–76
  Hayek on 89
  Oakeshott on 188–189, 206–207
  social democracy in a global
    world 152, 157
inequality
  capitalism 117, 120, 148
  and democratic participation 153–154
  Dylan songs 225
  liberal modernity 37
  and liberalism 3
  Marxism 106, 119
  and socialism 139
inflation 43
innovation 190, 193
Insanity Factory 227–229
Institute for Economic Affairs (IEA) 64
institutions
  Dylan songs 227–228
  Hayek on 96–97
  and knowledge 86
  Oakeshott on 185, 206, 211
  special interests 68
intellectuals 64, 114
interdependence 36, 46, 79, 120,
  146, 171
interdisciplinarity 11, 14, 104
interest rates 77
interests (versus doctrines) 66–70
international agencies 55

international division of labour 31, 146
international economy 40, 43, 47, 49, 55, 103, 144–145, 146
  see also global economy/global markets
international governance 149, 155, 156
  see also international state system
international market order 55
international organisations 114
international state system 36, 104, 111, 112, 120
internationalism 125, 141, 142–143
interventionism 31, 69, 78, 226
Irish Home Rule 169

J

Jacques, Martin 9–10
Japan 112, 113, 117, 122, 233
Jenkins, Roy 162
Johnson, Lyndon 5
Jones, Gareth Stedman 37
journalism 151–152
Jowett, Fred 174
Judeo-Christian tradition 215, 217
judiciary 207, 225

K

Kant, Immanuel 35, 36, 87, 88, 93, 95, 104
Kelly, Gavin 11
Kennedy, Steven 10
Kennedy Assasination 5
Keynesianism
  British economic policy 60
  doctrines 66, 76
  fiscal conservatism 54, 55, 56
  and Labour 162, 164, 165, 178
  legitimacy 74
  mass democracy 64
  and neo-liberalism 39, 40, 45
  social democracy in a global world 144
  technical experts 65
King, Mervyn 58
Knight, Frank 83
knowledge
  British economic policy 59–60, 61–62, 65–66
  Hayek on 81–99
  Oakeshott on 183
  social democracy 150, 157
  socialism 126
knowledge economy 27
Kojeve, Alexandre 106
Kristol, Irving 183
Kyoto protocols 241

L

Labour
  1997 election 11
  Brexit 178

Cole and 123, 125, 128, 136–138, 139
  in government 163–164, 166, 175
  MacDonald and the quest for a great Labour Party 162–179
  Oakeshott on 181, 185–186, 187, 209
  as Opposition 176
  quest for a great Labour Party 161–179
  and social democracy 162
  and socialism 135–138, 169–170, 175, 179
  universal suffrage 135
labour markets
  and alienation 216–217
  flexible labour markets 55
  and households 49
  international 36, 142, 146
  Marxism 69, 117, 118
  National Insurance Act (1911) 73
labourism 167, 168
laissez faire 40, 47, 54, 96
Lasch, Christopher 242
Laski, Harold 121
Lassalle, Ferdinand 135
League of Nations 28
left-wing politics 209
  see also Fabians
Letwin, Shirley 14
liberal political economy 30–32, 39, 47, 48–50, 52, 63, 238
liberalism
  and Christianity 26
  classical 40, 44, 45–47, 76, 85, 94, 198
  collapse of liberal economic order 142
  definition 24–25
  and democracy 93, 238
  Dylan songs 227
  Enlightenment 2
  and the fall of communism 24
  and Hayek 82, 83, 85, 93, 94, 98
  and modernity 106
  and nationalism 32
  and Oakeshott 181–182, 188, 189, 195–199, 211–212
  relation to neo-liberalism 42
  see also neo-liberalism
Liberals 72, 163, 168–170, 198
libertarianism 6, 75, 196
liberty 206, 211, 213, 238–239
  see also freedom
light touch regulation 55
limited liability 49
Linklater, Andrew 107–108
Lippman, Walter 141
List, Friedrich 47
Lloyd George, David 165
Locke, John 188, 195, 213
Lucas, Robert 44

M

MacDonald, Ramsay/MacDonald
    Government 162–179
Macmillan, Harold/Macmillan
    Government 5, 198
mandates 184
Mandel, Ernest 113, 115–116
Mandeville, Bernard 93
Manning, David 7, 182–183
Marcuse, Herbert 1, 3, 7, 242
market socialism 107
marketplace of ideas 66, 67
markets
    and alienation 216–217
    Dylan songs 228–229
    as ecosystems 98
    financial markets 145
    imperfect information 43, 81, 88
    interdependent with state 79
    and knowledge 84–92, 94
    Marxism 118
    neo-liberalism 46
    public choice theory 70–71
    social democracy 144
    and socialism 139
    and welfare 73
    see also global economy/global markets;
        labour markets
Marquand, David 161–179
Marqusee, Mike 225, 226
Marx, Karl
    and G.D.H. Cole 132–134
    influence on Dylan 216–217
Marxism
    after communism 101–120
    in Britain 47, 101–120
    Cole and 130–134, 137
    and Labour 171
    as 'post-Christian' 31
    public interest 71
    public policy 59
    socialism 33, 128
    special interests 68–70
    studying 7
Marxism Today 9–10
Maxton, James 172, 173–174
May Commission 164–165
McCulloch, J.R. 61
media 151–152, 157
Mellon, Andrew 54, 55
Menger, Carl 83
Middle Way 68
migration 146
Miliband, Ralph 69, 162, 170–171,
    172, 175
Mill, John Stuart 31, 195
miners' strike 53

Minogue, Kenneth 14, 203
Mises, Ludwig von 43, 52, 82, 86, 87
modernity 11–12, 27–34, 148, 192, 239
monetarism 44, 54, 74, 114
monism 31
monopolies 186, 198
Mont Pelerin Society 42, 189, 202
morality 85, 94, 96–97, 108, 136, 171,
    172, 205, 218, 230
Morris, William 123, 125, 133
Mosley, Oswald 165–166, 177
multiculturalism 153
multilateral cooperation 28, 35, 155
multi-level governance 28, 120, 155
multiple modernities 11–12
Mussolini, Benito 142, 204

N

Napoleon Bonaparte 2, 29
Napoleonic Wars 53
national debt 53
national economic management 74,
    144–145
National Health Service (NHS) 175
national identity 32
National Insurance Act (1911) 72–73
National Labour 164
nationalisation 143, 186
nationalism 2, 3, 32–33, 39, 112,
    118–119, 189–190, 239
nation-states 114, 142, 148, 154–156
    see also state role
NATO 163
natural law 184, 189
Nazism 131, 139, 142–143, 202,
    203–204
negative liberty 31
neo-conservatism 25, 26, 76, 183
neo-liberalism
    and classical liberalism 45–47
    context of modernity 30
    definition 24–25, 42, 237–238
    and the environment 242
    higher education sector 14–15
    lack of rivals to 34–35, 41
    many faces of 26
    public spending 44, 55
    resilience of 39–58, 239
    rise of 23–25
    and social democracy 145, 146
    strands of 42–45
    and the tax state 39–58
    transnational historical materialism 114
    western ideology 34–35
new Conservatism 76
New Deal 56
New Labour 10, 176

New Left 101
New Liberals 198
New Political Economy 11
New Right 76
New Zealand 42
Nietzsche, F. 25, 33, 196
'night of the long knives' 5
normative doctrines 60–61
Nozick, Robert 43
nuclear weapons 36, 240–241

O

Oakeshott, Michael 7, 76, 181–199,
    201–213, 237
Obama, Barack 55, 56
OECD (Organisation for Economic
    Co-operation and Development) 55
Olson, Mancur 67–68
One World 3
open economic systems 30
open left 13
Ordo-liberalism 42, 43, 45, 57, 238
organised labour 142
    see also trade unions
Orwell, George 202
Osborne, George 56, 58
O'Sullivan, Noel 76, 202, 203
outlaws 229–235
Owen, Robert 127, 128, 136

P

Pareto, Vilfredo 84
Paris Commune 135, 136
Parker, John 184, 185, 186, 188
Parkinson, Cecil 11
Parkinson, John 11
parliamentary socialism 134–139,
    172, 174
party systems 151
Paulson, Hank 55
Payne, Tony 11, 13–14
perfect information/markets 44, 66, 81,
    88, 92
perpetual peace 35–37
philosophy 6–7, 34, 82, 86, 89,
    181–199, 204
planning 86, 96, 184, 186, 205–206
pluralism 33, 66, 69–70, 128, 129,
    134, 139
Podoksik, Efraim 182, 202, 203
Policy Network 13
political economy
    definition 14
    and economics 65
    liberal political economy 30–32, 39, 47,
        48–50, 52, 63, 238
    and modernity 27

and public policy 60–62
in universities 9
Political Economy Research Centre
    (PERC) 11
Political Quarterly 12
political science 126
politics as a subject 4–15
Polyani, Karl 39–40, 41, 45
Popper, Karl 82, 86–87, 90, 92, 202, 206
popular sovereignty 63
populism 13, 177, 239, 241
positivism 87
    see also constructivism
postmodernism 25, 33–34, 105–106, 239
Powell, Enoch 7
price mechanisms 118
prison 224–225
privacy 73
private economy 52–53
privatisation 55
production versus consumption
    118–119, 120
profitability 116
Profumo affair 5
progress 2, 25, 31, 32–33, 76, 93, 96,
    239, 242
progressive politics 10–11, 13, 103, 143,
    147, 161, 167, 170, 177–178
progressive taxation 77
property
    and democracy 137
    and knowledge 86
    and Labour 171
    liberal political economy 32
    limited liability 49
    and socialism 127, 139
protectionism 143, 144, 146–147
Proudhon, Pierre-Joseph 127
public choice theory 44, 59, 69, 70–71
public goods 50–51, 70–71, 120
public households 50–53, 56–57
public interest 60, 62, 66–70, 71, 77,
    154–155
public policy 71–72, 95–96
public sector neo-liberalism 44
public spending
    individualism 77
    Labour 164
    neo-liberalism 44, 55
    public households 52
    social democracy 144
Puritans 208–209

R

race 27, 29, 36, 142
radical uncertainty 88
radicalism 82, 191–192, 242

rational choice 84
rationalism
  constructivist rationalism 92–95
  critical rationalism 92–93
  division of knowledge 85, 86
  Hayek on 85–86, 87, 92–95, 96–99
  households 50
  Keynesianism 64
  liberal political economy 31, 32
  Oakeshott on 181, 182–188, 189, 195,
    196, 199, 203, 206–207
  political economy 60
Reagan, Ronald/Reagan
  Administration 45, 240
realist traditions 37, 102–103, 105,
  109–111, 117–118
recessions 54
  see also Great Depression
Reddaway, Peter 23–24
redistributive policies 77
reductionism 70, 116
regionalisation 147–148
regulation school 115, 116
regulatory regimes 145
relativism 33, 239
rentierism 77
reproduction of capital 115–117
revenue tariffs 165–166
revolution 134–139, 171, 172
Ricardian socialism 127
Rights of Man 187, 188
rights protection 43
right-wing politics 177, 188
Robbins, Lionel 60
Roemer, John 107
Romanticism 32, 33, 125–126, 134, 182,
  216, 218
Romney/Ryan programme 45
Rothbard, Murray 43
Rousseau, Jean-Jacques 125, 139, 216
Russell, Bertrand 5
Russian Revolution 121, 122, 130–132,
  142, 171
Rüstow, Alexander 43, 238

S

Saint-Simon, Henri de 126, 128
Salisbury, Lord 32
Saville, John 255n26
scepticism 25, 33, 181, 194, 205–209,
  210, 211, 237, 239
Schapiro, Leonard 23, 38
Schumpeter, Joseph 51–52, 60, 61,
  63, 211
science 65, 85, 87, 92, 93, 95, 125–126,
  133–134, 148
scientism 93

Second International 121, 142, 143, 168
Second World War 112, 122
secularisation 32, 217
security 46–47
self-determination 2, 29
Sheffield, University of 8–9, 11, 13–14
Sheffield Political Economy Research
  Institute (SPERI) 13–14
Sinking Fund 53
Sismondi, Jean Charles Léonard de 127
Skidelsky, Robert 177
Smith, Adam 49, 83, 84, 94–95
Smith, John 171
Snowden, Philip 53, 77, 165, 166, 176
social democracy
  birth of 39
  and capitalism 144
  Fabians 64, 76, 77, 123, 125, 167
  in a global world 141–159
  Keynesianism 41
  and Labour 162, 177–179
  parties 142, 143
  socialism 122, 124, 126–127, 129,
    138, 139
  tax states 58
Social Democratic Party (SDP) 162
social justice 143, 153, 177
social policy 51
social sciences 81, 89–92, 95, 96,
  98–99, 101
  see also economics
social theory 90, 91
socialism
  and capitalism 24, 177
  civil association 77
  Cole and the history of socialist
    thought 121–139
  collectivism 63
  definition 126–128
  and democracy 124, 135, 137, 139
  gradualism 171–172
  guild socialism 124, 127, 129, 136, 138
  and knowledge 86
  and Labour 135–138, 169–170,
    175, 179
  market socialism 107
  and Marxism 107
  and modernity 2, 33
  parliamentary socialism 134–139,
    172, 174
  and totalitarianism 209
  United States 28
  societas versus universitas 195–196
  sound money 40, 47, 53, 56
  sovereignty 63, 119, 154–156, 188
Soviet Union
  collapse of 3, 23

Marxism 101–104, 107, 110, 112, 113
  socialism 122, 129, 130–132, 143
  totalitarianism 202, 239
  and the West 29–30
special interests 67–71
speculation 56
Stalinism 138, 202, 206
state role
  balanced budgets 44, 45, 49, 53, 55–56, 77, 164
  following Great Depression 54
  Hayek on 96–97
  individualism versus collectivism 63
  liberal political economy 52
  Marxism 103
  modern market economies 46
  neo-liberalism 42, 43, 55–56, 58
  Oakeshott on 182, 206–212
  social democracy 141
  socialism 124, 127, 128–129
  societas versus *universitas* 195–196
  tax states 46, 50–53, 55, 58
statistics 91
Strauss, Leo 184
subjectivism 89–90
supply-side economic considerations 42, 44–45, 55
supranational conceptions 154

T

Talmon, Jacob 202
tariff-reformers 74, 77
tariffs 47
Tawney, R.H. 121, 133, 198
taxation
  neo-liberalism 39–58
  supply-side economics 44–45
  tax states 46, 50–53, 55, 58
Tea Party 41, 55
technical experts 65
technology 36, 117, 148, 157, 242
Telo, Mario 11–12
Thatcher, Margaret/Thatcher Government 8, 45, 193
Thatcherism 9, 78
Thomas, Jimmy 172
Thompson, William 127
totalitarianism 31, 102, 201–213
trade unions
  Cole on 123, 124
  and Labour 165, 167, 168–169, 172, 173–174, 176, 177–178, 185
  special interests 68
Trades Union Congress (TUC) 167, 185
transnational companies 114
transnational historical materialism 114
transnational spaces 36, 114, 148–149, 154–156

Trotskyism 9
Trump, Donald 13, 241
truth 33
Tudor, Henry 7
2008 financial crash 12–13, 39, 40, 41, 55, 239

U

UN Charter 37
unemployment 72
uniform minds hypothesis 89
unintended consequences 34, 72–73, 85, 92–95
United Nations 28
United States
  alienation 216, 218–220
  communism 28
  Dylan songs 215–235
  fiscal conservatism 54
  and the global economy 112
  hegemony 113
  liberalism 2–3, 28, 143
  Marxism 102, 103, 112
  and modernity 28
  neo-liberalism 24, 25, 26, 34–35, 41
  public households 51
  social policy 51
  socialism 28
  supply-side economics 45
  and the West 25, 29
universal rights 36
universal society 108
universal suffrage 135, 239
universalism 24–25, 31, 32, 37
urbanisation 28
utilitarianism 31
utopianism 36–37, 96, 123, 136, 238

V

value-free science 61
Vietnam War 5, 226, 240
Virginia School 42, 44

W

Wall Street crash (1929) 53
Walras, Leon 84
Walton, Paul 8
war 111–112, 225–227, 240, 260n69
wealth creation 217
Webb, Sidney and Beatrice 123, 136
Weber, Max 211
welfare capitalism models 144
welfare state
  and capitalism 116
  and neo-liberalism 40
  public households 51
  and socialism 138
  universalism 144

Wertheimer, Egon 163–164
western ideology, definition 26
Wheatley, John 174
Whigs 182
Whitehead, A.N. 94
Whitman, Walt 216, 218, 219
Wilson, Harold/Wilson Government 5
Winch, Donald 65
working classes
  Conservatives 176
  Labour 168, 170, 173, 178

Liberals 169
Marxism 69, 105
  social democracy 141, 143, 147
  socialism 123, 127, 129, 133, 137–138
World Bank 35, 55
world government 36–37
world order 104, 112, 130, 141–142, 143
world systems theory 113–114, 116
Wright, Tony 12
WTO (World Trade Organization) 35